Commercial Robbery

Offenders' Perspectives on Security and Crime Prevention

For Karen, Emily, Karis and Oliver

Commercial Robbery

Offenders' Perspectives on Security and Crime Prevention

Martin Gill

Scarman Centre, Leicester University

BLACKSTONE PRESS LIMITED

First published in Great Britain 2000 by Blackstone Press Limited, Aldine Place, London W12 8AA. Telephone (020) 8740 2277 www.blackstonepress.com

© Martin Gill, 2000

ISBN: 1 84174 150 7

British Library Cataloguing in Publication Data
A CIP catalogue record for this book is available from the British Library

Typeset by Style Photosetting Limited, Mayfield, East Sussex
Printed and bound in Great Britain by Antony Rowe Limited, Chippenham and Reading

Contents

Acknowledgements   vii

Preface   ix

Chapter 1   Robbers and robbery in perspective   1
Crime prevention and the situational approach — Security management and crime risk management — The rational offender and the
criminal justice process — Research based on offenders' perspectives
— The sample — Structure of the book — Notes

Chapter 2   Getting started: preparing for robbery   24
What initially motivated robbers? — Preparing for the robbery: the
planning stage — Choosing the target — Physical security measures
— Repeat victimisation — Discussion — Notes

Chapter 3   Carrying out the robbery   62
Robbery styles — Are robberies lucrative? — Weapons, violence and
victimisation — Discussion — Notes

**Chapter 4   Robbers: the police, the sentence
and imprisonment**   89
Robbers' views on police and on the prospects of being caught —
Robbers and their sentence — Robbers and the impact of imprisonment — Discussion — Notes

Chapter 5   Case studies of robbers   ·   110
Billy — Dennis — John — Tom

**Chapter 6   Rethinking situational prevention:
                    where we go from here?**   148
Towards a typology of robbers — Are robbers rational? — Rethinking
situational prevention: the crime risk management process — Management techniques — Situational techniques — Social/political/
economic techniques — Concluding comments — Notes

Bibliography   183

Tables
Table 1.1   Clarke's 16 techniques of situational prevention
Table 1.2   Percentage of respondents convicted of robbing a specific
             target who had also robbed another type of target
Table 2.1   Robbers' reasons for committing their last robbery
Table 2.2   Time spent preparing for the robbery by target
Table 3.1   Number of robbers involved in last robbery
Table 3.2   Money robbers obtained from last robbery
Table 4.1   Robbers' perceptions of the likelihood of being caught
             prior to their last robbery
Table 4.2   Robbers' perceptions of the likelihood of being caught
             after their last robbery
Table 4.3   Sentence received by robbers and what they had expected
             to receive
Table 4.4   Whether robbers believed they would commit further
             offences on leaving prison
Table 6.1   The extent to which robbers displayed rationality indi-
             cators, by target
Table 6.2   The extent to which robbers displayed selected rationality
             indicators, by target

Figure
Figure 1   The crime risk management process in the context of the
             workplace   157

Index   199

Acknowledgements

There are many people who have helped me in the preparation of this book. The British Bankers' Association and the Building Societies Association funded the project, Sue Thornhill and Jane Jones offered good advice on the early direction of the study. I have received very helpful comments on various drafts of questionnaires and the text, especially from Estella Baker, Paul Barker, Paul Ekblom, Anthea Hucklesby, Peter Hamilton, Brian Pollard, Giovanni Manunta and John Vitols.

Over the time it has taken to write the book I have received some helpful tips from many people including Keith Bottomley, Mick Creedon, Dick Hobbs, Marcus Felson, Mike Levi, Rob Mawby, Ken Pease, Alan Trickett and also from colleagues here in the Scarman Centre, especially John Benyon. The approach adopted in this book has been greatly influenced by the work of Professor Ron Clarke. For this and for the advice contained in our exchange of e-mails about the content of Chapter 6, I owe him special thanks.

Various people worked on the project and provided helpful input. They include Peter Devereux, Sara Fovargue, Kevin Godden, Peter Francis, Julie Hill and Heidi Kubic. I gratefully acknowledge the contribution of Professor Roger Matthews in drafting questionnaires and conducting interviews with respondents. Chris Dunbobbin did an excellent job in helping to reanalyse the data and prepare the material for publication.

The research for this book involved spending a lot of time in prisons. I am grateful to all the staff at all levels who helped in various ways. And also the interviewees who answered questions and made this book possible. I spent a lot of time with some robbers and they provided very helpful insights into the ways they approach robbery and other crimes. They were sometimes amazed that no-one had asked them before.

Finally, a very special thanks to Karen, Emily, Karis and Oliver, four very special people.

Preface

This study is based on interviews with people in prison who have been convicted of, and/or have admitted undertaking, a robbery of commercial premises. It was sponsored by the commercial sector (and in particular the banks and building societies) who want to develop responses to the offence. It wasn't that they were short of ideas — a burgeoning security industry provides plenty of technical fixes — it was rather that they were uncertain how their attempts at security were being perceived by those who were robbing them. Nor were they certain that they were doing the right thing in the right circumstances. They wanted to know why they were being chosen as targets; and they wanted to know more about the people who robbed them, their motivations, their methods of planning and their attitudes to carrying out the offence. Given that they were concerned to stop robberies, they were keen to ascertain robbers' views on security measures and the police and prisons. They wanted to improve their understanding of the offence as a way of improving the response.

I shared these interests, albeit from a slightly different perspective. I had long been interested, indeed fascinated, by robbers. I had read several accounts of robbers (Read, 1977; McVicar, 1974) and this had helped to generate my early interest in studying crime and security. And on returning to academia in 1991, I was keen to launch a study into a crime that has received comparatively little academic attention. As a criminologist and as a teacher of security management, I had two additional interests. First, the theory of rational choice and the techniques of situational crime prevention, particularly their applica- tion to the world of security management. Second, the offenders' perspective on crime and security.

Situational crime prevention, as will be explained, draws upon the theory of rational choice, and situational techniques are techniques of security management; after all a security measure is a situational measure. Thus while the study of security (and for that matter the practice too), is limited by the lack of a theoretical framework (see Manunta, 1997), criminology offers the potential for rectifying this. Indeed, it is somewhat strange, at least to this writer, that security management issues have attracted such a small part of criminological interest (see, Gill, 1998). In the following pages, a range of crim- inological work covering environmental criminology, repeat vic- timisation and offenders' careers is referred to, and each could greatly enhance the theory and practice of security management. But a starting point is to seek to understand better the rationality of offenders and the extent to which they are influenced by different impediments, that is to say situational measures, when deciding whether and how to commit an offence.

A range of studies have shown that studying the offenders' perspec- tive can be a useful way of stimulating crime prevention ideas (see, Bennett and Wright, 1984; Levi, 1981; 1998). Yet, while there have been several studies of (commercial) robbery, and some have incor- porated the views of robbers, these have not been focused on evaluating the situational approach, nor on informing the techniques of security management. What follows is an attempt to evaluate the offence of robbery and to use this work and evidence from other studies to develop what is called the 'crime risk management process'. This is a book about preventing a serious crime in the business environment and, in the process, improving our understanding of the theory and practice of crime prevention. Some years ago Clarke (1980) advocated more research based on interviews with offenders which he felt might provide 'additional preventive benefits'. This study was undertaken very much in that spirit, with the focus on robbers of commercial premises.

Chapter 1
Robbers and Robbery in Perspective

Robbers have often exercised a romanticised appeal. They have been seen to be at the top of the crime ladder, the most respected of a disrespected world. Tales of robbers have provided the inspiration for many a book and film, and biographies and autobiographies of robbers are popular reading amongst the general public. Robbers can even attract considerable public sympathy when they are caught and punished. The infamous American robber Jesse James is a case in point. He attacked banks and railroads but neither were popular in the eyes of the public; the former because of the difficulty of getting credit, the latter because of the high prices charged for freight (Macdonald 1975). And in Britain, the enormous public sympathy for the Great Train Robbers of 1963, who robbed a Royal Mail train, is said to have been one reason why those caught and found guilty soon after the offence received such severe sentences (Reid, 1977).

Yet, robbery is a very serious offence and very traumatic for victims. In Britain robbery carries a maximum sentence of life imprisonment. The essence of robbery is the use or the threat of force to steal.[1] However, in the legal classification the offence includes street attacks (commonly known as 'muggings'), and raids on premises — indeed the merging of the two in official statistics makes it difficult to identify trends. In England and Wales the problem reached a high point in the early 1990s.[2] The number of robberies in which firearms were reported to have been used increased fairly steadily between 1985 and 1993, more than doubling in frequency from 2,531 to a peak of 5,918. In 1993 42.4% of all notifiable offences involved firearms.[3] 1994 saw a dramatic fall in the number of such incidents and there was an additional fall in 1995 to 3,963 and to 3,029 in 1997 (Home Office, 1998; see also Broadhurst and Benyon, 2000). The escalation of offences up to 1993 was reflected in the numbers imprisoned for robbery. Indeed, in 1995 13.6% of the male prison population were serving sentences for robbery compared with only 8.1% ten years earlier (Home Office, 1996). Official concern has been matched by public anxiety, and Matthews (1997) has argued that the offence of robbery is a public barometer by which levels of crime are measured.

Research has shown that the people involved in street robberies (sometimes referred to as 'muggings') differ in type from those who raid commercial premises (Gill and Matthews, 1994). Street robberies have been the subject of a range of studies (Banton, 1985; Hermann, 1991; Hall, et al, 1981; Lejenuce, 1977; Poyner, 1980; Pratt, 1980; Wright and Decker, 1997), but these are not discussed here; this book is about robberies of commercial establishments, that is crimes against businesses. In fact, there have been a number of studies focusing on robberies of commercial premises (although not always exclusively) and in a number of countries including Australia (Challenger, 1988; Marsden, 1990; McRoberts, 1992), Canada (Canadian Bankers' Association/Montreal Urban Community, 1987; Gabor et al, 1987), Croatia (Dujomvic and Miksaj-Todorovic, 1994), Hong Kong (Vagg, 1996), Netherlands (van Koppen and Jansen, 1996a,b), Nigeria (Ekpenyoung, 1989), South Africa (Maree, 2000), United States of America (Conklin, 1972; Feeney, 1986; Macdonald, 1975), and the United Kingdom (Mclintock and Gibson, 1961; Morrison and O'Donnell, 1994, 1996a,b; Walsh, 1986). Moreover, robbery is an offence that is discussed in the context of organised crime (Birbeck, 1980) and gun crime (Broadhurst and Benyon, 2000; Harding and Blake, 1989).

Some of these studies have presented the offenders' perspective (see Feeney, 1986; Morrison and O'Donnell, 1994; Walsh, 1986) and offer an important insight into the mind and behaviour of robbers. However, there has been relatively little emphasis on crime prevention. True, both Austin (1988) and Ekblom (1987) offered valuable insights into the prevention of robberies of building societies and post offices respectively, and a range of crime prevention ideas are discussed by a range of authors as will be pointed out in the following pages. The present study is different insofar as it uses robbers' experiences as a source of ideas on the theory and practice of situational crime prevention. It is based on the premise that to prevent an offence it is necessary to understand the behaviour pattern of the offenders; in particular their motives, their planning and their methods of carrying out the crime, their resources and not least their levels of rationality.

This chapter provides the background to the theories and the research which are presented in the remainder of the book. It begins with a review of work on the rational offender and situational prevention as they relate to broader ideas on crime prevention and security management. It then moves on to consider the methodological issues associated with studying offenders in prison. In fact the robbers were interviewed and the content of the interview and the characteristics of the sample are discussed prior to providing an outline of the structure of the book. First though, the theory of crime prevention, and in particular situational prevention, is discussed along with its relationship to security management.

CRIME PREVENTION AND THE SITUATIONAL APPROACH

The term 'crime prevention' is fraught with definitional problems (Crawford, 1998). A basic definition is that crime prevention aims to stop, reduce or contain crime. In reality the theory and practice of crime prevention are more complex. As Pease (1994: 660) has argued, '(a)ll theories of crime are also theories of crime prevention', and that adds up to a lot of theories. Or, as Gilling (1997: 3) notes:

> Different theories imply different modes of intervention, relying on different agents (such as criminal justice professionals, or the general public) and different techniques, applied at different stages in the genesis of crime, and at different sites.

Both 'crime' and 'prevention' attract a variety of interpretations (see Gill, 1996). Not surprisingly, there are many ways of classifying crime prevention. One that is prominently referred to is based on the work of Brantingham and Faust (1976). They developed their model from a public health paradigm and argued that crime could be tackled at three levels. 'Primary prevention' is directed at the conditions in society that generate crime and seeks to rectify them; 'secondary prevention' is directed at the early identification of individuals at risk of progressing into crime and intervening to reduce the risk; and 'tertiary prevention' is directed at the prevention of recidivism.

The classification has its critics (van Voorhis, 1986). As Labb (1992) notes, one of the principal problems is that many types of prevention overlap. This consideration and the laudable aim of wanting to evolve a system helpful to practitioners led Graham and Bennett (1995) to develop a different three-way classification: criminality prevention, situational crime prevention and community crime prevention. Their study does not appear to have attracted as much attention as it deserves, although their decision to exclude the criminal justice system (while including the police) limits its usefulness. Certainly, as far as robbery is concerned, the severity of sentencing is potentially a major factor in deterring some people from offending.

Partly to overcome the limits of previous attempts at classifying crime prevention, Ekblom (1996;1997) has been working to develop a holistic model which could provide the basis for a discipline of crime prevention. For Ekblom (1994: 194), crime prevention is 'intervention in mechanisms that cause criminal events'. Some causes are defined as 'distal', such as events in an offender's childhood, others as 'proximal', that is those that influence the offender at the point of committing the offence. Ekblom's work is extremely helpful in bringing together the various models focusing separately on the offender and on the criminal event. Identifying the type of mechanism that is most appropriate for elucidating the cause of an event is the key to Ekblom's ideas. His model is thus useful as a means of thinking about evaluation and as a way of diagnosing crime problems. The real weakness is the lack of research on the issues he identifies.

As far as this study is concerned a classification which identifies the various stages of the offence and specifically includes the situation is the most helpful. In his critique of shifts in British crime prevention strategies, Bright (1991: 62) identifies three principal perspectives in the debate about crime prevention:

> a belief in the preventative effect of law enforcement and the criminal justice agencies; situational crime prevention in which

opportunities for committing crime are reduced by modifying the design or management of the situation in which crime is known to occur; and social crime prevention, which aims to prevent people drifting into crime by improving social conditions, strengthening community institutions and enhancing recreational, educational and employment opportunities.

One of the main inspirations for crime prevention work focusing on the criminal event was the belief that schemes aiming to impact on motivation and the causes of crime have failed (see, Martinson, 1974). In fact, these criticisms were certainly overstated (see, Currie, 1985) and were in part a product of vague objectives (Bright, 1991). But the British Home Office were in search of alternatives and found inspiration in a strange but important source. In the 1960s British houses were converted to natural gas, which was much safer than its predecessor (which contained dangerous levels of carbon dioxide), and an option for those wanting to commit suicide at home was removed. The number of suicides decreased. Since removing an opportunity for suicide had reduced its occurrence, could the same be true for crime? In other words, could the situation be manipulated in such a way as to reduce the likelihood of an offence taking place? The advantage of switching away from the offender to the event as the primary point of focus was that it lent itself to practical crime prevention measures. While it is a complex matter to seek to change the behaviour of an offender, there are a whole range of measures that can be implemented to change the situation the offender faces. Moreover, such measures may be easy to implement and cheap and one can be seen to be doing something practical about the crime problem.

Over the years a number of theories have emerged which focus on the criminal event. These include lifestyle theory, where the risks of people's victimisation are linked to the type of lifestyle they adopt (see, Garofalo, 1987; Hindeleng et al, 1978). Thus changes in lifestyle, such as the route people take to work or their means of travel or their leisure activities, can affect the risk of victimisation. This approach is closely related to routine activities theory, which has had a prime but not exclusive focus on predatory crime (see Felson 1986;1998). This theory suggests that at least three elements need to converge in space and time for an offence to be carried out. They are a likely offender, a suitable target and the absence of a capable guardian. However, the potential of an 'intimate handler' who can exercise a check on offenders' behaviour (Felson, 1986) and the notion of 'crime facilitators', which is borrowed from the situational approach (see, Clarke, 1992) and includes such things as weapons and getaway cars which render a crime possible, provide ideas for the future development of the theory. The overlap between lifestyle and routine activities theories is considerable, which has led one commentator to suggest that ultimately they will merge (Pease, 1994). Others see potential for them both to merge with situational crime prevention (see, Clarke, 1995), while Garland (1996) considers them 'the new criminologies of everyday life'. Meanwhile, Ekblom (1996, 1997) has attempted to integrate them all. Situational crime prevention has certainly developed through these theories.

Situational crime prevention derives its intellectual framework from the rational choice perspective. As Clarke and Felson (1993) note it is more accurate to consider it a 'perspective' than a 'theory' because it is essentially a way of organising an array of ideas and perspectives from which theories can develop. The perspective incorporates both the offender's decision to become involved[4] and the choice of target and the method of committing the act. In brief it posits that an offence is committed because offenders make a decision at the scene of the crime and that this decision, to a lesser or greater extent, is based on a consideration of the relative advantages and disadvantages of the act. Thus, the potential offender will make a 'rational' decision and if he or she believes the crime will be successful then it will be carried out; if not he or she will not press ahead. Clearly, if the offender is pre-determined to commit a crime then he or she will not be put off from committing it in any but extreme circumstances.[5] While the rational offender may decide not to tackle a relatively secure target and turn elsewhere, finding a new target will take time and effort and involve further exposure to risk. So not all offences that are deterred are displaced.

The issue of displacement has attracted considerable attention within the criminological literature. In fact concern about displacement is not a reason to reject situational crime prevention, not least because displacement often does not take place (see Laycock, 1985 and for review Clarke, 1995). And even where it does it can be benign — for example, if the displacement is to a less serious offence or enables it to be confined to certain areas (see, Barr and Pease, 1990). It is generally seen as malign where the crime merely shifts to another (more vulnerable) target. Yet, I have heard many comments at meetings over the years by security managers arguing that their main job is to protect their organisation. Some have taken this a stage further to argue that if the effect is that their rivals are attacked instead, then all the better. Jacques (1994) reported that one company refused to take part in his study of ram-raiding because it did not want to give rivals a competitive edge.

While there are a range of examples of effective situational measures (see, Clarke, 1997; Welsh and Farrington, 1999), more research is needed on what works. As Clarke readily acknowledges, many of the studies he uses to support claims that situational measures are effective are based on a flawed methodology, and 'the successes claimed in any individual study may be open to question' (Clarke, 1995; 110). Moreover, he recognises that successes are sometimes limited, often because of displacement effects or because the measures themselves are faulty or inappropriate. Indeed, crime prevention initiatives can have negative consequences (Grabosky, 1997) and research has found that some measures work in the interests of offenders. Wiersma (1996) reported that signs of a safe in some businesses attracted burglars because it indicated that there was something worth stealing. Wojcik et al (1997) reported that in Poland ground floor accommodation with window security bars provided a ready-made ladder for burglars wanting to reach second and third floor flats. The danger of not researching security measures adequately is clear. Also, while there is a growing body of evidence which supports the claim that offenders are to a lesser or greater degree rational, the evidence is conflicting (for example, see Bennett and Wright, 1984; Clarke, 1992, Cornish and Clarke, 1986; Ferreira, 1995; Wright and Decker, 1997). Elsewhere, Trasler (1986, 1993) has argued that situational prevention is less applicable to the prevention of expressive crimes. And there is need for more work on its application to a wider range of offences.

The perceived focus of situational crime prevention on locks and bolts is associated with the least attractive aspects of crime prevention fuelled by a concern that homes and businesses are being turned into fortresses and thereby destroying community frameworks (Crawford, 1998). Some point to the class bias of the approach. For example,

Heal and Laycock (1986) note that those most likely to benefit from crime prevention measures are the more affluent and they highlight the need for this to be balanced by provision for those unable to afford such measures. Further criticisms of the situational approach focus on its failure to tackle the root causes of crime and see it as offering, at best, a partial answer to the problem (see, Garland, 1996; Hughes 1998).

The situational approach is continuously undergoing revision. Clarke and Homel (1997; see also Clarke, 1997) have recently enhanced their classification of situational techniques by adding a new objective of 'removing excuses'. This is a response to the realisation that many offences take place because opportunities present themselves in everyday (working) life (see also Gill, 2000). The response argues that there is a need to remove the justification for people to make excuses for their behaviour and incorporates a range of techniques. For Clarke, there are sixteen techniques of situational crime prevention which he divides into four sets of objectives shown in Table 1.1. These are measures which increase the effort needed to commit the crime; measures which increase the risk of the offender being caught; measures which reduce the reward in the goods obtained; and measures which deny the offender the justification for blaming others by inducing shame and guilt and remove the chance for them to make excuses.

Table 1.1   Clarke's 16 Techniques of Situational Prevention

Increasing Perceived Effort	Increasing Perceived Risks	Reducing Anticipated Rewards	Removing Excuses
1. Target Hardening	5. Entry/Exit Screening	9. Target Removal	13. Rule Setting
2. Access Control	6. Formal Surveillance	10. Identifying Property	14. Strengthening Moral Condemnation
3. Deflecting Offenders	7. Surveillance by Employees	11. Reducing Temptation	15. Controlling Disinhibitors
4. Controlling Facilitators	8. Natural surveillance	12. Denying Benefits	16. Facilitating Compliance

Perhaps surprisingly, there has been little attempt to apply these techniques to the world of security. Yet most form part of standard security procedures. Indeed, a classification of the techniques of security management or crime risk management could be based on that of situational crime prevention as devised by Clarke. The central themes, of the need to increase the effort and risk for offenders and to reduce the reward and to deny offenders resources, as well as to remove excuses, are all parts of what most good security managers and crime risk managers do. The more one can understand the perception and decision-making patterns of offenders the more chance there is that appropriate measures can be applied.

SECURITY MANAGEMENT AND CRIME RISK MANAGEMENT

'Crime risk management' is easier to define than either crime prevention or security management. It carries much less intellectual baggage, and bridges the gap between criminology and security management. Crime prevention is not the same as security management; while security management will always incorporate crime prevention the reverse is not the case (see, Gill, 1998; Manunta, 1998). Indeed, the very word 'security' causes confusion (Cahalane, 1998; Manunta, 1999; Post and Kingsbury, 1991, see also Manunta, 2000). Security managers' roles vary and frequently include responsibility for both security and safety issues.[6] On a conceptual level, Manunta (1997) has sought to differentiate between security and safety; and he deploys a very helpful but quite complex argument to show that a state of security exists where there is an intended threat, and that safety refers to protection against unintended threats, this is somewhat at variance with the use of the term 'community safety'. In any event the techniques used to respond may be the same. Nalla and Newman (1990: 84) argue that much of the difference between what is defined as criminal and what is viewed as an accident will depend on the state of mind of the person involved, but they 'may have similar situational circumstances' and therefore similar techniques are needed to respond.

The subject area of security management may include the study of accidents, hazards, risk, disasters and much more, as well as management and criminology.[7] The subject is concerned with the protection of assets from threats; hence the overlap with criminology when the threat is crime. The two subjects share an interest in 'crime risk management': a process of identifying the threat of crime, understanding and interpreting that threat, and then managing the response and ensuring the responses are adequate and maintained over time by appropriate monitoring and evaluation.[8] In short, crime risk management has been used to define the aspects of security management that deal with crime and where appropriate the terms have been used interchangeably in this book (see, Gill, 1998).[9]

There are a number of advantages in interpreting the situational classification in the context of 'crime risk management' or 'security management' rather than 'crime prevention'. Earlier it was noted that situational prevention has been criticised because it does not tackle the root causes of crime. This is true. But for security managers, charged with the responsibility of protecting company assets, tackling the root causes of crime is neither practical nor within their remit (and this will apply to many others too). This is not to suggest that this is not important. What follows will show that tackling robbery will require attention to social policy; some robbers live a life of drink, drugs, unhappy relationships and crime and return to it after periods in prison. Social crime prevention is crucial and better ways need to be found of tackling social problems. There is a need to persuade the commercial sector that it has a vested interest in contributing to research geared to understanding the causes of and potential remedies for a range of social issues. Traditionally the commercial sector has been slow to offer financial support to such initiatives, which it sees as a government responsibility (Bright, 1991), but this attitude is long out of date.

The point is that, at present at least, security managers do not spend much time tackling social problems in the course of their normal duty. This is not a negative point (although it ignores the causes of crime), it is a positive one (in that it provides a framework for people to do their job of preventing victimisation better); it is not a case of choosing one crime prevention approach at the expense of the other because security managers rarely have the choice. The lack of a recognised framework of techniques has limited the extent to which security practitioners can interpret and understand what they do. The security world has a crucial role to play in protecting people; it is precisely because the security world is accountable to those who pay, rather than society generally, that it merits attention. The big companies can afford more effective security and if the consequence is to displace offenders on to less protected targets then it is important to trace this development and provide a response. Businesses contain people and their victimisation is important; and given the legal requirements governing the care of those at work, the need for a security strategy should become a more prominent part of criminological enquiry.

In the UK the security industry has a low status. This is partly to do with the lack of statutory regulation (George and Button, 1994). Indeed, one can be forgiven for believing that the most important credential for a senior appointment as a security manager is a pension from the police or military. Despite aspirations for the world of security to be a 'profession' (Simonsen, 1996), it clearly lacks the credentials (Manunta, 1996). Garland (1996) has argued that crime control has shifted away from state agencies to those 'poorly equipped' for the task, and private security may be cited as an example. Because the practice of security has not been theoretically elaborated, many of the claims it makes, such as the success of closed circuit television in reducing crime (see Horne, 1996), are disputed (see Beck and Willis, 1995; Ditton and Short, 1998;1999; Gill and Turbin, 1998;1999; Norris et al, 1998; Painter and Tilley, 1999; Short and Ditton, 1995).

The study of security management/administration and crime risk management is becoming more common at the advanced level; security-related research is becoming more identifiable (e.g., Beck and Willis, 1995; Felson and Clarke, 1997; George and Button, 2000; Gill, 1994;1998; Jones and Newburn; 1998), and two scholarly journals exist in this subject area.[10] Yet it is badly in need of a theoretical framework which will enable it to become, and be seen as, more than a (small) part of criminology and to a lesser extent management (see Nalla and Newman, 1990). Not only is this needed to enhance the status of the subject as an academic discipline; it is also needed to guide practice which frequently lacks respect and credibility. Evaluating the extent to which the key elements of the situational approach are relevant to the practice of private security is one objective of this book.

THE RATIONAL OFFENDER AND THE
CRIMINAL JUSTICE PROCESS

Understanding the rationality of robbers is important for other reasons
than being able to help inform situational crime prevention. For the
rational offender situational measures are just one way in which
conditions can be manipulated to render an offence less desirable or
likely; the criminal justice process is another. And assessing offenders' views of the threat posed by the criminal justice process offers
another approach to understanding the ways in which offenders can
be considered rational.

The preventative and deterrent capacity of the various parts of the
criminal justice process will be addressed in more detail in Chapter 4.
The idea is that catching and prosecuting offenders will prevent crime.
This will act as a deterrent to some and rehabilitate others, bringing
about a change either by the threat or the reality of punishment. So
the argument goes, the rational offender will consider the consequences of his or her actions, the threat of punishment, and decide not
to proceed, or will stop after the punishment or help has been applied.

Recently, Ekblom (1997) helpfully clarified the preventative functions of the criminal justice process as: deterrence, influencing the
offender to believe that the threat of sanctions is real; frustrating
offenders' preparation by taking action against them or by influencing
the crime situation; intervention during the execution of crimes;
reaction in the form of arrest, cautioning, punishment, incapacitation
or rehabilitation; and reinforcing the moral order. Such a definition
provides a useful point of analysis for a book about offenders'
perspectives in that it affords the opportunity to ask offenders whether
they consider that the criminal justice process affected them in these
ways. Again, where the offender makes some sort of rational decision
there is potential for measures to have an impact on whether the
offence takes place. This is certainly an area where more research is
needed and this book aims to examine the rationality of robbers by
considering the issues which they say influenced them when they
considered committing their last offence.

The various perspectives on crime prevention all have their place.
As Labb (1992: 247) has observed, 'No single approach to crime
prevention has proven to be acceptable in all situations.' Indeed, a
search for a single cure is likely to be in vain; because crimes have

different causes and are committed in different situations they must be combated in different ways (Kühlhorn and Svensson, 1982). This is no less true with regards to situational crime prevention. As Clarke (1995; 121) notes:

> Much detailed thought has to be put into the design and implementation of measures. They have to be carefully tailored to the settings in which they are applied, with due regard to the motives and methods of the offenders involved, to the costs and acceptability of the solutions proposed, and to the possible unwanted consequences in terms of displacement or escalation.

Herein lies a problem for security in that it has tended to operate in a theoretical vacuum. In attempting to develop a framework with the situational approach as a basis, this book will consider robberies of commercial premises. In essence it aims to assess the rationality of commercial robbers, and to this end it will consider the motives of offenders and the specific issues affecting the decisions taken at key points in the process of preparing and committing a raid. Attitudes to the dangers posed by the different types of security measures and the criminal justice process will be covered. Thus it will consider offences from the offenders' perspective — an approach which is fraught with difficulties.

RESEARCH BASED ON OFFENDERS' PERSPECTIVES

Studying crime from the offenders' perspectives, while an under-used approach (Burrows, 1997), is not new. A number of studies have incorporated offenders' views on such diverse topics as fraud (Gill et al, 1994; Levi, 1981;1998), burglary (Bennett and Wright, 1984; Butler, 1994; Wiersma. 1996), and robbery (Gill and Matthews, 1994; Gabor et al, 1987; Morrison and O'Donnell, 1996). While Walsh (1986) has argued, quite understandably, that it is 'absurd' not to listen to what offenders have to say, asking offenders questions about why they offend and relying on what they say as being accurate is fraught with difficulties. There are good reasons why even when asked 'factual' questions offenders should not be completely candid. Polsky (1971) has summarised at least some of the relevant concerns. He identifies broadly four issues, two related specifically to offenders and two related to the general problem of interviews. In the first case he raises concerns about sample bias and the danger of a false (and perhaps forced) cooperativeness leading to corrupted data. Hirschi (1986) adds that care is needed to find supporting evidence for what is said in offender interviews. Second Polsky laments the limits of the interview method in providing data divorced from the context in which people experience their lives, and the difficulty of checking the validity of findings (see also Crawford, 1998; Wright and Decker, 1997). Polsky (1971: 123) has written:

> Data gathered from caught criminals, for reasons in addition to and quite different from sampling bias, are not only very partial but partially suspect. These are data that are much too heavily retro-spective; data from people who aren't really free to put you down; data often involving the kind of cooperativeness in which you get told what the criminal thinks you want to hear so you will get off his back or maybe do him some good with the judge or parole board; data from someone who is not behaving as he normally would in his normal life-situations; and, above all data that you cannot supplement with, or interpret in the light of, your own direct observation of the criminal's natural behaviour in his natural environment.

As Levi (1981) has argued, Polsky probably overstates the difficul-ties of prison interviews and certainly underestimates the ease of establishing the validity of alternative methods, as many a book on research methodology points out. As Levi notes, one advantage of the prison setting is that it does leave scope for 'serious soul searching' and this certainly adds validity to prisoners' accounts. Levi was able to limit concerns about the validity of his data because of sampling bias by double checking some accounts with other fraudsters (some of whom had knowledge of similar crimes) and others outside prison. Levi sought to overcome the false cooperativeness factor by assuring interviewees that as a student he was too poor to help them financially and had insufficient status to help them in the matter of parole. To encourage trust he affirmed at the outset that the interview was confidential, and he 'did not use tape recorders and wrote down the absolute minimum during the interview' (p. 329). Interestingly,

Bennett and Wright (1984) in their study of burglars took the opposite approach; they used a tape recorder for the whole interview to enable them to record information accurately. They felt that this was necessary given that they were discussing complex issues.

So in seeking to resolve the same problem of prison-based interviews — the difficulty of gaining valid data — Levi limited his note-taking while Bennett and Wright used a tape recorder. While Levi prioritised building trust with interviewees and saw notes, etc., as an impediment to that objective, Bennett and Wright were concerned about missing information about complex issues and so used a tape recorder. Bennett and Wright believed they had been at least partly successful, in that burglars often admitted offences for which they had not been convicted.

There is no way of ensuring a representative sample because there is no way of identifying the population represented. Robbers are not always caught (there is no way of knowing how many have carried out just one robbery and stopped, although from the available research it seems that this applies to only a few); they are not always convicted even if they are caught; and even those convicted will not always be convicted of all the robberies they have carried out. Moreover, since not all robbers who are caught and convicted will be sent to prison (although this is rare), a study based on prison interviews is further biased.

What is important is that interviews can identify issues, and it may be instructive sometimes to note the numbers answering in a particular way. This may identify trends which can be supported or explained by other evidence or explored in future studies; and there are ways of limiting the criticisms, for example, by conducting interviews with a diverse group of robbers in a range of categories of prison. The purpose of the present project was to better understand the issues which are seen by robbers as relevant to the planning and carrying out of their robberies. The more interviews that are conducted the more likely it is that issues will be identified. And, following the same logic, the more prisons one visits, the more likely it is that one will uncover different types of robbers. In reality of course, all types of robbers in all prisons could refuse to an interview (and as noted earlier some robbers may not be sent to prison). But what is a reasonable number of interviews?

In this study 341 robbers were interviewed in 18 prisons (mostly Category B and dispersal prisons). In two prisons it was possible to cross check details of those interviewed with information about the robbers in that prison.[11] There was a slight under-representation of robbers serving longer sentences in the interview sample compared with the numbers of robbers in the prison as a whole. Perhaps more than anything, this confirms the wisdom of concern about sample bias and supports the idea of concentrating on issues. Throughout what follows, where statistics are given this should be borne in mind. The statistics may be interesting, or even be indicative, but there is no way of ensuring that they are typical of all robbers.

It is perhaps worth noting how the robbers to be interviewed were selected. At the time of the study inmates were sometimes classified by the most serious conviction for which they were currently serving. So if they were convicted of robbery and kidnapping then the robbery conviction would be less apparent. Moreover, prisoners' files were bulky documents and it was surprisingly hard to identify previous convictions. Had this been the aim it would have been a very time-consuming process. Moreover, as noted earlier, robbery is an offence which includes what is commonly referred to as 'mugging' or street robbery as well as robbery of commercial premises. There was thus often no way of telling whether a person would fit the criteria for interview just by reviewing the database and files. Some robbers were accordingly overlooked at this stage and there is no way of knowing how many.

A letter was sent to all inmates who were recorded as having a conviction for robbery explaining the purpose and focus of the project. If they had committed a robbery of commercial premises and were prepared to be interviewed they were invited to contact a nominated individual in the prison. This approach certainly put some people off. Inmates were often suspicious of outsiders by nature. It has to be said that the response rate also reflected the level of support given by prison staff. Some prison officers distributed the letters and advised inmates not to co-operate with 'those university people'. In other prisons the member of staff who was the appointed liaison approached robbers individually to explain the role of the project and this induced more to co-operate. The fact that in some prisons response rates were very low was not simply because there were more street robbers in those prisons.

Some of those who initially agreed to be interviewed moved to another prison or were released before an interview could be arranged;

but once researchers arrived at a prison and word got around a few more came forward. Interviews generally took place in the prison, in an empty office, cell or waiting room, and were invariably conducted on a one-to-one basis. Interviewees were advised that they did not need to mention exact dates or the names of any individuals, that if they did not want to answer a question they could just say so and the interviewer would move on to the next question, and that they could leave at any point. Fortunately no-one did withdraw. Indeed, despite the advice many did mention names and provided other information they did not want disclosed. At the outset interviewees were reminded that the interview was to be conducted in complete confidence and that their names would not be recorded. In fact in a few cases their names were not known to the research team. They had agreed to be interviewed and prison staff just sent in the next one from the list they held. The problems here were that lists were sometimes lost or not administered properly; staff finished shifts having failed to record who had been interviewed and the research team had no way of knowing!

The interviews usually lasted over an hour but often a lot more and rarely less. Interviews were semi-structured to ensure that key points were covered and that there was ample opportunity for discussion of complex issues and any interesting points that emerged. The research team carried a tape recorder to interviews, but rather than recording everything and collecting an immense amount of data on tapes which take a long time to transcribe and analyse, the recorder was only used in the interview where the robber made particularly interesting points. If something particularly complex or interesting emerged, the inmate was asked to repeat it on tape. This rendered the data more manageable. In addition, a whole day was spent with seven robbers who offered particularly thoughtful insights and four of these are discussed in more detail in Chapter 5.

Several methods were employed to ensure the accuracy of the data collected and to reduce the opportunity and need for offenders to lie. The stress on confidentiality and the fact that there was no need to record names was one aspect to this. The point of this is to say to the robber, 'there is no need to lie, it's all in confidence and if you are unhappy with a question just say so and we will move on'. As will be shown, quite a few robbers were reluctant to answer some questions, especially the more organised cash-in-transit robbers, but better they refuse to answer than lie.

On a number of occasions it was possible to speak to robbers who had been on the same robbery and to cross check their accounts; the findings were encouraging in that for the most part differences related only to small details. Moreover, the interviews were not short and enabled interviewers to ask detailed questions from a number of angles; so it was not easy to lie continuously. No doubt it did happen, but the cross checks were encouraging. It is suggested that the data collected represents, fairly well, the views and experiences of those robbers who were interviewed; and these included robbers from a wide variety of backgrounds who adopted a variety of robbery styles against different types of targets over many years. There may well be gaps; the reader will need to decide for himself or herself how large these are, and whether they are acceptable. At the very least this book offers an insight into the ways of the robber.

THE SAMPLE

Of the 341 interviews carried out, 340 were with men. Over half the interviewees were in their twenties, and a quarter in their thirties. Just under a fifth were married; the majority were single and slightly more than half had children. About a sixth had served in the armed forces and approaching one third said that they had been in care. Over half the sample claimed to have some educational qualifications. Mostly these were gained at school but some were vocational qualifications, including those gained in prison. Over half of those who gave details on the total length of time they had spent in prison claimed they had served more than 5 years, although less than 1 in 10 had served more than 5 years of their current sentence.[12]

Many started offending when young. Nearly a sixth had received their first conviction by the age of 12 and nearly one-third were convicted for the first time between the ages of 12 and 15. Approaching three-quarters had received their first conviction by the age of 18. Just over half of all respondents said they had been convicted of assault, slightly more of car crime, and more than six in ten of burglary (see also, Kapardis, 1988). Many fewer, about one in eight, said they had been convicted of street robbery. Robbery was commonly an offence committed at some time in their criminal career but few were exclusively robbers (see Gunn and Gristwood, 1976). About a third were aged 18 or under when they first committed a robbery and another third were aged between 19 and 24; slightly fewer were older than this. Despite this, about a fifth were 18 or under when they were first convicted for robbery and approaching 4 in 10 said they were over 24 when they received their first conviction. This data, confirmed by the interviews, suggests that offenders progress to robbery which is frequently an offence committed by older offenders. Most carry out more than one robbery before they are caught.

The main part of the interview focused on the offence itself. The interview schedule was divided into five sections each containing a set of questions which were similar in purpose but focused on a different type of target. These targets were banks, building societies, post offices, cash-in-transit vans, and other commercial premises.[13] In each section robbers were asked specific questions about their last robbery of this type of target and more general questions about any other robberies of this type of target. Because of time constraints and because it would have made the interview repetitive each robber was only questioned about a maximum of two target types. Since a large part of the funding for the project was provided by banks and building societies, robbers who had raided these premises were always asked about these robberies.[14] If they had robbed a bank, a post office and a cash-in-transit van, they would be interviewed about the bank robbery and the other most recent raid.[15]

As the following table shows, most robbers admitted they had committed more robberies than they had been convicted of. Even allowing for the inevitable reluctance of some to admit to robberies for which they had not been convicted, it is striking to find that so many had, at some point in their career, robbed other types of target.

Table 1.2. Percentage of respondents convicted of robbing a specific target who had also robbed another type of target

	Banks	BS	PO	CIT	CP
Bank	–	43.3	39.0	35.1	32.9
BS	32.0	–	29.8	20.4	32.9
PO	32.3	33.0	–	27.7	47.3
CIT	42.9	19.4	40.6	–	42.2
CP	13.8	19.4	24.2	14.8	–

(For example, of those respondents who had been involved in a bank robbery, 43.3% had also been involved in a building society robbery.)

This table suggests that those respondents who said they had been involved in cash-in-transit robberies were most likely to have been involved in robberies of other types of target. Those respondents who said they had been involved in robberies of commercial premises appeared the least likely to be involved in other robberies. As will be shown they tended to be more amateurish; they did less planning and preparation and made less gain than the more professional robbers who tackled the more difficult targets.

These issues are discussed more fully below with the help of a number of variables which are helpful in distingushing between the 'amateur' and 'professional'. These include the level of planning, reflected in questions about visiting the target beforehand, the wearing of a disguise and special clothes, the monitoring of the police at some point in preparing or carrying out criminal activities and the extent to which they had taken account of the existence of police Rapid Response Units in their planning, whether a gun was carried, and the level of reward. However, there are problems in using these 'ideal types' of amateur and professional for crime prevention purposes (and there are problems in using other typologies too). So while they will be used to differentiate between robbers, suggestions will be made in the final chapter as to how a more helpful typology might evolve.

The final part of the interview (covering the whole sample) included a range of questions about the police, courts and prison, about motivations and attitudes to victims.

STRUCTURE OF THE BOOK

This book presents offenders' perspectives on robbery of commercial premises with the aim of using the data derived from interviews to develop the theory and practice of (situational) crime prevention, or what has been termed 'crime risk management'. The next four chapters discuss the data derived from the interviews. The literature has been referred to only in as far as it is necessary to support the points made. It is the robbers who are quoted at length. The theoretical work is saved until the end.

In Chapter 2 the ways robbers prepare for a robbery are considered together with their motives for carrying out the offence, the type and levels of planning they undertake, and the type of factors the interviewees took into consideration when choosing their last target. In Chapter 3 the ways robbers conduct a raid are considered and in particular the type of issues they need to take into consideration, their thoughts at the time and their use of weapons. Chapter 4 reviews robbers' perspectives on the criminal justice process, in particular the police, sentencing and prisons, and the extent to which the threat of the police and the experience of imprisonment acted as a deterrent. In Chapter 5 four case studies, each based on one robber's account of his offending are presented. While this chapter moves away from the orientation towards crime prevention, it will provide an insight into the offence of robbery and the careers of those involved and discuss how they acquired the motives and resources (including neutralisation techniques) and applied them to robbery situations; this will provide the basis on which good preventative strategies need to be based.

Chapter 6 attempts to draw the data together. It looks more closely at the rationality of offenders. It takes a critical look at the situational approach and posits a reconstructed situational classification taking account of broader issues in what is termed the *Crime Risk Management Process.*

[NOTES]

[1] In England and Wales the offence of robbery is now defined by section 8 of the Theft Act 1968 as follows: 'A person is guilty of robbery if he steals, and immediately before or at the time of doing so, and in order to do so, he uses force on any person or puts or seeks to put any person in fear of being then and there subjected to force.' Although it is common to speak of 'armed robbery', this is not a legal classification; it includes offences relating to possession of a weapon and robbery. In the text 'armed robbery' refers to a raid where a weapon (including an imitation) was carried.

[2] It was about this time that financial institutions agreed to sponsor the project discussed in this book, and the Home Office a parallel study (see, Morrison and O'Donnell, 1994).

[3] The research on which this book is based began in 1992.

[4] Professor Ron Clarke, who has done much to spearhead the situational approach advocates using the term 'motivations' to refer to the reasons for committing crime, and 'motives' to refer to the reasons leading up to a specific offence. That the approach ignores 'motivations' has led to widespread criticism of it as will be shown.

[5] It is possible to imagine, in theory at least, premises that were totally secure and impenetrable (for example, Fort Knox).

[6] Some managers responsible for security do not include that word in the title. For various reasons 'security' is sometimes viewed as having a negative image, and sometimes as being an inappropriate description of the role which may include other duties ranging from personnel work, facilities management and audit. Some are called 'loss prevention' managers emphasising their key function to the organisation. Whether these terms just reflect current trends, or are an indication of where security management will go in the future remains to be seen.

[7] The subject matter of security, and an attempt to define its boundaries is a central concern of an international working party to evaluate the 'Body of Knowledge' for security management. This has been initiated by the American Society for Industrial Security. It is anticipated that the findings will be published in the *Security Journal*.

[8] Some consultants now describe their area of interest and expertise as 'crime risk management', and until recently the Scarman Centre at Leicester University offered a distance-learning course in this subject, the MSc in Security and Crime Risk Management.

[9] Similarly, 'situational measures' and 'security measures' are used interchangeably throughout the text.

[10] The *Security Journal* (which has recently merged with and absorbed the *International Journal of Risk, Security and Crime Prevention*) and the *Journal of Security Administration*. Another publication, *Crime Prevention and Community Safety: an International Journal*, also includes relevant papers.

[11] This was done by analysing prison files; a time consuming process since they were often bulky documents and not kept in good order.

[12] This will be explained in part by the type of prisons which were selected for interviews.

[13] A range of premises were included here including shops such as convenience stores, off-licences and garages. Mostly, these represented easier targets than the other types specifically questioned about.

[14] This is another reason why the sample is not representative and the data is biased towards those who have robbed banks and building societies.

[15] Of course, some robbers would only talk about robberies for which they had been convicted. It had been the intention to focus on the most recent robbery in order to collect the most up-to-date information about the offence. Certainly, many robbers spoke about their last robbery even if they were not caught. But some will have only discussed those for which they had a conviction.

Chapter 2
Getting Started: Preparing for Robbery

Understanding why people commit an offence is fraught with difficulties. They may not know or there may be a combination of reasons which they are uncertain about or unable to articulate. Or offenders may be embarrassed or lie when asked. But an understanding of motivations is important as a basis for thinking about crime prevention. It has long been recognised that committing an offence involves a variety of decisions including an initial commitment to carry out a crime, a decision about which target and a decision about method. Sometimes these decisions merge, and sometimes they are made separately and actions are only undertaken after careful deliberation, as shown by Bennett and Wright (1984) in their study of male domestic burglars. Understanding the way an offence is committed and the influences on decisions made at various points in the process is important in terms of evaluating the potential effect of situational measures. The potential benefits of situational crime prevention are based (amongst other things) on the premise that the decision to commit the offence is determined by something in the situation and that offenders make a free or rational choice.

The emphasis of this study was on the type of issues that influenced robbers' decision-making at the scene. This includes the factors that they took into account when deciding to commit a robbery and how they prepared or planned their last raid, how they chose the target, taking into account its design and location, and the type of security measures that were present. However, the chapter begins with a review of robbers' accounts of what initially influenced their decision to offend. They were asked to state whether any of a list of 'reasons' explained why they committed their last robbery: all respondents cited at least one reason.[1] This insight into motivations tends to show that decisions about committing robbery are often made away from the scene and that, while situational measures cannot influence this initial decision in most cases, they have a greater impact at the preparation and carrying out stages (chapter 3).

WHAT INITIALLY MOTIVATED ROBBERS?

Questions to robbers about why they committed an offence produce a consistent, but not very remarkable, finding that the main motivation for robbery is money (see Kapardis, 1988). For example, Walsh (1986) found that 81 percent of those he interviewed considered that obtaining money was their principal motive. In fact the materialistic motivation was evident in most answers (this includes robbing to finance drug addiction or drinking). The money obtained was in most cases used for personal non-essential consumption, rather than basic or 'life' needs; and the rewards were not always high. Feeney (1986) quotes a number of robbers who simply did not know why they had robbed, but who refused to cite the need for money.[2] On this evidence it appears that while some robbers have clear ideas about why they committed an offence this is not always the case. What is needed is further elucidation of this aspect, in particular linking motivation with other issues.

To this end respondents were asked to state whether any of a range of factors had been influential in their decision to commit their last offence. Their replies are shown in Table 2.1. They were told they could mention as many as they believed appropriate. In addition, other questions were included to elicit additional information on this issue, such as the influence of the media. During the interview no attempt was made to distinguish 'causes' from 'triggers', although evidence emerged in the comments that interviewees made. And it was possible to identify links between the various motivational factors.

Table 2.1.   Robbers' reasons for committing their last robbery

Response	Yes		No/No Reply		Total	
	No.	%	No.	%	No.	%
Money	274	80.4	67	19.6	341	100.0
Unemployment	140	41.1	201	58.9	341	100.0
Excitement	121	35.5	220	64.5	341	100.0
Drugs	98	28.7	243	71.2	341	100.0
Friends	81	23.8	260	76.2	341	100.0
Alcohol	64	18.8	277	81.2	341	100.0
Power	43	12.6	298	87.4	341	100.0
Family	21	6.2	320	93.8	341	100.0
Revenge	21	6.2	320	93.8	341	100.0

The table indicates that the findings tend to mirror those of previous research in that the vast majority (80.4%) of the sample said that they committed their last robbery for financial reasons. There was a strong link between the need for money and claims that unemployment was a reason for the last robbery ($x^2 = 23.4$ p<0.01), although not all of those who were unemployed considered this to be relevant and not all unemployed people linked their offence to the need for money.[3] Elsewhere in the interview, in the context of detailed questions about the last robbery, respondents were asked to explain how they had spent any money they had obtained. There were four (overlapping) types of response here: robbers claimed that they spent money feeding an addiction (in particular drugs but also alcohol and gambling), on everyday expenses, on providing for their future, and, most common-ly, that the proceeds were spent on living the 'high life'. This was sometimes linked to spending on recreational drug use:

'I don't know where I spent it . . . In the fast lane somewhere.'

'Champagne, women and clubbing.'

'A different car and a few parties. And I done a bit of coke and cannabis.'

'I blew it on drugs and going out.'

'Clothes, a music centre, drugs, and a fucking good time.'

'I went to Holland and Denmark and spent it on drugs and women.'

'Two thousand pounds would last me a couple of days, 'cos after feeding the family, buying clothes, shopping, take the missus out, going out raving and all that partying, that would be about it.'

Many who spent their robbery earnings in this way had not initially intended to do so. Some had originally been motivated by a 'need' for money to meet expenses, for example, to pay off debts, but changed their mind after the robbery had taken place. Many respondents seemed to feel that frittering away the money was acceptable because it was not really theirs anyway. Others viewed their gain as a reward to be spent on pleasures rather than necessities; some had been so stressed by the experience that they felt they deserved a spending spree:

'The idea was to pay off my debts, but once I got the money I thought if I pay off the debts they might get suspicious. So I paid some debts but the rest of the money burned a hole in my pocket.'

'I planned on using the money originally as just recovering money that my father gave me that I'd spent. I'd convinced myself that banks were robbers anyway, you know? But that was just something to make myself feel a little bit better. It never worked out like that, just blowing it on my drinking habits, cannabis habits and just going out quickly and getting rid of the money as quickly as possible because I felt so bad about it.'

Second, robbers claimed that they spent the money on everyday living expenses:

'I regard robbing as a steady job; a wage. If I stole £3,000 today, even to me, even though I've gone through a few quid, that is a lot of money. So what I'd do is I'd break it up into multiples of £250, and at the end of each week allow myself £250, with whatever else I earned that week. I just want a decent living now. I don't want to have to wait 10 years to have coving up and the ceiling artexed. I don't want to wait 2 years for a tumble drier and a washing machine.'

'Normal living: clothes for the kids, nights out. It's the same as you except you'll save for three or four months to buy a suite for the house, I won't.'

'I used it to pay household bills.'

'Just everyday living expenses.'

Third, some of these respondents used the money to safeguard their future, or to fund legitimate projects. One interviewee told how he robbed a bank with a relative to provide enough money to start a business. The robbery was successful and within six months his business had begun to flourish. He had no intention nor need to return to crime but his relative was caught and 'grassed' him up. His business closed because he was sent to prison but he felt that the experience had taught him that he could survive and he was determined to start again with legitimate funds when he finished his sentence. There were other examples:

'I invested it; bought some property in the Isle of Man.'

'I saved most of the money.'

'It was basically just so that I could get a couple of thousand pounds so that I could buy two transit trucks and go out and do a bit of scrap dealing.'

'I was doing mobile discos, like advertised in the papers, for ordinary parties. The money got spent on that, and wasted in my opinion, looking back now. But I was very committed in what I was doing, trying to build it up.'

It is significant that over a third of the sample claimed that they were motivated by excitement. While it is has long been recognised that crime can be exciting (see West and Farrington, 1977), the strength of the link here is interesting, albeit that it was of secondary importance. Many regarded the 'buzz' they felt when committing robbery as merely a welcome bonus:

'Money to live, but I also got a buzz out of it. You don't do it for the excitement but the buzz is there.'

'First of all, the money. After a while, the buzz, the excitement, massive surge of adrenaline. It's so good, this excitement.'

Excitement was generally mentioned by the more professional robbers, the ones who plan more and obtain bigger rewards, although some amateurs claimed that robbery could be exciting; often alcohol played a part here. Some respondents suggested that the excitement they felt when committing robberies was addictive:

'I'm sure it's like being addicted to drugs. It's a funny old buzz. It's like being addicted to adrenaline. It's a wonderful feeling, it really is, and then once you've carried the thing out and you leave, within 10 or 15 minutes it's gone. It's gone completely, and you're looking for the next one. It doesn't matter that you have money, you're off and you're thinking what about that one? What about that one?'

'I liked robbery. Not just robbery but crime. Fuck me, it's hard to draw away from like a fag.'

'I was addicted to the excitement and power.'

Many of the respondents who cited power (and there was a strong link here with those citing excitement[4]) as a reason for committing their last robbery said that they particularly enjoyed the feeling of being in complete control of the situation, with power of life or death over their victims:

'When you do coke you get a rush out of it, but when you got a gun in your hands, people are listening to you, they're doing as they're told, you're in full control. It's just brilliant, you're just there, you are the man, you're like God. I think they know if they don't listen then they could be shot, they could be killed, they know you are the one that's going to control the moment.'

'I do enjoy it sometimes seeing someone back down when there's a gun sticking in his face, it does make you feel good.'

There has been considerable debate about the link between drugs and crime.[5] Therefore it was instructive to find that while over half (56.9%) of all respondents said that they were taking illegal drugs during their last period of offending, fewer than three-tenths (28.7%) of the sample said that drugs were relevant to their last robbery. While over one-third (34.3%) of respondents admitted to drinking heavily during their last period of offending less than one-fifth (18.8%) said that alcohol was a relevant factor in their most recent robbery. Those who cited drugs as a reason for the robbery appeared the more desperate. Some robbers added that they never took drugs while on a raid in case it impaired their judgement. Those who admitted that drugs were a factor in their decision to commit the last robbery shared many characteristics with those who said that alcohol was relevant; they tended to be the more amateurish robbers. For many money was needed to fuel their addiction:

'Cocaine was costing me £60 a gram, and I was buying up three or four grams a night. I hit a building society on a Monday afternoon, depending on how much I'd got, I'd buy say 3 grams on the Monday. I knew somewhere to get a hit on the Thursday, I'd buy another few grams on the Thursday, and so on and so forth. It was just getting out of order, I felt myself losing all control of myself, with the cocaine.'

'There are all sorts of ways [to finance a crack habit]. From what I've learnt in prison the way people supply their crack habit is through burglary, street robberies and the sort of crime which I've committed which is armed robbery.'

'It's our choice, it's my choice to go on it, take it, no-one's forcing me. But once you're on it, I don't think the courts realise the power of the stuff. It's just like, you know, you inhale it and you get a high, and then it's gone. That's how quick it is. And you need it. I mean, I don't think the courts really register drug abuse as a valid reason for crime.'

'It wasn't money I needed specifically for cocaine, it was the fact that up to that time, the time of the robbery, I'd got myself in a great deal of debt, plus I looked like losing my business 'cos I'd been using too much money, hard earned money, on cocaine. So I saw it as a means to an end, just to pay off the immediate things and get myself back on my feet. You just kid yourself. It's psychological, because you know if you go and nick twenty-five grand, it was £23,000 that we got from Birmingham, you know yourself in your heart that a good amount of that's going to go on cocaine anyway. It's just supplementing your need.'

Some respondents said they used the proceeds from their robberies to fund drug deals. Dealing in drugs was widely regarded as a more lucrative and less risky activity than armed robbery, but robbery could be a useful means of raising the relatively large sums of money necessary to set oneself up as a dealer. Most interviewees claimed that they had had no intention of giving up robbery in favour of drug dealing on a permanent basis but had used the proceeds from their robberies to buy drugs which they then sold on for a profit. For these more professional robbers, drug dealing was a means of inflating their gains from crime:

'I needed money to invest in anabolic steroids which were used by people to keep fit. You can invest five grand and make over ten grand.'

'I was selling cocaine by the kilo. Yeah, do a robbery and then buy £5–£10,000 worth of fucking coke or heroin, then you flog it . . . You get £30,000 . . . It just multiplies.'

'Yeah, most money, particularly where I come from in London, most money got illegally from armed robberies will wind up in some sort of drugs deal. Definitely, there's no question about that.'

'A lot of people move through armed robbery into drugs. You get to my age and you think, I don't want to be running up and down the streets looking for cars that's gone 3 seconds earlier and stuff like that. What you want to do is get involved in something else. You want to turn some money over and get a good profit and the only obvious thing nowadays is drugs.'

'I needed the money for a big scam which I had in my head which was drug related.'

'What a lot of armed robbers are doing, or have been doing, is doing robberies to finance drug deals.'

'On some scales there is a tie in between armed robbery and drugs. There are some people who are dependent on drugs and go out to pay for drugs, or you got a lot of people who deal in armed robberies to get finances to buy lots of drugs.'

Following this logic, eradicating addiction to drugs could reduce or even eliminate the pressure for some people to commit robberies. But there were other ways in which alcohol and drugs were linked with robbery. Some respondents claimed that they had committed the robbery while under the influence and had been unaware of their actions until later. For example:

'We done it when we were on mushrooms and when we came off we realised what we'd done.'

'Yeah, well we were just on crack . . . I didn't care, no mask, nothing, just ran in, get the manager, ran him out the back, perfect description. I weren't going to get away with it, but that didn't matter I suppose at the time. It's crack that is, it's terrible.'

'I went in to enquire about how much it would cost me to get some caps done on my teeth . . . but I was a bit out of my head on drugs. It was near closing time, and I was sitting there, and then the bird behind the counter, she started like counting the money out on the till. With the effect of the drugs, I was transfixed by the money. It was just a case of me getting up, walking over, giving her a slap on the face and taking the money.'

One robber admitted that alcohol had been his downfall in a different way. He was aiming to commit what would have been his second robbery; he drove his car to the bank and once there decided that he needed a drink if he was to have the courage to carry out the raid. In the event he imbibed too much and became drunk, crashed the car and was arrested for conspiracy to rob. He was later charged for his only other robbery. But the need for Dutch courage was mentioned by a few robbers:

'Coke gives you confidence and it makes your adrenalin work for you. And it makes you insensitive . . . I think that crime and the drugs go hand in hand.'

'Drink has been in all of the robberies. It gives me a bit of Dutch courage.'

'Sometimes it helps to have a drink when committing a crime. It helps your nerves.'

Amongst the more amateurish robbers alcohol was just one feature, along with drugs, unemployment, and the influence of friends, which characterised a lifestyle where crime was accepted and where opportunistic robberies were regarded as an easy way of obtaining money (see also, Kapardis, 1988). Some of these people were motivated by revenge, often born of resentment of previous treatment by some part of the criminal justice process rather than by individuals or businesses — although there were some unhappy ex-employees. There was a difference in the explanations given for the influence of friends and family. While robbers associated with fellow robbers, and these would often be friends, it was not common to involve family members; but this did sometimes happen (see Chapter 5). Thus while the role of a friend might be to suggest an opportunity for a robbery or even to issue an invitation to take part in one, the influence of the family had more often to do with a lack of money to take care of basic family needs:

'I needed money for the kids' Christmas presents. I was under pressure from the wife to get some money, so I decided to go out and rob somewhere.'

'I did it for money which the family needed.'

'I needed money to pay the mortgage. The bailiffs were coming that morning.'

'I needed money for the family. I'd just got married, and Christmas was just round the corner.'

On the other hand the absence of a family served to reduce the reasons for not committing a robbery (see Chapter 4). Some noted that the absence of a family (about a third of the sample had been in care), or the existence of a family that had set a bad example had led them to a life of crime. As one robber noted 'I was a battered child for years and years and years . . . it turned me into a little bastard.' Being surrounded by criminal activity in the family environment from an early age was blamed by some for leading them astray:

'There's me dad working in the docks. He'd be coming home with sheep skins, pulling all things out of his trousers what he smuggled out, and a lot of his friends used to hi-jack lorries, bring home things like 50 tellies for me old man to sell, or loads of jeans and that, and they'd all be up in the spare room. There was crime going on in the house. I grew up seeing crime, and everyone who was anyone in my area was a robber.'

'I was put in care 'cos the police first got me at 7. My mum used to collect me from the police station, give me a belt round the head and everything in front of the police, but as soon as we was outside the police station, round the corner, she used to give me a cigarette.'

'Where I came from, all the people I looked up to were armed robbers. Families spanned the years, dynasties of them. You couldn't wait to be invited to be one. Then once you have tasted the high life it's hard to give up unless you have another source of income.'

During the interviews robbers were asked whether the media had ever affected their offending in any way and just over a third claimed that it had, albeit in different ways. Some felt that the media gave the impression robbery was easy to commit and/or glamorised the off-ence, reinforcing impressions that some had formed themselves of local robbers they had met or heard about. Several interviewees had gloated over reports of their offences in newspapers which had helped to confirm their status as 'real' criminals. Robbers had been in-fluenced by films they had seen. Some robbers admitted that they had received ideas from the media, not just about whether to commit a robbery but also about the best way of carrying it out. And factual programmes gave an insight into police strategies. Indeed, factual television crime shows, ironically often designed to help catch

offenders, were most likely to be influential in this way.[6] The British
television series Crimewatch was mentioned frequently:[7]

'The media, the press used to do a lot for my ego. The BBC television
series, Crimewatch, sends men on robbery sprees, you know? I used to
look in papers every time I'd done a robbery . . . I'd thrive on it all.'

'I suppose I did it partly to get my name in the papers. I didn't have a
great deal of friends and I suppose I thought people would turn round and
say "That's him." It sounds crazy now.'

'They made it look easier for me to go and rob a building society. The
media done a lot for me. The papers as well. The way they say like a man
walked in broad daylight, he took such and such and walked out with
£5,000. Well, you know that he's got away clean. You know, they're
offering a reward, they don't know nothing about it.'

'I seen it on Crimewatch, on the local television news, in the evening
papers . . . It was just showing the video cameras from inside, and it
showed that they couldn't really identify the people from the video
cameras, and how easy it was to get the money . . . I suppose it did give
a model of how to rob them.'

'They actually show people robbing banks and building societies, and it
just goes to show how easy it is if you've got a little bit of nerve. I used
to watch them programmes all the time, thinking well, if they can do it, it
looks easy, I'll do it.'

'I saw some robberies on Crimewatch. They seemed really easy. Just
whack a gun on the till and they give you the money. It seemed so easy.'

The current debate which is polarised around whether media causes
violence is in danger of missing the more subtle point that the media,
in all its forms, can reinforce images and ideas and introduce new
ones about the commission of crime, not least in the minds of those
who are marginalised and desperate.

To sum up, while people commit robbery for a range of reasons,
the main one is money, although the uses to which this is put are
varied. The more professional and organised robbers obtain greater
sums and at the same time enjoy committing the offence. Drugs are
sometimes a factor and some invest the proceeds of their crimes in
drug deals to increase the yield. The more amateurish robbers obtain
less money, some are addicts to alcohol and drugs and they are
generally unemployed and more likely to be influenced by friends;

robbery and crime are a part of their lifestyle. Clearly situational measures will influence these two groups in different ways. Since another distinction between them is their attention to planning, it may be helpful to consider this in more detail.

PREPARING FOR ROBBERY: THE PLANNING STAGE

The level of planning varies considerably; much depends on the character of the people involved and their commitment to offending generally and to robbery in particular, and their state of mind (for example, the influence of alcohol and drugs). As Letkemann (1973) has noted, some robberies require managerial, social and organisational skill; and not all offenders have the inclination or the ability to carry out such offences (see also, Lukenbill, 1981). Within the literature on robbery there has been quite an extensive discussion about planning by 'professionals' or 'planners' on the one hand and 'amateurs' or 'opportunists' on the other (see Conklin, 1972; Walsh, 1986). At one extreme Roebuck (1967) found from his study of black armed robbers that 15 out of 32 made detailed plans; but most research has found a larger 'amateur' or 'opportunist' element. For example, Walsh (1986) discovered that while nearly a quarter of robberies were planned over several months to years, most were planned over days to weeks, and less than a quarter were planned in just a few minutes. A similar trend emerged from the findings of Gabor et al (1987) who reported that approximately a fifth of robbers they spoke to claimed to have undertaken no planning whatsoever, while in two-fifths of cases preparation spanned several days or weeks, with plans sometimes being quite detailed. Feeney (1986) found that half his sample of Californian robbers did not plan at all and a third planned on the day of the robbery only. Robberies of commercial premises were more likely to be planned. In general the findings suggest that those who plan are likely to reap greater rewards (e.g. Walsh, 1986) because they tackle the riskier targets (Einstader, 1969; Roebuck, 1967). Macdonald (1975) reports that those who robbed the Boston office of the Brinks Incorporated stole $23 million and made five dry runs.

Robbers were asked to discuss what they thought were the most important considerations when thinking about carrying out a robbery.

They were asked about the type of planning they undertook, for example, whether they or accomplices visited the scene or kept it under surveillance. They were questioned about the ways in which they obtained information about the target and in particular the features of the target, if any, that attracted them to it. Specific questions were included on the location of the premises (whether it was situated on a corner, and on a main or pedestrian-only street), its size and whether the fact that the inside of the premises might be visible to passers-by, the gender of staff or the presence of customers affected them. And they were asked for their views of the security measures (closed circuit television cameras, security screens and alarms) designed to counteract the threat they posed. Clearly, if we understand the influence of these components of planning we gain an insight into the feasibility of reducing or stopping robberies at the planning stage.[8]

The process of planning

There are problems in attempting to classify planning. The findings from this study suggest that while some robbers spent a considerable amount of time searching for a target they did not consider this to be 'planning' but a normal and on-going activity; they were committed to offending and so were always looking for targets. Others did nothing more than keep watch on a premises for a few minutes before the robbery and claimed they had planned it. Moreover, quite detailed planning could be undertaken quickly, while a considerable amount of time could sometimes be spent to achieve very little. Some robbers claimed to have spent a month planning when all they had done was buy a weapon or stolen a car while others, admittedly the minority, devoted themselves completely to the task over such a period.

These limitations need to be borne in mind. When the results are analysed further, robbers who spent more time planning were more likely to say they undertook tasks associated with planning. These are the more professional robbers. For example, those who planned for more than one day[9] were found to be more likely than those who planned for less to visit the target beforehand themselves (67.2% compared with 34.8%); to keep the target under surveillance (66.2% compared with 37.8%); and to conduct the robbery having received a tip (26.5% compared with 14.8%). Moreover, as can be seen from

Table 2.2, the level of planning varied with the target. The findings are consistent with previous research in showing planning for robberies of 'softer' targets (building societies and commercial premises) to be less than for robberies of 'harder' targets (cash-in-transit vans and banks).

Table 2.2.   Time spent preparing for the robbery by target

	Bank	Building Society	Post office	Cash-in-transit	Commercial premises
			Per cent		
Up to a day	34.2	60.4	46.0	12.8	58.4
Day to a week	14.5	22.8	23.8	17.0	15.4
Over a week	40.8	12.9	27.0	63.8	14.1
No reply	10.5	4.0	3.2	6.4	12.1
Total	100.0	100.1	100.0	100.0	100.0

Many of the robbers who were classified as having 'prepared for up to a day' had in fact hardly prepared at all. The following comments are quoted at length to illustrate the point:

'First we went into town on a Sunday morning . . . we went driving around looking for a place to rob. The only place open was an off-licence so we went in there. My mate checked it out first. He came out and said it was safe. We asked for cigarettes and as she turned around, we got our knives out and just told her to open the till and give us the money. She was just scared, so I went round the counter (and) helped her empty the till.'

'(My) mate come round about the third night after I done . . . one of the other robberies . . . and said did I want to do another one. So we went round and got a gun off one of my mates . . . walking past this supermarket, newsagent thing, and my mate says "Shall we do this one?". I said "No, I got a bad feeling". So we hung around outside for a bit and I said "fuck it", so I pulled my balaclava down, just went steaming in there with a gun, (we) made about 3 people lie on the floor, got the money, legged it out.'

'Well, what happened was we come to a stage, me and my co-defendant, where we had no money. I just got married, and we got a bit desperate. We did go to do a launderette over, just rip the cash boxes out, but the launderette was packed, too many people in there. So on the way back my co-defendant suggested robbing a petrol station. I thought he was joking, but he wasn't and so I just said ''yes''. In the end and we went ahead with it, and that's about it.'

'Just walked down the street and found this building society closest to the underground.'

'Just did it on the spur of the moment. I see it was empty, I had a firearm and so I did it there and then.'

'Never really prepared at all. Just sus out the bank that day, walk in there first, have a look around about half an hour before then go back and rob it.'

'This one wasn't really planned. It was just we were walking down the street, with my mate and we (had) seen it, we went in there, just walked in, walked up to the counter and said ''we'd like to make a withdrawal'' She said ''how much'' and we said ''the fucking lot'' and she put the money on the counter and we walked out.'

Clearly, preparation is often not deemed to be necessary because the target is viewed as easy (see Broadbent, 1999). This point will be returned to later. It may be helpful to crime detection that some robbers visited the premises shortly before the robbery; they may have been caught on a camera so that there may be scope for matching images of robbers caught on camera with visitors to the premises (indeed the vicinity) in the hours before the offence. Some robbers though did plan meticulously, as the following dialogue illustrates. In this example, the robbers kept watch at the same time each week in the lead-up to the attack, which suggests that investigations taking this into consideration are likely to prove fruitful in some cases:

'First of all you do your spotting which is your initial ground work trying to find out how much the bank is carrying . . . when there's a delivery of money coming in at a certain time, or someone who goes in regularly and pays in from a shop say. Sometimes you may just go round various banks with a tenner . . . wear something extremely bright, you might wear normal clothes say and a bright yellow beret or a pair of blindingly day-glo trainers 'cos what happens is it draws people's attention to that. When people say ''what did he look like?'', ''he had a yellow beret on'' they don't look at your features 'cos your memory tends to go with the thing that's made the most impression, that's one little trick. You go in and stand in the queue with a tenner and you just go to the counter for change, but while you're in there you're watching every counter and watching who is paying in what, what's going on behind the counter. You sometimes spot the delivery, or it might take three weeks, you might have to send another member of the team in the following week at exactly the same time to see if the same person's paying the same amount in. Then once it's done twice the third week you send someone else in, three times it's a definite and the fourth one you hit it . . . once you've got the information, when you ask them for the money you make sure they know you know the money's there. You say "listen you get a delivery every morning at 10.30 on a Thursday we know just give us the money"; you're not going to get fucked about.'

'My friend walked into the building society to withdraw some money for himself, whilst he was in there one of the cashiers was counting the money out on the counter, he met up with me later in the pub and told me about this. We had a discussion about it and I asked him to go into the building society the same time the following day, they were doing exactly the same thing that day, this carried on for about 2 or 3 or 4 days, on the fifth day I decided to take pot luck, walked in there the money's all sitting on the counter, and that was it, it was just gone.'

Nearly twice as many robbers who planned for more than a day (67.2%) claimed that they visited the scene beforehand compared with those who planned for up to a day (34.8%). While just over a quarter of those who robbed a building society said they had, a third of those who discussed their last commercial premises robbery said the same. About a half of bank and post office robbers and over three-quarters of those who discussed a cash-in-transit robbery did so. These answers need to be set in context. Many robberies were committed locally and thus the fact of having visited a premises does not necessarily mean that the robber visited it for the sole purpose of committing a robbery. Some robbers chose their targets because on a legitimate visit to the premises they found security to be slack or identified some other reason why it was a good target. Hence the need for continuous attention to security. However, a high proportion of robbers of building societies and commercial premises claimed that the visit took place on the same day. This may be further evidence of the lack of planning on the part of robbers of these types of target. By contrast no robbers of cash-in-transit vans claimed that they visited the scene on the day of the robbery; most who gave details claimed they made several visits, often over a week before the day of the raid. A very similar pattern emerges from the answers to a question about accomplices visiting the scene beforehand.

A variation on this theme is the extent to which the target was kept under surveillance. Again nearly twice as many robbers who planned for more than a day (66.2%) claimed that they kept the target under surveillance beforehand, compared with those who planned for up to a day (37.8%). Once again, cash-in-transit robbers were the most likely to say that they did, 57 per cent replied in the affirmative here, compared with a much lower proportion of commercial premises robbers (33 per cent) and a slightly lower proportion of robbers of other targets (banks, 48.7%, building societies, 46%, post offices, 46%). And once again cash-in-transit robbers were the most likely to say that an accomplice kept surveillance on the target. A greater proportion of robbers of building societies, post offices and commercial premises carried out surveillance on the day of the raid. Robbers of cash-in-transit vans were the most likely to say they carried out regular surveillance. An important point was made by just a few robbers, who said that they avoided keeping watch on the target in case they were seen. Thus a decision not to maintain surveillance on a premises does not necessarily mean that robbers did not consider it important or that it is indicative of a lack of planning.

Sometimes planning is helped by the receipt of information about a target. Often this will come from friends and acquaintances. One bank robber claimed 'another person had a team to do it, but they let him down so they passed the tip on'. Occasionally information came from a member of staff who participated in the robbery. For example, one interviewee had been a trainee grocery store manager (in his early twenties) and had no previous convictions. One day somebody he vaguely knew came into the shop and started a conversation. Initially the man broached the idea of the back door being left open to facilitate a burglary but by the end of the conversation the trainee manager had agreed to 'play victim' in a robbery the following evening. The manager was unable to explain why he had agreed to this other than that it seemed a good idea at the time; he liked his job, he didn't need the money and he liked his employers. The following evening the robbery took place and within a week one of the perpetrators 'grassed' on them all. As soon as he was arrested he admitted the offence and was later sentenced to four years in prison.

Cash-in-transit robbers were the most likely to get information for a robbery from a member of staff. Sometimes security guards or others were bribed for information, but sometimes staff approached robbers (see Chapter 5) with a deal which might involve the robber keeping the stolen goods, and the owner of the company claiming on insurance policies for losses incurred in the 'robbery'. However, where information was supplied by staff it was usually done unwittingly. Associates, friends and relatives of robbers talked about the lack of security in their places of work on the availability of money and robbers seized on this information and used it as an aid to choosing a target; hence the need for discretion. Typical examples of this were:

'My sister-in-law worked down the bank and she told me that they had been told if they were robbed to hand over the money. She told me this and I got the idea.'

'(I heard about it) from a member of staff who disliked the boss and she was in it for the money too.'

In a slightly different way one robber recalled how he had heard the chairman of a building society invite him to commit robbery:

'About three or four years ago the chairman of the (name) Building Society was having a television interview with the police because a series of robberies had occurred and, er, he stated that it was building society policy to hand over the money to anyone who asked for it, so obviously ... I started laughing. It's giving people a chance to rob ain't it? Basically he's saying come into our building society, ask for the money and we'll give it to you.'

Macdonald (1975) found from his early American research that some people devoted themselves to planning robberies but took no active part in the raid itself. In general, there was scepticism about tipsters amongst the robbers interviewed; accepting tips depended on knowing the people concerned and believing that they had a good reason for not wanting to participate. Sometimes people providing a tip are paid in the form of a 'drink' (a (usually small) payment) as opposed to a 'whack' (a share of the haul). As one bank robber summarised:

'Well, there was one fella, we used to call him Mr 10 per cent, he was always setting himself up as an armed robber, but he wasn't. He used to find bits of work and then come and say, "here, found a nice one in the High Street, there's got to be £75,000 there," and if you do it he's got to have his 10% for doing nothing.'

So while for some robbers planning was non-existent, for others it amounted to no more than trying to identify an easy target. For the more ambitious, choosing a target was itself a part of a planned offence.[10] But what is it about the target that makes it attractive to robbers? A clue is given by the responses to a question about the most important considerations when planning a robbery. It prompted numerous references to the escape route. Some elaborated here and spoke about checking the getaway, obtaining vehicles and acquiring safe houses. Other important considerations included the need to stay calm; to get the money; to ensure all team members understood their roles and carried out the plan effectively; to obtain disguises or weapons; to understand the security measures at the target and know the whereabouts of the police and police station; to check the victims and gain an idea (usually just by looking at them) of whether they were likely to be 'have-a-go-heroes'; to avoid getting caught; and to check the premises to ensure there were few or no customers. Some robbers answered in a different vein, believing that the most important consideration was to be 'professional' (although the meaning of this varied) and to prepare mentally ('getting the bottle to do it' was referred to) which in some cases meant consuming alcohol to build up courage.

But the importance of not getting caught were recurring themes in conversations with robbers and these were important considerations in choosing a target to rob. More details were obtained by asking robbers specific questions about this issue.

CHOOSING THE TARGET

Because some robbers had not prepared for the robbery, the choice of target was opportunistic; or it was the first one they encountered or it was chosen at random. When asked why they chose the last target they robbed, a few robbers mentioned that it was the only one in view at the time they wanted to do the robbery, e.g. a petrol station late at night. However, answers from those identifying specific features can be classified in five overlapping ways. First, many chose the target because something about it made them think it would be easy. Comments were sometimes not precise and based on general perception or 'feel' or 'instinct' or 'common-sense'. Some based this decision on the fact that the target was empty or quiet, or it looked as if it would contain money often for no other reason than it was big:

'I was driving past and it looked affluent, like it had a lot of money in there. If you wanted to open an account then this is where to go.'

Second, some robbers identified specific features which they liked about the design and layout of the target. This includes a lack of security features:

'Because it was easy at the time. The till was 10 feet inside the door and no-one was there, just walk in and then run.'

A third, and much smaller category were robbers who chose a target because they wanted revenge on the owner/manager. Some indicative comments included:

'Some friends asked me to do it to get revenge on a shopkeeper who had informed the police about their involvement with cannabis.'

'One of my friends had gone in drunk, they had sacked him and he wanted revenge so he told us about it.'

Fourth, some people chose the target because details of it were known to them. Sometimes this was because it was local or had been robbed before (discussed below at p. 53). A few mentioned that they had received a tip or had been given inside information (especially cash-in-transit robbers):

'This one was always being robbed and we thought it was easy.'

Fifth, robbers favoured the location. A few said they chose a target in a location where they would not be known. Others offered a different reason, preferring, for example, premises located on corners or main roads. But most comments focused on accessibility and getaway routes. Typical comments included:

'It was convenient to my shop. I could do the robbery and arrive back at my shop in 20 minutes. Hence, an alibi.'

'I suppose it was close to home. I knew the getaway area so well so I wasn't going to get caught. That's how you start, around your manor. Then you can't keep hitting places in your own manor and that's how you get caught, bad getaways and all that.'

'I wanted one in a quiet street, in (a) built up office block where there is plenty of wages and a good getaway route. I just drove by it one day and thought, yer, that's it.'

Later in the interviews robbers were asked more specific questions about the location and layout of the target, such as whether it was on a corner, a main road/pedestrian street, what was the size of the premises, where the teller (money) was located within the premises and whether the inside could be seen from the street. In a different way the presence or absence of customers and the gender of staff affects some robbers, as do security measures.[11]

There are no (publicly available) statistics on the number of banks, building societies and post offices which are situated on a corner and this limits analysis. In the last robberies discussed by interviewees, about a quarter of building societies, about two-fifths of post offices but over a half of banks were located on a corner. While this was generally viewed as unimportant, over a half of the building society robbers claimed that the corner location had been relevant to why they had chosen the target. The main reason was summarised by one bank robber:

'I had 5 directions to go, it was perfect, a bad place to put a bank.'

Others noted disadvantages:

'It was a disadvantage really, because on a corner they stand out more and it was watched from both sides, you have to keep watch both ways.'

About two-thirds of the banks, building society and post offices robbed were located on a main road and about a third of the robbers in each category claimed that this was a relevant consideration in why the target was chosen, principally because it was advantageous to the escape. There were very few robberies of premises located in pedestrian only streets, probably because fewer premises are located here. Mostly robbers saw premises located in pedestrians streets as unattractive, although some stated that the main reason for choosing a target here was that it made the escape easier. This is not a contradiction. Different robbers see different advantages in certain locations: if a robber intends to escape on foot, a busy pedestrian street can be an advantage, and a busy (but not jammed) main road can help if the escape is by car.[12] What is striking is that the ease of escape was once again viewed as a priority. Some typical comments included:

'Not a high street because it's packed all day long. I'd never have done it with people in it.'

'I try to do them in really busy areas so you blend.'

'Don't like precincts, too many police and harder to get out.'

While most robbers stated that the size of the premises was largely irrelevant to them, over a quarter of bank robbers, a fifth of building society robbers and over a tenth of post office robbers considered size to be relevant. Some favoured smaller premises because they believed that they would be easier to control and more quiet and that there would be less security; others larger premises because they assumed they would yield more money. These points emerged in response to a question about choosing the day of the robbery. The most common days chosen were Thursday and Friday. Where a robbery was planned, the two salient issues affecting the day and time were the perception of the amount of money available and the level of customer activity. The ideal target was one full of money but empty at the time the robbery was being carried out. Yet there were contradictions. For example, some banks, building society and post office robbers preferred to attack towards the end of the day after customers had paid in, while others preferred mornings before money had been paid out! Similarly, some chose periods of the day because they believed the premises would be quiet while others avoided these same times because they felt they would be busy. And often these robbers were referring to similar targets in similar locations (see Broadbent, 1999; van Koppen, 1996a; 1996b).

It is possible that interior design and layout are a more important consideration for robbers. This point was not asked about specifically although respondents were asked which teller(s) was chosen in the last robbery. By far the most common response was the one nearest the door. Again, ease of escape was given as a reason. At least one robber had considered layout in more detail and offered the following insight and clue for internal design:

> 'Straight banks are the easiest, 9 times out of 10 I'll operate on my own. Then you get L-shaped banks which go round a corner, (then you) usually (need) 2 people 'cos you can't watch both ways and the door. Whereas on one I can come in and stand just inside the door.'

Are there any features of layout that would make you avoid it?

> 'Yeah, any bank with revolving doors, 'cos they lock them. Other doors they do lock automatically but it's very easy to deal with them 'cos all you do is take a piece of 3 by 2 and drop it so if the door goes bang the lock goes.'

Revolving doors have been used as a deterrent measure, for example, in Puerto Rico (Rodriguez, 1995). Another robber claimed that a good way for a premises to avoid being robbed was by installing queuing rails between the counter and the door because this would frustrate the escape. Another robber advised companies to play music; he felt that this would affect his concentration.

From other research based on interviews with offenders it has been shown that what particularly worries shoplifters are 'people factors' (see, Butler, 1994). It was argued that while physical measures could identify individuals, it was people not technology that made arrests. In the course of the research robbers were asked questions about the presence of customers in the last premises they robbed and the effect this had on the robbery. As a starting point robbers were asked whether they could see inside the premises from the street. This could be viewed in two ways. On the one hand it would enable robbers to check the scene prior to the raid. On the other hand it would make it possible for passers-by to witness the attack and raise the alarm and thus has been advocated as a good robbery prevention measure (Macdonald, 1975). Yet, while 64.4% of building society robbers compared with 43.4% of bank robbers and 42.9% of post office robbers claimed that the premises were visible from the street only a minority of each said that this had been a consideration in choosing the target. However, over a quarter of building society robbers thought it was relevant.[13]

Many respondents pointed out that the robbery took place quickly and that passers-by did not tend to look inside premises anyway.

Others pointed out that even if passers-by were watching they would not necessarily realise a robbery was in progress. As will be shown in the next chapter, many robberies involve offenders demanding money at the counter and someone would have to look closely to discern anything unusual about their behaviour. One bank robber, for example, had queued up with others and when he came to the front had passed a note to the cashier demanding money. He indicated that he had a weapon under his jacket and waited for his bag to be filled up before walking calmly out of the bank with the money. Overall, opinion favoured the premises being visible from the street since it provided an opportunity to check that the premises were 'safe'; this was viewed as outweighing the danger of a passer-by noticing what was going on and intervening. But views were expressed on both sides, as the following quotes indicate:

'Had it been possible to see inside I would have thought twice about doing it.'

'Well, I could see the layout, how many cashiers there were, where the camera was situated and whether there was going to be anyone in there.'

Some robbers stated categorically that they always at least tried to avoid customers being present, since they are potential witnesses and may frustrate the escape. For others the presence of customers was inevitable and had to be taken into account in the planning stages, usually by involving more accomplices and/or by demanding that customers lie on the floor. Some robbers preferred there to be customers present: a few even intended to take customers hostage or steal from them as well. But more commonly robbers answering in this way felt that staff were more likely to agree to hand over money if they believed customers might be threatened. A few robbers said that customers were a part of the plan to steal money; for example, a shop robber pointed out that he needed to wait for a customer to buy something for the till to be opened, at which moment he struck. Some typical comments on the presence of customers included:

'I just told her straight, "don't muck about and you'll be OK. If you fuck about I'll kill you". I wouldn't have but they don't know that.'

'I wouldn't have robbed it with witnesses.'

The evidence here would suggest that owners of premises where priority is given to security should not make the inside visible from the street. Added to this is the earlier finding that some robbers chose the target they did only because they happened to be walking past and looked inside. In reality of course there are other considerations for owner/managers beyond those of security, not least the need to make the premises attractive and welcoming to customers. This illustrates the potential for conflict between the demands of security on the one hand and sales and marketing on the other; the very features that attract the honest customer also attract the attention of the thief and robber (see also Beck and Willis, 1998).

Whether the staff and victims of the robbery are male or female appears irrelevant for the majority of robbers. The few who claimed that this was relevant preferred female staff because they felt they would be less likely to resist. Against this, some said they felt uncomfortable upsetting women or felt that women panicked more, rendering the robbery more difficult to control. A few robbers claimed they liked to scare men. Some typical comments included:

'I don't think I'd have done it had it been a woman because I am not into frightening women. I like to think that but you don't know do you?'

'I like 1 or 2 to be male because I get a buzz at them shitting themselves, it's better when you're telling the lads.'

'I wouldn't have done it with males because I am a born coward, they might resist.'

PHYSICAL SECURITY MEASURES

According to the robbers interviewed, most banks and building societies, but very few of the post offices, had closed circuit television cameras installed.[14] Clearly this was not a deterrent in most cases, although some of the interviewees stated that they would always avoid premises with cameras, some adding that the abundant supply of targets without CCTV encouraged this approach. A few robbers admitted that they had been caught on camera and said that this had been instrumental in their capture and/or prosecution.[15] In practice though most robbers considered the presence of CCTV inevitable; as one noted, 'it's a bonus if there's no cameras'. Those who robbed building societies and commercial premises were more likely than others to say that they did not realise CCTV was present. This was true for over a fifth of the former and a third of the latter — another reflection of their lack of planning.

Some interviewees stated that the presence of cameras changed the way they did the robbery, principally in encouraging them to wear a disguise. A few claimed that they made a point of not looking at the camera. Others mentioned poor picture quality as a reason for not worrying or took the view that most cameras were fake. One robber claimed that cameras were an advantage because they added to the risk and sense of adventure that a robbery provided, and another felt that they lulled staff into a false sense of security (see, Beck and Willis, 1994). Some robbers claimed that they smashed cameras or otherwise put them out of operation and one team tried, and failed, to find the video in order to steal it.

For the most part though the presence of cameras was taken for granted, and the response typically took one of three forms. The robbers ignored the cameras altogether; they attempted to destroy the cameras, in one case by firing shots at them and in others by spraying them with car paint and shaving foam; or they wore a disguise or hid under a scarf, hat or balaclava. Generally robbers dismissed CCTV frequently citing poor quality images. Some typical comments about CCTV included:

'I suppose the disguise was more for the cameras than the staff.'

'I didn't know they were there until after I had been caught and I was shown the photographs.'

'It was the first thing I looked for. If it had them I wouldn't have done it.'

'I don't care if there's cameras, you can always change your appearance.'

Most robbers, and especially bank robbers, claimed that they wore a disguise but those who had robbed a cash-in-transit van were frequently reluctant to answer. A range of disguises were used by robbers including balaclavas, hats, stockings, baseball caps, crash helmets, gloves, scarves, spectacles or sun glasses, wigs, masks, false beards, false tattoos and different hairstyles; and some grew a beard or long hair which was shaved soon after the robbery. Gloves were worn to avoid leaving prints at the scene. Some wore several layers of clothing to make themselves look bigger and confuse witnesses (and cameras). This had an additional advantage in that the top layer could be discarded easily after the robbery to reduce the risk of identification. Some argued that by looking bigger or by covering their face they appeared more threatening; this made it less likely the victim would resist. Only a minority wore garments specifically for the robbery. Track suits and/or track shoes made it easier to run, overalls or a boiler suits were favoured because they could be easily removed, and reversible jackets so that they could alter their appearance. Some wore clothes they could burn or discard after the robbery.

Some robbers wore 'ordinary' clothes so that they did not distinguish themselves whereas others wore bright coloured garments to distract attention from the face. One robber wore black clothes because he considered it more intimidating and others because they were conducting the robbery at night. Some wore a baggy jacket so that they could hide a weapon. One team dressed as security officers in order to rob a security van.

Security screens were very common in banks and post offices that were robbed, but less so in building societies. Where there were screens most robbers knew about them in advance, although over a quarter of robbers of building societies and commercial premises didn't realise they were there nor a sixth of bank robbers. While a few interviewees claimed that they would not rob a premises that had screens, for most, security screens, like cameras, were viewed as inevitable in financial institutions. A few of those interviewed considered screens an advantage because they prevented staff from attacking them; they ensured that staff could not confront them and complicate the robbery and the escape. For example:

'It was important, for my safety as well as the people working behind the counter. I felt safe there, and it cut the risk down of say, somebody jumping over the counter . . . I felt safe.'

There was some evidence, albeit from only a few interviews, that the presence of screens encouraged robbers to become more threatening and violent. Some argued that it would have had an impact on the way they decided to conduct the offence:

'It would have made a difference if screens were there. Had there been I personally would have captured them as they came in and gone behind the screens with them.'

'To a certain extent it made me appear more aggressive in case they didn't take any notice.'

Screens played a part in frustrating the robbery. A few robbers stated that when they had demanded money the staff had reacted by just lying on the floor. In another case a cashier refused to give the money and the robbers felt they had little choice but to leave empty-handed. Such a policy may work where staff have faith in the strength of the screen and where robbers do not aim to take hostages.

At the time of the research rising screens were just beginning to be introduced. A few robbers claimed that they had found ways of circumventing the system but those interviewed who had encountered a rising screen had generally been unsuccessful. Some robbers claimed that the existence of this threat deflected them on to other targets:

'I look in the bank to see if there are security guards or to see if there are large shutters in there . . . you know, some of them have large shutters that go up? If they have got them I don't bother doing them.'

There is no doubt that rising screens present a serious challenge to the robber but the experience of one interviewee suggests that there may be problems for staff too:

'I had a terrible problem with the screens, they got a remote control of some sort which they can, well, they supposedly should use before you get through the counter. So anyway they are activated from the cashier's side, from somewhere. So anyway, they were activated too late, you know? I already jumped the desk, so I was their side, so I was filling the bag with money and . . . all of a sudden there's this terrible noise, bang, and I thought a weapon went off, possibly my partners. All of a sudden I look up and I couldn't believe, I mean, I thought something was wrong. Because this shield came up so quickly, I didn't see it. So I started to walk around and the whole picture had changed. I didn't know, I was shocked for about 2 or 3 seconds. I didn't realise what happened. They came down and I could see my partner was like me, in a state of shock, so, I shouted to one of the girls, the one who pulled the note from the till, and I say ''look you silly cow, get me out of here, otherwise there will be trouble''.

> She was just on the floor saying nothing. So I told her it would be bad for both unless they got me out of here . . . so she starts to feel panicky and er, in the end I pulled the door and managed to open it.'

Again there is evidence that some measures may increase the amount of violence used to ensure a robbery is successful. Indeed, Rodger (1996) noted that rising screens are being overcome by 'steaming', where a group of robbers quickly jump over the counter before staff have had a chance to raise the screens. This increases the level of aggression shown in the robbery.

Alarms were regularly sounded in raids, particularly in robberies of post offices (39.7%), cash-in-transit vans (27.7%) and banks (25%), and much less so in robberies of commercial premises (17.4%) and building societies (13.9%).[16] Most robbers expected the premises to be alarmed and those that had thought about the robbery beforehand were generally psyched up not to be shocked by an alarm being activated. In any event many companies have a policy of only sounding an alarm once the robbers have left the premises so as not to panic them and risk injury to customers and staff. Some robbers knew this but since speed of escape was a priority anyway it did not appear to affect their approach to the raid. Others pointed out that they could never be sure that the premises did not have a silent alarm and that it was sensible to work on the assumption that there was one.

While Ekblom (1987) found that alarms stopped raids, this was true for only a minority of robbers interviewed in this study. Some claimed that the alarm was only sounded as they left the premises but some admitted they had been thwarted:

> 'Me and my co-accused, we went to the petrol station late at night, and er, wore balaclavas and with baseball bats, and er, my co-accused ran into the shop up to the counter and I stood at the door 'cos it was an electric door and there's a switch to lock it. So I stood at the door, my mate ran up to the counter and the man had some money in a safe. My co-accused swung his bat at the counter and asked for the money. The man just pressed the alarm bell, stepped back and we ran off. That was it.'

Yet in the majority of cases where an alarm was sounded robbers claimed that they obtained money. Clearly, the numbers are small here but in about a third of robberies of cash-in-transit vans and commercial premises, a quarter of post offices, and about a tenth of banks and building societies robbers failed to obtain money. For the first three categories of premises this is considerably higher than is the case overall. Alarms can play a part in stopping robbers getting money.

Robbers were asked to imagine that they were engaged in a robbery and an alarm sounded, and to state what they would do. The reaction was mixed. The majority claimed they would carry on with the robbery, often with more urgency; others said they would abort. One robber claimed that alarms were not a principal concern, only police sirens. Another admitted that the alarm had made him panic and caused him to brandish his knife. Once again this raises the concern that sometimes security measures induce more violence and make an injury more likely.

Finally, robbers were asked about time-delay safes.[17] Most robberies did not involve access to a safe and hence many had not made it their business to find out about it. This was less true of robbers of commercial premises and post offices (where about a sixth did so) than robbers of banks and building societies. The main effect on the robbery was that it required access behind the counter.

REPEAT VICTIMISATION

There is one other feature that is important when considering how robbers choose their targets, and this concerns repeat crimes. Earlier it was noted that some robbers chose their targets because they had some knowledge of them. There is a growing amount of research that suggests repeat victimisation is common (Ashton et al, 1998; Ellingworth, et al, 1997; Gill and Pease, 1998; Pease, 1998). During the interviews robbers were questioned about repeat robberies. They were asked whether they had previously robbed the premises and 19.1% admitted that that they had, principally because they had found it easy the first time. Moreover, 18.5% admitted that they had robbed premises that they knew had been robbed by someone else, again because they felt it would be easy. Some typical comments include:

'It was easy so I went back 10 days later.'

'A factory and shop twice. It is easy, it's about 25 minutes before the (factory) alarm goes off, and the shop didn't have one. They didn't learn.'

'If you get a good result you go back a second time.'

A number of interviewees noted that they hadn't realised that the place had been raided before until after the event, and some avoided going to a place that had previously been victimised. One common reason was the belief that the security would have been improved as a consequence of the first raid. But it seems that these robbers may have overestimated the security consciousness of victims.

Thus at least part of the reason why some targets are chosen is because robbers have conducted a raid there before or because they are aware that others have done so and been successful. Further analysis revealed that it was the more professional robbers who were the most likely to claim that they repeated robberies of the same target (see Gill and Pease, 1998). This is important and draws attention to the wisdom of installing security measures soon after initial victimisation.

DISCUSSION

Robbers were able to give reasons why they had committed their last robbery and these brought out some differences between professionals and amateurs. While for both groups money featured prominently, professionals obtained larger sums and were sometimes inclined to invest their haul in drugs to sell at a profit; amateurs stole more to meet immediate needs. The more professional robbers enjoyed committing the offence and found it exciting while, for the more amateurish group, robbery was one feature of a lifestyle which included unemployment and membership of a group which drank a lot of alcohol and took drugs.

Not surprisingly professionals and amateurs differed in the degree to which they planned the offence. Some robbers do not plan; they notice a target and rob it immediately. The motivation here is closely linked to the opportunity. Had an opportunity not presented itself it is doubtful whether the offence would have been committed. This is where situational measures can have an impact on the initial decision to offend. Other robbers plan, in as much as they search for a suitable target; but this can take minutes rather than hours or days. Some robbers are always planning, in that they are always on the look-out for a suitable target in much the same way that many people look for bargains when shopping. Some robbers planned in detail but this did not necessarily take a lot of time.

Those who planned more, that is they spent more time setting up the robbery and visited the scene and kept it under surveillance, were the most likely to tackle the riskier targets. It was found that those who spent less time planning were more likely to visit the target just before the robbery. Those who were aiming at larger hauls spent more time planning and were more likely to visit the scene at the same time as the planned robbery a day or more in advance. This may offer clues to investigators. It underlines the importance of ensuring that staff are always security conscious; those who plan and those who act on impulse are attracted by the same thing, the sight of any easy target.

Sometimes robbers received information from people who did not take part in the robbery; but there is scepticism about them. Sometimes robbers plan raids and seek to identify a person who can be bribed. Some of the more professional robbers had attempted to bribe security guards and/or had been approached by guards or employees because they wanted money or revenge.[18] Sometimes staff had been indiscreet and robbers had seized the opportunity to learn more about a potential target.

The minority of robberies which are based on inside information are preventable; at least two lessons can be learned here. First, companies need to ensure they recruit the right staff; vetting and training are crucial. Ensuring that staff are treated fairly will help minimise the chances of their feeling isolated and aggrieved and seeking revenge in ways that include robbery. Security guards appear to be especially vulnerable since in the UK the security industry is not subject to statutory regulation. Low pay and poor standards are common and the presence of large numbers of offenders amongst their ranks is seen as inevitable (Button and George, 2000; George and Button, 1996). Second, staff need to be trained (on a regular basis) in the importance of discretion in talking about security matters outside the workplace; a security strategy is important. Some robbers are constantly on the lookout for a target and are always seeking information which could facilitate a robbery.

But how do robbers choose their targets? In short, they claimed to look for premises that were 'easy' and the most important consideration was the escape; that took priority over the money or goods to be seized. Success meant avoiding leaving evidence at the scene and ensuring that they were not caught. While this was the aim of almost all robbers, those who planned their robbery took greater care to ensure that these objectives were met. While, robbers said that they sought a target that was 'easy', a range of specific questions was asked which gave an insight into robbers' perceptions of features which made a target more or less easy.

While a quarter of building society robbers said that the location of the premises on a corner had affected their choice of target, and about a half of these saw it as an advantage, this was not viewed as a priority by most robbers. Indeed, some saw disadvantages in such a location. Certainly, there is insufficient evidence here to show that premises located on corners were viewed as easy targets, although for a minority it was a factor. Similarly, while location on a main road was common, few saw this as specifically relevant; but those who did noted that it assisted the escape. Similar points were made by robbers who chose a target in a pedestrian street: escape was a priority and the premises they chose had features which assisted this. Main roads were better for those escaping by car; and crowded streets for those escaping on foot.[19] It is likely to be the case that location has an influence but is rarely the decisive factor.

Location is important for the robbers' escape once they have left the premises but first they have to get outside the building. Hence it was argued that impediments such as revolving doors, queuing rails and L-shaped design (which may prevent the robber from keeping sight of and control over the exit) were helpful crime prevention measures because they made the escape from the premises more difficult. Clearly, there is a whole range of other physical measures that could have an impact here. In a different way the presence of customers deterred some; because they were worried about their role as witnesses and/or because they were concerned that some might be have-a-go-heroes. But there are no simple solutions. This is another example of a double-edged sword, with a few robbers viewing the presence of staff on premises, especially in banks and building societies, as offering an opportunity for taking a hostage. This lends force to Clarke's (1995) warning that security measures need to be tailored to meet local needs.

This study did not seek to evaluate the effectiveness of security measures (see Tilley, 1998), merely to assess robbers' opinions of them. Physical security measures can work; CCTV and security screens deterred some robbers, and some were caught on camera, which led to their imprisonment; and some screens were instrumental in stopping raids. Alarms led some robbers to abort their attack. But the findings suggest that robbers were generally not deterred by knowledge of such security measures. Mostly, robbers expected premises to have some types of security equipment installed. But CCTV could be negated by disguises, screens by adopting a method of robbery which rendered them superfluous (such as the most common method, demanding money at the counter), and alarms by psyching oneself up to expect the noise and being prepared to abort the robbery soon after they were sounded.

Some measures, and especially screens, were sometimes viewed as an advantage principally in keeping the biggest danger, people, out of the way. Some comments indicated that the presence of security measures increased the amount of violence robbers were prepared or 'needed' to use in carrying out their raids; cameras were attacked, as were screens; and the sounding of an alarm panicked some. The findings suggest that caution is needed in evaluating the effectiveness of security measures. Some robbers argued that the effect of cameras being present was to encourage them to wear disguises. This made them more menacing and no doubt the experience of victimisation was all the more harrowing; but it also made it more difficult for victims and witnesses to identify robbers. While it requires a logical jump to argue that the absence of cameras should make disguises less likely and make possible better victim and witness descriptions, this is a possibility and will be discussed in the final chapter. Whatever security measures are deemed to be appropriate need to be implemented soon after the initial victimisation since some robbers return to rob again, or other robbers decide to do so.

The fact that escape was the main concern was highlighted in the many comments robbers made about the need to avoid confrontation. There were three principal considerations here. First, confrontation could result in injury to the robber. Second, confrontation could result in the robber getting caught. Third, an injury to the victim might increase police efforts to capture them and almost certainly result in a bigger sentence if they were convicted. Where robbers believed they might come into contact with people they were more likely to take weapons. This issue will be discussed fully in the next chapter.

There was very little planning for the majority of robberies discussed by the interviewees. Targets were perceived to be easy and, as one robber remarked, 'it is only a matter of asking for money from those who have been told to give it to you'. Making the target less soft, making money less available and advertising the fact, and making the escape more hazardous offer clues to prevention. On this level Clarke's (1997) techniques for situational prevention appear convincing. But it needs to be recognised that some robbers stole for very little money and were oblivious to the risks involved. And some planned their offence carefully or were so determined that it would take a fortress to thwart them. It is perhaps comforting to note that they probably represent the minority. It is no longer true that robbers represent the elite of the underworld; all too often robbers are desperate people for whom robbery offers an easy opportunity to gain small sums of cash quickly.

While it has been argued that location does not in itself appear to be a priority, it is an important consideration in so far as it affects the escape. Premises in a one-way street, near a police station, without immediate access to alleyways or tube stations, with a revolving door, with a counter a long way from the door and obstructs such as queuing rails in between and with cameras, (bullet-proof) screens and alarms would be bad places to rob. Premises located on a corner and a main road, with alleyways and/or a tube station near-by, situated some distance from a police station, with easy access and exit, a short distance between the counter and the doors, normally busy but empty at the moment the robbery was to be conducted, without screens, cameras and alarms would be good targets for a robbery. There was thus evidence to suggest that the principles of situational crime prevention offer a good basis for thinking about crime prevention and this will be addressed again in the final chapter. However, situational measures were shown to have a potentially dangerous effect in increasing the amount of violence robbers were prepared and felt they needed to use in conducting their raids. This is an example of malign displacement. A better evaluation of these issues requires an analysis of the way that robberies are carried out.

[NOTES]

[1] This was a general question. It would clearly be a jump to interpret the reasons given as typical of all offences, although many noted that they were. As will be shown later, there were links between certain types of reasons and levels of planning.

[2] In a different way Clarke and McGrath (1992) examined whether the newspaper reporting of bank robberies led to increases in copy-cat robberies during the following week. They examined police robbery statistics for New South Wales during 1987–1989 and newspaper reports from two tabloids during the same period. They concluded that there was no evidence of copy-cat offending.

[3] In this chapter chi square tests have been calculated by comparing the variable with the rest. Thus, here those who cited unemployment as a reason were compared with those who did not. In fact, 48.3% of those who claimed they robbed for need of money also stated unemployment as a reason compared with only 13.8% of those who did not claim money was a reason.

[4] $(x^2 = 50.9 \ p < 0.001)$.

[5] The link between drugs and alcohol as motivating factors appeared to be strong. Those influenced by alcohol were more likely to admit to having been heavy drinkers during their last period of offending $(x^2 = 82.3 \ p < 0.001)$, and to have taken illegal drugs during this period $(x^2 = 6.5 \ p < 0.05)$ and drugs was much more likely to be cited as an influence on the last robbery $(x^2 = 33.7 \ p < 0.001)$. Moreover, unemployment was also viewed as more relevant amongst those influenced by alcohol $(x^2 = 6.2 \ p < 0.05)$ and so was the influence of friends $(x^2 = 5.6 \ p < 0.05)$, and this group were more likely to claim that they found the raid exciting $(x^2 = 6.0 \ p < 0.05)$ and that this had influenced their offence. Thus while money was the main reason, not helped by being unemployed, drugs and alcohol were clearly prime reasons for why the money was wanted in a context where friends were sometimes an influence and where robbery could be exciting. The lifestyle amongst a significant part of this group bordered on the criminal and crime of some sort was perhaps inevitable.

[6] Nevertheless some people admitted that the programme had been instrumental in their capture.

[7] 'Crimewatch' is a programme shown monthly (not Summer) on national television in the UK. It contains reconstructions of crimes, including robbery, and appeals to the public for help.

These reconstructions and other features such as video recordings of offences gave some robbers insights into robbery and even encouraged some to consider the offence.

[8] There is clearly a considerable amount of overlap between the content of chapters. For example, choosing whether to carry weapons can be considered part of the planning of the offence but this issue is discussed in the context of how robberies are carried out (Chapter 3). Similarly, the account taken of the police can be considered as part of planning but this is discussed in the context of robbers' attitudes to the police (Chapter 4). These aspects will be drawn together in the final chapter.

[9] Although planning times vary and are not necessarily related to what has been done to prepare for the robbery, there was a link. Those who had planned for more than a day were more likely to say they carried out a whole range of planning activities and thus this aspect has been included in the analysis in this chapter.

[10] In discussing the decision-making processes of burglars, Bennett and Wright (1984) note how some burglars made a decision to commit a burglary having encountered a suitable target by chance (which they called 'opportunistic'); some searched for the target and committed the offence immediately (which they called 'search') while others planned the offence having found a suitable target (which they called 'the planned offence'). Such is the case with robbers interviewed in this study although it was not designed to collect data in the same way as in Bennett and Wright's work.

[11] Responses are only given to bank, building society and post office robbers since these questions were not appropriate for most cash-in-transit robberies and many of the general category of commercial premises robberies.

[12] Some robbers escaped on foot to a place where they had a car parked; this was especially important for those robbers who were using their own vehicles.

[13] Five of the 33 (15.1%) bank robbers, 18 of the 67 (27.7%) building society robbers and five of the 27 (18.5%) post office robbers claimed that this affected their choice of target.

[14] The question specifically referred to close circuit television cameras as opposed to other types. However, it has been pointed out to me that robbers would often not know the difference. This needs to be borne in mind although the perception of the robbers is important here.

[15] In the interviews robbers were asked how they were caught and 3.3% mentioned CCTV.

[16] There is some missing data here. The percentage who said that alarms were not activated were as follows: post offices (57.1%), cash-in-transit vans (51.1%) and banks (63.2%), and much less so in robberies of commercial premises (75.2%) and building societies (71.3%)

[17] Although the question was originally aimed at ascertaining robbers' views on time delay safes it seems probable that robbers concentrated on access to 'safes' rather than 'time delay safes'. This needs to be borne in mind.

[18] In most cases the circumstances discussed here were not explored and so it is not possible to comment on the extent to which the robbers' grievances were real, much less the extent to which they merited retribution on the scale of robbery. But the concern that disaffected workers can become a security threat is a real one and begs consideration.

[19] During conversation some robbers noted that targets located in one-way streets were undesirable. One robber claimed he had found a bank that was 'perfect' but had to reject it when he realised it was located in a one-way street; it made the getaway too dangerous in that there was effectively only one escape route in a car.

Chapter 3
Carrying out the Robbery

Although robbers carry out their offences in different ways, their aim is invariably the same: to obtain as much money as possible, in the shortest possible time and with the minimum hassle; and to avoid capture. While Gabor et al (1987: vii) have argued 'there are probably as many ways of robbing people of their money as there are of making money legitimately', in practice most robberies of commercial premises involve demanding money or goods at a counter, often while showing a weapon. Ekblom (1987) in his work on post office raids found that the most common variations on this pattern involved taking a hostage, breaking into closed premises and waiting for staff to arrive and attacking as money was being delivered or collected (Home Office, 1986). Some robbers are 'wheelmen' or getaway drivers, others only become involved in as much as they provide information on which the idea of the robbery is predicated (Conklin, 1972), while the role of some robbers on 'inside jobs' is to 'play victim'.

A key issue in discussions of robbery is the carrying and use of guns. Victim reports suggest that two-thirds to three-quarters of British commercial robberies involve firearms. Ekblom (1987) found that two-thirds of screen attacks on post offices involved guns, while Austin (1988) found firearms were used in 65 percent of raids on building societies. A Home Office (1986) report noted that firearms were carried in 70 percent of bank raids. These figures are double those of the 1950s (McClintock and Gibson, 1961). However, more recent evidence provided by Morrison and O'Donnell (1994) and based on interviews with robbers suggest that the danger is exaggerated, in that only a third of those they interviewed carried a gun capable of discharging a lethal shot. Their evidence suggests that many 'weapons' cited by victims and witnesses are imitation or unloaded weapons.

Moreover, most of the research evidence suggests that robbers are not intent on causing injury and that a weapon is carried to ensure that injuries are in fact avoided; people are less likely to challenge if they believe that they will confront a weapon (Feeney, 1986; Harding and Blake, 1989; MacDonald, 1975; Walsh, 1986). Cook (1979) reports that those carrying a less lethal weapon, such as a knife or a cosh, are typically more violent. Other American writers agree:

> The more lethal the weapon the less likely victims were to undertake either threatening or non-threatening tactics, and the more likely they were to agree to the demands of the robber.
>
> (Skogan, 1978: 65)

> If the offender is carrying a knife, he uses physical force about two times in five; and if he has a firearm, he uses violence about one time in five.
>
> (Conklin, 1972: 116)

Similarly, in a British context, Morrison and O'Donnell (1994) have shown that even where a loaded gun is taken along to a robbery, it rarely results even in minor injuries (See also O'Donnell and Morrison, 1997). However, there is very little research on robbers' attitudes towards gun use and to their victims and the extent to which they see force as an important part of conducting a raid.

This chapter seeks to fill some of the gaps in our knowledge by reviewing robbers' accounts of how they carried out their attacks. If crime prevention and security are going to be effective a much better understanding is needed of robbers' attitudes to their actions and behaviour during the act itself. This process may provide ideas for how future raids can be stopped. But it is also important to gain an insight into ways of reducing the levels of violence and ways of deflecting offenders on to less serious tactical approaches (Barr and

Pease, 1990). The chapter begins by reviewing why robbers chose to attack in the way they did and their thoughts as they were committing the offence. It then moves on to consider the issue of weapons and violence and provides evidence that brings into question official data on the number of real guns used in robberies. Moreover, it looks at why robbers say they used weapons and the circumstances in which physical injures occurred, which includes a review of robbers' attitudes towards their victims. This chapter seeks to identify what robbers do and how, and attempts to understand robbery from the perspective of the offender as a means of informing crime prevention.

ROBBERY STYLES

At the beginning of the interview robbers were asked to describe in general terms their last robbery. Given the numerous comments cited in the previous chapter about robbers' lack of planning, it was not surprising to find that in the last robbery the most common method deployed was a demand for money at a counter: this was true of banks, building societies and post offices, although in the latter there was a greater likelihood of robbers getting behind the counter. Demanding money at the counter was viewed as the easiest way of conducting a raid and a point reflected in many of the comments about this issue. For example:

'There was only one female there, and it looked just like taking candy from a baby. Basically . . . there was no screens there, there was just nobody, just her in the shop on her own, one counter which was about waist high.'

'I were afraid when I went into the bank, I didn't think, you know I didn't think I'd do it, and then I just went up to the counter and gave her the note, and I just couldn't believe it was happening 'cos she was so calm, just giving me the money, you know? She didn't laugh or think "oh he aint serious", because if she'd just challenged me I would have run. She didn't, she just read the note, straight away she just put the money in the bag.'

'We were just driving around North Wales, going through villages and we came across a building society without a counter. So I parked the car, my co-defendant went in and came out 2 minutes later and that was it.'

'They just gave me (the money) straight away. Until I saw her put money in the bag I couldn't believe how easy it was. I was just like a normal customer with a scarf around my face. This is why I think there will be more bank robberies in winter, because you have a scarf to cover your face.'

'The first one I done, I come out (of) there and I was in shock. I was in shock (at) how easy it was, I found it very hard to believe what I'd just done. It was that easy it was a joke.'

'Well on the night it was about 6 o' clock and me and two of my friends decided to do a robbery. So that night we went down to the petrol station and we had three masks and two imitation guns. My first friend went in, me and my other friend ran in after, and there was a woman behind the counter and there was a man standing next to the door. We told them to put their hands up above their heads, and give us the money or we'd shoot them. The woman opened the till, the bloke stood up against the door with his hands above his head. She gave us the money, she pressed the alarm button, the alarm went off, we ran out down the road.'

'I had a canvas bank bag that I had change in . . . I walked into a bank, put that under the (screen) and as they looked at it I pulled out a hand gun, pointed it at her. Then I motioned towards the till and said "fill that up", she filled that up.'

It is slightly ironic that these robbers were being interviewed in prison and yet claimed to have found their offence relatively easy to carry out. But this is a characteristic of robbery, which makes it one of the most important challenges for security and crime prevention: robbery is a relatively easy crime to carry out.

Getting behind the counter sometimes enabled robbers to reach safes but more usually gave them access to cash in tills or at teller positions. Sometimes it was relatively easy to jump the counter; on other occasions it was necessary to trick staff or pressure them to open the security door, and some, particularly post office robbers, smashed the screen. In all, three robbers of banks and post offices and one of building societies admitted taking someone hostage and one bank robber broke into premises when staff were not there and left before they arrived. Robberies of cash-in-transit vans usually involved taking money from the guard as it was being delivered or collected but in some cases involved stopping vans. In such types of attacks, where robbers were physically close to victims (be they customers, members of the public or staff), they needed to exercise additional control over the environment.[1] This was normally facilitated by the use of weapons (discussed later) or by involving accomplices.

As can be seen from Table 3.1, the number of robbers who were involved in raids varied with the type of target. Apart from building societies, raids normally involved more than one robber. Raids on cash-in-transit vans were unlikely to involve just one robber due, at least in part, to the sophistication of the target (see also, Morrison and O'Donnell, 1994).

Table 3.1   Number of robbers involved in last robbery

	Bank No.	%	BS No.	%	PO No.	%	CIT No.	%	CP No.	%
One	19	25.0	55	54.4	9	14.3	6	12.8	41	27.5
Two	22	28.9	24	23.8	22	34.9	15	31.9	55	36.9
Three or more	27	35.5	11	10.9	28	44.4	23	48.9	42	28.2
Missing	8	10.5	11	10.9	4	6.3	3	6.4	11	7.4
Total	76	100.0	101	100.0	63	100.0	47	100.0	149	100.0

The way robbers conduct a raid will depend on a number of factors. First, as was shown in the previous chapter, it will depend on the amount of planning they have done (see Walsh, 1986). Second, it will depend on their skills and robbery can require skill (see, Luckenbill, 1981) although this is not always the case (Gabor, 1988; Matthews, 1997). Some robbers, and a few who had a military background, were introduced to robbery because they knew how to use a gun. A good driver may be sought as a 'wheelman' but most robbers felt 'bottle' and reliability were more important attributes for this role. Indeed, interviewees regularly highlighted the crucial role of the getaway driver (another indication of the robbers' priority of escape). One robber described how he hired a taxi to wait for him while he carried out the raid (the taxi driver had no idea that his customer was a robber). It then took him several miles to a point where his accomplice was waiting with another taxi. This was the accomplice's only role in the robbery but he received half of the haul. The interviewee had no misgivings about this, for him escape was crucial and if they were caught they would both receive prison sentences. Also, as many robbers noted, when they went into premises they liked to be sure that their getaway vehicle would be waiting for them and equal shares were the most common way of ensuring this.

This was not always the case though. Some robbers mentioned that they paid drivers a percentage. Their justification was that if they were caught they would argue that the driver was just driving them to the target and was ignorant that their aim was to commit robbery. Even so, some robbers had been convicted despite such a plea.

Third, method will be dictated, at least to some extent, by experience. While it is now accepted that some offenders progress to robbery in their criminal career, it is also true that robbers start off on softer targets and progress to the more ambitious ones as they acquire confidence and knowledge (for example, see Ekblom, 1987). There is a flip side to this. Some of the robbers interviewed who had committed a single robbery adopted inappropriate approaches. One bank robber, who was in his thirties when he undertook his only robbery reported how he made an appointment to see the manager and then during the interview pulled out a gun and demanded a quarter of a million pounds. He had considered this a reasonable amount to take from a bank and was not aware that his method was unorthodox and his expectations unrealistic. Another (very experienced) robber also made an appointment to see a building society manager under the pretence of wanting a loan. He described how he conducted the robbery and how experience helped him to reap a big reward:

'I explained that I was at work, that I was during me dinner hour, I needed an appointment with the manager 'cos the only day off I got was a Saturday, and I got an appointment for the next Saturday, and I gave a fictitious name, and a fictitious reason. Er, I got the appointment for half 11 Saturday morning, mainly because I know that building societies close at 12 'o' clock. So (the following Saturday) I parked me car . . . Anyway, I waited till about quarter to 12 and I jumped from the car into the building society, explained I'd been caught in traffic, and I was terribly sorry, and I was settled in, they brought me in to the manager's office. I explained to them about I'd just arrived from Ireland, I was waiting for money to be transferred, I intended to buy a house and we went through all the implications of it. Then he just waffled on, he told me about interest and mortgages, etc., etc., etc., and by that time it was about 12:10, by then all the girls had cashed up, and they were ready to put the money in the safe, and the place was closed down, there was no customers.'

You planned it like that, just to let him waffle on?

'Yeah, let him just carry on, I didn't want anybody in the place, right, and at the same time, you get a lot of people that rob building societies, they go to the counter, they stick a gun into the girl's face, and they get their personal drawer, they may get two or three drawers, but this way, you're actually robbing the place, you're getting everything and there's very little chance of you having to hurt anybody, because when you got the manager under control, consequently he got the rest of the staff under control. What he says goes. So, I waited 'till about 10 past 12, one of the girls came in and said ''Mr so and so, we're ready'', and that's when I took my gun out, I told him I'd have everything, he opened the safe, I took the money from the safe, put it in my briefcase, went to the counters, emptied the drawers, put that in my briefcase, pulled out the phone, put them in the office, when I left the key was still in the door because they were waiting for me to leave so they could lock it after me. Consequently it was all there so I've gone out locked the door behind me, dropped the keys in the bin, went round for my car and away I went.'

Fourth, method will be influenced by a robber's expectation; raids at the counter are easier to conduct but they are much less likely to reap huge rewards than, say, emptying the contents of a (recently filled) safe or for that matter a cash-in-transit van. The issue of expectations is sometimes linked more to the choice of target than the type of robbery, although of course the two factors overlap. As Ekblom (1987) notes, raids on delivery vans are more likely to be lucrative but they require greater skill and more planning. Many robbers have quite modest aims:

'Me and three of my mates we pulled up at the garage forecourt, and er, I went in the shop to get some cigarettes, and when she opened the till I put my hand in my pocket and told her to give me the money . . . I did it on the spur of the moment it wasn't planned, I wanted cigarettes, he wanted a drink.'

Fifth, the style of robbery adopted will be influenced by the state of mind of the robber; those who are desperate, and this includes many of those who were suffering from addictions, need money immediately and even the lure of relatively small amounts can be sufficient to make a robbery worthwhile (Morrison and O'Donnell, 1994). Thus, less complicated approaches would be preferred.

Sixth, a robber's method will be influenced by his/her personality; some robbers were prepared to use violence or to associate with those who were. Some, despite the seriousness of the crime they commit, make a distinction between generating fear and inflicting physical harm. Some robbers took hostages. As one experienced robber explained, when reflecting on a career in crime:

'Mostly, what I do is grab someone else, put a gun against their head, and they like open the till. Ninety nine out of a hundred they do it.'

The purpose of taking a hostage was that it made the threat all the more apparent, and in these robbers' view allowed the offence to progress more efficiently, often enabling them to increase their haul. One robber reported how his normal method was to attack a manager as he/she was leaving the premises and then force him/her back inside at gun point to make him/her open the safe. The robber argued that this approach was less risky because he knew there was only one person on the premises — and that individual was under control — and more lucrative because it enabled him to gain access to the safe. This approach renders violence more likely and can only be contemplated if one is prepared (or associates with others who are) to inflict injury.

Seventh, method will be influenced by resources. Some of the more ambitious robberies require a considerable amount of funding to buy equipment or a safe house, bribe staff, and to support a gang while it prepares for the raid. Many of those who acted because an opportunity presented itself to rob premises at the counter did not have the resources (for example, accomplices, weapons, getaway vehicles, local knowledge, places to store money), even if they had the inclination to attack, say, a security van.

In essence, being in control and being able to conduct the robbery quickly were important considerations for robbers. Indeed, when they were asked how long they spent inside the premises on their last robbery few said longer than five minutes, and about a half of building society robbers said they took up to one minute. Over a third of bank, building society and post office robbers claimed the robbery took from one to three minutes. By all accounts robberies tend to take place fairly quickly (see also, Morrison and O'Donnell, 1994). However, for the robbers these minutes often seemed like a very long time indeed. One man who had been caught on his first robbery told how he had bought false number plates which he planned to fix to the car while his accomplice went into the building society to demand the money.

But his accomplice completed the raid before he had had a chance to append the plates.

The interviewees were asked what their main thoughts were during this short but fraught period. Two responses were especially common: they were thinking about getting the money and/or the escape. In addition some noted the importance of keeping control and high-lighted the need to keep a careful watch on customers and staff. In fact keeping control is essential to a successful robbery and later it will be argued that productive ideas for crime prevention can come from thinking of ways of impacting on robbers' ability to exercise control of their environment. In their answers many robbers made reference to the 'buzz' or rush of adrenalin occasioned by the carrying-out of the crime, and not infrequently robbers admitted to being nervous. Some comments included:

'To be perfectly honest I was shitting myself.'

'I was psyched up, nervous, tense.'

'I have never known such a rush of adrenaline. I don't know what I was thinking.'

'My personal thoughts when I go into the bank is to be as calm as possible. Try not to make myself look nervous, don't shout, make myself be understood and clear, to get as much cash as you can in the allotted time, and then just go and be as calm as possible without causing too much disturbance.'

'It's like a buzz. The adrenaline flow is unbelievable. You do shit yourself. The first one is the worst. It don't get any better, you just get used to it.'

'To get as much money as possible without making them panic. Not to look at the cameras, talk aggressively and as soon as I got the money to get out straight away.'

'The worst part is pulling the gun out, once you've pulled the gun out it is normal. It is a bit anxious but you just concentrate on getting the money.'

'Hurry up, I was under pressure, 'course I was. I knew the old bill might come in and the gun wasn't loaded. But it's not really pressure, it's a buzz, like taking speed.'

'The teller delayed. I was very nervous. I had to step up the aggression. I tried to scare him. He was a bit aggressive back, he argued with me.'

'Hard to explain. When I do a robbery I change. I respond. I know I can respond to any irritation, I can hit people, anything. That's why I don't do so many robberies. I plan them . . . I get a buzz out of it.'

'I wasn't thinking. It was as though it was happening and there was nothing I could do, as though I just had to do it.'

'Just getting in there and doing it to the best of my ability and getting what I want without anyone getting hurt.'

'A real buzz, no drug can give you the same buzz. Looking and concentrating all the time, but when you see the money you think of the new car tomorrow.'

'I was scared, very nervous, I was shaking. That is why he set the alarm off, he could see that.'

'Confusion, very nervous, especially when my mate pulled a knife out.'

'I was quite surprised at what I was doing, and very worried, but pleased it was going OK.'

The main objective of robbery is to obtain money. The manner of demanding the money varied. Some passed a note across the counter, usually with a bag, others demanded the money aggressively, sometimes showing a gun, while others asked gently, keen not to panic the victim to such an extent that he or she could not carry out the orders. The most common way was to demand 'give me the money'. In most cases the money was handed over without resistance, although a minority of robbers, as will be shown, claimed that they only obtained the money after they had threatened or assaulted victims.

ARE ROBBERIES LUCRATIVE?

Robberies are lucrative for some robbers and not for others. It was the more professional and organised robbers, of banks and in particular of cash-in-transit vans, who obtained the highest rewards, as Table 3.2 shows.

Table 3.2   Money robbers obtained from last robbery

	Bank No.	%	BS No.	%	PO No.	%	CIT No.	%	CP No.	%
Nothing	6	7.9	4	4.0	11	17.5	11	23.4	17	11.4
Up to £1,000	8	10.5	22	21.8	9	14.3	3	6.4	73	49.0
£1,001–£5,000	15	19.7	49	48.5	19	30.2	3	6.4	22	14.8
Above £5,000	39	51.3	15	14.8	20	31.7	29	61.7	22	14.8
Missing	8	10.5	11	10.9	4	6.3	1	2.1	15	10.1
Total	76	100.0	101	100.0	63	100.0	47	100.0	149	100.0

A minority of robbers admitted that they did not obtain any money in their last robbery. Cash-in-transit robbers were the most reluctant to answer the question. Indeed, there was a high non-response here, but of the 46 who answered 11 (23.9%) said that they failed to get money. This compares with 11 out of 59 (18.6%) of post office robbers, 17 out of 134 (12.7%) robbers of commercial premises, four out of 90 (4.4%) building society[2] and six out of 68 (8.8%) bank robbers. There were several reasons. Some, as indicated previously, were stopped by a security measure; sometimes victims refused to hand over the money (or were too much in shock to do so) or duped them; sometimes victims attacked robbers and thwarted the attack; and a few robbers, for a variety of reasons, were caught in the act. Some typical comments here include:

'Pure bloody obstinacy from the teller. One day I was literally 500 yards from the police station and I'd spotted it, timed it, knew where I had to go and everything, only a building society, crashed in, "fill the bag", "no — we're being robbed". I just had to go, what could you do? I couldn't bleedin shoot her. I just went, I was terrified at the time, but when I got out of the way and sat on the bus I just laughed.'

'He just ran into the back living room. He shut the door behind him so we went. We weren't going to hurt anyone involved, we just wanted the money.'

'Well we went in with a broken stick underneath my coat and I demanded the woman to hand over the money but the woman was so frightened she couldn't hand over the money to me so I panicked and ran off.'

'Walked into the building society, there was one customer, told him to get in the corner, told the cashier to give me the money and then I heard a voice say "no don't give him anything", he ran back in and then dived behind the furniture, so I left.'

'What happened was I pulled out a gun . . . There was just one girl in there, no customers, and she was on the step ladder putting some videos on the shelf. So we says "where's the money" so she got down and opened the till, but apparently the manager had been around quarter of an hour before and taken the money and all we were left with was 14 one pound coins. So I just took that, we couldn't take any more.'

'It was like, er, Sunday night about half past 7, and I had a combat mask, I walked into the petrol station, pulled the knife out, tapped (it) on the counter, threatened the cashier, told him I wanted money, which he (gave me). I put the knife away, I ran outside. That's when he pressed the bell, the police were on that road as luck would have it and they just caught me there and then.'

'We was on drugs . . . we ran out of money, and we got talking about how we were going to get some money. One of my friends said there was a shop down the road and it seems easy. So we walked down, we had balaclavas, I walked into the off licence, and it just happened. As soon as the geezer saw me he came running at me with a crate of lager. So I retaliated, took the money and went, and I got caught half way down the road.'

But most robbers did benefit from their robbery because most victims, often working to employers' instructions and following official advice (Health and Safety Executive, 1993), gave the money when it was demanded. Even comparatively small sums were satisfactory for the needy robber. One who started robbing banks when his wife left him explained that the amounts varied but were not large:

'My ex-wife up and fucked-off like, I asked her back, I asked her back, I was hounding her and I had no answer at all back off her. She left me, had my nippers off me. I had to fight them over access, right. I had access on a Monday, a Wednesday, and a Saturday afternoon. I still asked my ex-wife back, out of work I was as well, and so I held up a bank. I made a mask in my house, my ex-wife knew I was holding up these banks, after the first one I think I had £1,750. A month after that one, I was still out of work, still asking my ex-wife back, handing her money, and I held up another bank. I held it up, I had the money. I fucking held them fucking all up as well, I only made £995 out of the second one. The third one now,

I held it up, and made £447, and the fourth one I held it up again and I think I had about £900 odd out of my fourth one. My ex-wife had £800 of that money and her sister rang up the law and said I was holding up banks. Then my ex-wife moved back into the house and I'm here inside.'

Most robbers said they would divide up the money with accomplices immediately and start spending it soon after: many would start spending it the same day and most within a week. But, what is important here is that robbers were prepared to conduct raids for relatively small sums. This was rational because it was viewed as an easy way of obtaining money quickly, with a low risk of detection. One feature that could make the robbery easier was the use of guns and violence, but this could cause complications too.

WEAPONS, VIOLENCE AND VICTIMISATION

It will already be clear that weapons are commonly used in robberies although research by Morrison and O'Donnell (1994) found that only 33% of weapons carried in raids were capable of firing a lethal shot, either because weapons were imitation or because they were unloaded or not loaded with live ammunition. The findings from this study are similar although there were variations by target, as the following summaries illustrate.

- Of the 70 bank robbers who answered the question on whether they carried a gun, 53 said they did, nine were imitation and 44 were real guns: 40 of these robbers admitted the gun was loaded and 35 with live ammunition. This is important because it means that of the 53 who may have been identified by victims as having a gun, 35 (46%) had a weapon that was capable of firing a lethal shot. Of the 11 who claimed that they did not carry a weapon, six reported that they had an associate with a weapon capable of firing a lethal shot. Of the six who had a weapon other than a gun no-one had an associate who had a gun which was capable of firing a lethal shot.

- Of the 93 building society robbers who answered the question on whether they carried a gun, 67 said that they did but a much higher number than for bank robbers, 27, said it was an imitation. Of the 40 who claimed the gun was real, 29 said it was loaded and 24 of these with live ammunition. Of the 67 who may have been reported by victims as having a gun, 24 (35.8%) had a weapon that was capable of firing a lethal shot. Of the 13 who did not have a weapon, one had an associate with a weapon capable of firing a lethal shot. Of the 13 who had a weapon other than a gun, no-one had an associate who had a gun which was capable of firing a lethal shot.

- Of the 61 post office robbers who answered the question on whether they carried a gun, 40[3] said that they did and 29 said that it was a real weapon and 10 claimed that it was an imitation. Most of the real weapons (20) were loaded with live ammunition (17). Of the 40 who may have been reported by victims as having a gun, 17 (42.5%) had a weapon that was capable of firing a lethal shot. Of the five who did not have a weapon, one had an associate with a weapon capable of firing a lethal shot. Of the 18 who had a weapon other than a gun, two had an associate who had a gun which was capable of firing a lethal shot.

- Only 37 cash-in-transit robbers answered the question on whether they carried a gun, 20 said that they did and 17 said that it was a real weapon, and three claimed that it was an imitation. Most of the real weapons (16) were loaded with live ammunition (15). Of the 20 who may have been reported by victims as having a gun, 15 (75%) had a weapon that was capable of firing a lethal shot. Of the 11 who did not have a weapon, six had an associate with a weapon capable of firing a lethal shot. Of the six who had a weapon other than a gun one had an associate who had a gun which was capable of firing a lethal shot.

- Of the 136 robbers of commercial premises who answered the question on whether they carried a gun, 55[4] said that they did and 27 said that it was a real weapon and 27 claimed that it was an imitation. Over half of the real weapons (18) were loaded with live ammunition (11). Of the 55 who may have been reported by victims as having a gun, only 11 (20%) had a weapon that was capable of firing a lethal shot. Of the 37 who did not have a weapon, two had an associate capable of firing a lethal shot. Of the 46 who had a weapon other than a gun two had an associate who had a gun which was capable of firing a lethal shot.

While the number of non-responses complicates the interpretation of the findings,[5] it is clear that in a large number of cases where robbers admit taking guns they claim that the gun was incapable of firing a lethal shot, either because it wasn't loaded or it wasn't loaded with live ammunition. This proportion varies markedly from target to target. The more professional and organised robbers were more likely to carry loaded guns. Thus, bank and cash-in-transit robbers were more dangerous than robbers of commercial premises. And even when robbers of banks and cash-in-transit vans were not carrying a weapon capable of firing a lethal shot, further questioning showed that they were more likely than robbers of other targets to have an associate who did.

Other weapons mentioned by interviewees included a cosh, axe, stick, golf club, hammer, screwdriver, baseball bat, iron bar, CS gas and other instruments used to appear like guns including a water pistol and fingers (which raised under a jacket can look like a concealed firearm). Thus victims are likely to perceive the danger to themselves to be greater than it is according to robbers' accounts.

Several reasons were offered for carrying a replica gun. For some it was all they had or all they could obtain, but a common comment was that they did not want to risk hurting someone and so preferred a replica (see also Morrison and O'Donnell, 1996). There were a variety of reasons offered as to why weapons of some sort were not carried; some believed that they were unnecessary in that the task could easily be achieved without them;[6] others claimed that their role in the robbery rendered weapons unnecessary (they were drivers or their accomplice had a weapon). For some the decision to commit a robbery was made without thought of a weapon or time to acquire one; while some were concerned that the use of weapons could lead to a serious injury either to themselves or to victims. Where a weapon was carried, the type varied with the target. Bank and building society robbers were more likely to carry a hand gun or pistol than a rifle or shot gun but in raids of post offices the preference was reversed. These were by far the most common weapons in robberies of banks and building societies. Knives were sometimes used by robbers of post offices and commercial premises (see Broadbent, 1999). Cash-in-transit robbers were as likely to carry a hand gun/pistol as a rifle/shot gun but were unlikely to carry any other weapon.

When interviewees were asked why they carried a weapon on the robbery there were four types of response. First, some were permanently armed and carrying a weapon was as normal as wearing clothes. Thus, the carrying of a weapon is not necessarily indicative of a planned raid or of a rational offender making a decision about the best method of attack. Second, a few people carried weapons because they believed there was a risk of encountering armed police and it was therefore viewed as an appropriate countermeasure. Third, it gave certain offenders confidence and in some cases made them feel invincible. It will be recalled that some people gave as one reason for committing the robbery the excitement and sense of power it generated. As one robber recounted:

'I had this gun in my hand, I was literally buzzing on it. With a gun in my hand I had that power, you know at the time? It was like everything in that post office I could have had, you know? Even anything from chocolate to cigarettes I could have had. I could have had the whole lot, because I had that gun, I had that power . . . they had to give me what I wanted. I had that gun, I was like the man in there. I was on that power trip, you know? I felt the big man, the top man, you know? This is a gun, you know it can kill? Give me, give me, give me, you know? So there was a lot of power there and excitement, definitely.'

Fourth, and this applied to the vast majority, it was assumed that it would make the robbery easier by reducing the likelihood of victim resistance. Getting even real weapons was relatively simple; there was a plentiful supply on the black market and most of those who wanted a gun knew how they could obtain one easily. A few robbers had obtained firearms from burglaries they had carried out and one robber claimed that his gang only turned to robbery from burglary having obtained weapons in this way.[7] Thus while there is much merit in 'controlling facilitators' the challenge is to stem the flow of firearms onto the black market.

Many re-iterated the point that the purpose of a weapon was to avoid conflict and that they would back down rather than risk injuring someone. Some put limits on the level of violence they would be prepared to inflict. Some typical comments included:

'When we went in there I had a knife on me. I could have got more out
of him by threatening him with a knife . . . but I didn't. If he'd refused to
open the till all I would have done was try to open it myself and run out
of the shop.'

'If you go into a place and you start pointing a gun at people, and
threatening what you are going to do and what you are not going to do?
Obviously you are going to frighten them to death. That ain't the point . . .
you go in there to get money, as quiet as you can, as least noticed as
possible, because the last thing you want is confrontation; you want to get
in and get out. You don't frighten nobody . . . customers, you can't have
them screaming and panicking you don't want that, that's the last thing
you want. You don't want to bring no, er, no notice to yourself at all. You
want to get in and get out. The less people that see you . . . the less
evidence they got against you.'

'I've never consciously set out to hurt people to get money, ever, and
er, . . . sometimes you come away from a place or a van alone and think
"poor bastard must be terrified". But there again I draw the line at certain
things. I would not contemplate pouring petrol over people, or locking
them up in a strong room, with maybe 24 hours air left and it's over the
weekend, stuff like that. That would worry the life out of me. Yeah, I'd
never set out to hurt people, I never have done getting money, but I do
consider other people's feeling, strange as that may seem.'

Many claimed that they were genuinely sorry for the trauma they
had caused the victim. For example, when asked whether they had any
sympathy for staff who had witnessed (and been victimised by) their
robberies slightly more than two-thirds of the total sample claimed
that they had. Less than one-third claimed to be sympathetic towards
customers; but many robbers had avoided customers and others
pointed out that they had conducted the robbery in such a way that
customers would not have realised it was in progress. Some expressed
considerable regret, as the following dialogue illustrates:

'Well my dream is, if I win the pools or something, I would like to pay
people back all the money what I have took off them. The simple reason
is, right, I robbed it for the cause of my family, right? And I did not hurt
the public or no-one else, so if I ever did get a chance just to prove to
them that I am not bad, that's the thing, you see what I am saying?'

So, afterwards do you think about the victim?

'I always think about the victim, because the simple reason is like, I feel
hurt inside (I worry that they might think) I'm going to come and get them,

or I'm going to blow them away or something. But that's not (true) in my case. In my case I would like to go back and explain to them my circumstances, and the reason why I done the job.'

A few robbers had written to victims apologising for their actions and others wanted to do so but were generally advised not to. It was feared they might cause more anxiety and remind the victim of their trauma.

Some of those who were not sympathetic claimed that they had no intention of causing any harm, often not realising that the victim had no way of knowing this. Others felt they had given staff and customers something to think and talk about, a distinguishing event in an otherwise routine life, and clearly underestimated the trauma they caused. A few suggested that employees working with money must expect to be robbed and that this risk was reflected in the amount they were paid. Again here, there were frequent comments by robbers to the effect that if the victim complied with their demands they would be unlikely to get hurt and thus any injuries were their own fault. For example:

> ' 'cos they're choosing a job where there's a lot of money involved, that's their risk. They don't have to choose that job, maybe there's a lack of jobs, but they're trained in handling. If they give the money over straight away they're not going to get hurt, nobody's going to get hurt . . .'

What about the fact that they're scared?

> 'Everybody gets scared in their life at some time anyway. It's just something that you've got to get over. I've been scared in my life, by a lot of things, but I got over it. It's part of life.'

Some robbers believed they had a good reason for not feeling sympathy with the victims. A few claimed that the organisations they had robbed had inflated the amount they had stolen.[8] They reasoned that this was because they wanted to gain more from their insurance companies. But for robbers the sentence they received was more severe as a consequence. Similarly, a few complained that victims had dramatised the impact of the crime in court with the result (the robber believed) that the sentence was heavier than it might have been. For example:

'I haven't got any sympathy because (the) two females (were) involved in
this particular robbery, and this incident, and when it came to court to give
evidence they were crying and it added 12 months to my sentence. They
were so dramatic, you could tell it was just a show put on.'

There is plenty of evidence that robbers underestimate the impact
of their crime. This may offer encouragement to those undertaking
therapeutic work with robbers.

In practice most robberies do not result in physical injuries.[9] They
appear particularly uncommon in bank and building society robberies.
During the interviews two robbers admitted shooting and seriously
injuring — one a police officer and one a security guard; and one
robber of a jewellery shop admitted that he and an accomplice had
shot two people, one fatally.[10] Others admitted hitting customers or
staff with clubs or coshes and staff and customers were pistol-
whipped. One robber fractured someone's skull, and another broke a
victim's leg and caused other injuries by driving his car into him. A
few robbers admitted injuring and killing dogs. Others recalled that
they had pushed victims and one robber had tied someone up. A big
fear for robbers, and a major reason for avoiding confrontation, was
that they might be injured themselves; this could result in their not
getting the money, frustrate their escape and lead to evidence being
left at the scene.[11] One robber injured himself on broken glass as he
jumped across the counter and a few mentioned that they had been
hurt as, together with accomplices, they jumped into getaway vehicles. One robber in his eagerness to get away from the scene ran
into a lamp post and bruised his forehead.

There are at least three (overlapping) reasons why physical injuries
occurred in the robberies described; accidents, by-stander intervention
and to make the robbery easier. First, accidents can cause quite
serious injuries, especially where a gun is discharged. It was this fear
that prompted some robbers to avoid carrying a weapon that could
discharge a lethal shot; but many had not considered this a possibility
or that their accomplices could fire accidentally. But this is hardly
realistic. As pointed out above, many robbers admitted to being
nervous when they committed the offence and to being in a rush to
complete the robbery as quickly as possible. Given this, it is wise
policy for staff to be advised to hand over money when it is
demanded. One robber described how he caused serious injury in an
accident:

'Unfortunately the firearm was discharged by accident because the victim reacted, he recoiled actually against the gun and, er, I happened to have my finger on the trigger guard and a shot was discharged, and he was seriously hurt. Of course the job was spoiled. I felt sorry for the chap, I didn't mean to shoot. If I'd wanted to I had 15 rounds in my magazine, plus a 357 magnum in my holster, and er, so it was just an accident, and again if it was my intention to hurt, to kill, I wouldn't have felt sorry. But he recovered.'

Second, injuries occur because the victims or 'have-a-go-heroes' intervene. These often brave people were viewed with considerable resentment and even disbelief by some robbers. Robbers did not understand why they should risk their lives to prevent the theft of money or goods that invariably did not belong to them. Many robbers noted that had they been at risk of serious injury in similar circum- stances they would part with the money and preserve their life. As one remarked, 'that is straight people for you'. Others pointed out that people are warned that a robbery is in progress and argued that those who intervene and are hurt are merely receiving their just deserts. Certainly, any sympathy for injuries inflicted on victims was blunted by the view that their actions had been unnecessary. For example:

'She got hurt, yeah, I think I do feel a bit sorry for her, she shouldn't have (been hurt), but then again she shouldn't have done what she done by trying to cling on to one of my mates and if she hadn't have done that she wouldn't have got hurt . . . It's not as if it was her money. If it was her money I could understand her fighting for it. It's the post office's (money), who owns the Post Office? . . . I asked this in court like and no-one can give me an answer. Who owns Post Office Counters Ltd, whose actual money am I taking? I'm not taking anybody's that I know.'

'On one or two occasions the bloke's got a right-hander, or shoved to the ground when he's not done as he's told, you know what I mean? But not smashed up or shot. Certainly not shot.'

'Nine times out of 10 they ask for it . . . you don't hurt no-one unless you've got to. In other words you only hurt them if they're not doing as they're told or if they're trying to arrest you.'

'I'm going to speak frank here, you know what I mean? If . . . someone had a go, and I had a gun I'd shoot them, 'cos there's no way I'm going to let one man or two men or three men take me and get 15 years for armed robbery. I would shoot them . . . if a person comes and grabs hold of me I'd shoot him down.'

Third, a few robbers claimed that it was part of their strategy to cause injury so as to make the robbery easier to conduct. Earlier it was shown that weapons extract compliance from victims. Some robbers took this a stage further and inflicted violence to induce fear as a means of reducing the likelihood of resistance to their demands. In one case a robber reported how he attacked a newsagent with a golf club and then demanded that he be shown to the safe. More commonly robbers stopped short of physical injury and used aggressive words or gestures, including pointing a gun and brandishing a knife at victims. Some, as noted in the previous chapter, were violent towards cameras and screens and it was argued that security measures can lead to violence.

The overwhelming conclusion that emerged from the statements of the robbers interviewed was that the causing of injury was undesirable on almost all counts. It would attract unfavourable police attention and a longer sentence if they were caught; and even the threat of violence could result in some people being scared and shocked and unable to hand over the money. More importantly, it could result in the robber being captured and some admitted that they had been injured themselves. For the most part robbers felt that violence could only be justified if it was deemed necessary to avoid being caught or if it helped to get the money; and then it was usually linked to the intervention of 'have-a-go-heroes'. In some cases injuries were the result of accidents. This is an inevitable consequence of the nerves and pressure that robbers feel in a conflict situation and a danger that many underestimate. Indeed, while previous research has highlighted the finding that weapons are unlikely to result in injury, it has perhaps played down the reality that robbers are nervous, that accidents will occur and that this danger is frequently under-estimated by robbers. Robberies are emotionally charged events, robbers are nervous and volatile, often desperate and usually very determined.

Thus, while robbery is by definition violent the question for consideration is how can the level of violence be reduced and in particular what scope is there for reducing the chances of physical injury? These issues will be addressed next.

DISCUSSION

This chapter has considered a number of issues relating to the way robbers carry out their raids. It has been shown that robbery is a fairly easy crime to commit, and although the rewards may not seem high, they are frequently sufficient to meet the expectations of the robber. Indeed, even quite small amounts can prompt a robbery because offenders believe that a target is soft. There are perhaps four stages in the process of carrying out a robbery that merit consideration here. Initially the robber must take control of the environment. Second, he/she must obtain the money or the other goods. Third, he/she must escape. Fourth, he/she must avoid leaving behind evidence which can lead to capture.

A primary consideration for the robber is to control the environment in which the raid is taking place. For some this aim will be evidenced by such visible signs as customers being told to lie on the floor and staff being held at gun point. For others it will be a case of ensuring that no customers are present or that the premises has screens so that they are separated from staff. Taking control meant ensuring that potential 'have-a-go-heroes' were kept at bay and that those who were in possession of the money or goods, that is the victims, complied with their demands. Different robbers did this in different ways. For some the requirement was to be as calm as possible, to ask rather than demand or threaten. For others, threats, intimidation and even assaults were a means of exercising control. Either way, weapons could be carried to help achieve the objective. The findings broadly confirm those of previous research that the objective of taking a gun was to reduce the chances of injury. For a few carrying weapons was a normal activity. Clearly, part of the answer to the problem of robbery would be to increase the chances of people being caught for carrying weapons, perhaps through increased police activity; or to influence offenders' lifestyles so that they do not see it as necessary to carry weapons.

It is tempting to suggest that reducing the availability of weapons (controlling facilitators) should be an aim. But for such measures to be effective there would have to be a dramatic impact on the supply of guns to the black market. Controls on the legal supply of guns miss the point. People wanting to conduct a robbery generally do not apply for a gun licence. They do not need to do so because there is a plentiful supply on the black market. It was a striking finding from the many conversations about this issue how easy guns are to obtain. Thus while legal controls may have some effect on the slippage of guns to the black market, they are not likely to have a dramatic impact on reducing the use of guns in robbery (see Greenwood, 1972). Perhaps a better approach would be to tackle the illegal trafficking of firearms (Taylor, 1994).

Some offenders carried weapons because they believed the police might be armed. In the UK, where arming of police is still a matter of public concern, this finding is important. Weapons gave some people confidence and many said that the main reason they took a weapon with them on a robbery was that it made the robbery easier to conduct; nearly all claimed that the purpose of carrying a weapon was to reduce the chances of an injury occurring. Robbers were often sympathetic to victims, but there was a tendency to underestimate the impact of the crime. Some said that they were not sympathetic to victims because they had no intention of hurting them, not realising that victims had no way of knowing that and every reason to believe the opposite. There may be some scope for building on this aspect in rehabilitative work with offenders in prison. However, according to robbers some victims exaggerate the impact of the offence in order to secure a more severe sentence. Some reported incidents where they felt victims had feigned injury and others claimed victims inflated losses in order to claim more from insurance companies and as a consequence made the crime appear worse than it was.

Nevertheless, injuries did occur and it was suggested that there were principally three reasons for these. First, robbers or their accomplices injured people by accident. In a few cases guns were discharged accidentally and in one case a robber described a raid in which a victim died. There are strong arguments for discouraging robbers from carrying guns which can discharge live ammunition, but most don't anyway. In any event, the majority of injuries involving weapons were the result of people being struck. It is tempting to suggest that in such cases robbers can expect longer sentences if caught but, as will be shown in the next chapter, there is not much scope for optimism about the effects of this approach. As long as there are robberies there will be accidents and injuries. A better pointer to the prevention of injuries during robberies was the second finding here, that accidents occurred because of the intervention of 'have-a-go-heroes'. The advice offered by the Health and Safety Executive (1993) and the police that by-standers should not intervene has much to commend it.

Some people use physical violence gratuitously as a means of intimidation. Fortunately, this applies to only a minority and it is questionable whether many of these robbers are behaving rationally. As stated above, there are many good reasons for not using violence. It is important, therefore, to improve security so as to make the targets less attractive to robbers and to make robbery less attractive as a way of obtaining money.

In a different way, robbers' ability to take control is aided where they are informed about the environment of the robbery. Knowing such things as where the money is, how much there is, what security is present and how it can be circumvented and where the escape routes are help to ensure that a robbery is successful. What robbers fear is the unpredictable, the things that they cannot control and that could lead to them getting caught. Robberies take place very quickly, and during this time the robbers too are under pressure. Many interviewees spoke of a buzz and a rush of adrenalin which they found exciting but their primary objectives were to get the money and escape. The ideal robbery was one in which the robbers quickly obtained the money and escaped without any injury or physical contact. The longer the robbery lasted the more risk to the robbers and the greater the threat to their control of the environment. So what crime prevention ideas emerge from these findings?

There is a big overlap between measures which reduce a robber's ability to exercise control and those which frustrate the escape — between increasing the effort and increasing the risk (Clarke, 1997). One of the major concerns of the robber is to ensure that he or she is able to get away speedily. Thus revolving doors, queuing rails and longer rather than shorter distances between the counter and the doors merit consideration. In addition, a few robbers are caught and convicted with the assistance of CCTV pictures. Some robbers we spoke to pointed out that members of staff posed a threat. Some interviewees who had robbed financial institutions mentioned that mortgage advisors or loan managers in the foyer were a threat, but others argued that they merely offered easy targets as hostages. Similarly, in a few branches the manager's office had a door which led into the foyer and this worried some robbers because it was a feature that was difficult to control — they could never be sure who was behind it.

A second priority for the robber is the seizing of the money or goods. According to the sample they were usually successful. Many of the robbers took the view that they were involved in an act,

robbery, in which their objective was to get *their* money. They were
usually very determined and given this, combined with the fact that
they had more power than the victim (a weapon, the threat of force,
etc.) and the element of surprise, the high success rate is not
surprising. Moreover, many employees were under instructions to
give the money when it was demanded in a robbery.

But not all robbers were successful and it is worth pausing on the
reasons for these failures to see what lessons can be drawn for crime
prevention. Some robberies failed because of victim or bystander
intervention, but it is clearly undesirable to recommend tackling
robbers as a means of capturing or deterring them. Some robberies
failed because victims had faith in security measures, for example,
security screens, and therefore refused to hand over money. (Some
companies advise staff to lie on the floor as soon as a robbery begins
and good security screens can prove an effective prevention measure.)
Of course screens are more suitable for some environments than
others, and many feel they conflict with the marketing objective of
providing a customer-friendly environment (see Beck and Willis,
1998). But where they exist there are advantages in training staff in
their effectiveness to provide them with the confidence to render the
measure effective. Security is getting better but it is only as good as
the employees using it. However, as indicated in the last chapter,
screens present their own problems, not least in rendering violence
more likely.

Robbery is normally not very lucrative, and sentences (relative to
economic advantage) were severe. It is tempting to suggest that
attention should be drawn to the low rewards from robbery when set
against the possible sentence. However, many robbers were desperate
and the gains were important for them at the time. Moreover, since,
as will be shown in the next chapter, robbers did not expect to get
caught, there does not seem much merit in trying harder to get across
the message that crime does not pay.

However, some robbers were disappointed and in two main ways.
First, some obtained much less money than they aimed to get. A few
put this down to bad luck; often robbers would not know how much
was available at the target for them to steal. Procedures which reduce
rewards, for example, the retention of only a minimal amount of cash
in tills, are desirable: some outlets arrange for anything more than a
float to be sent to underground safes. Some robbers who carried out

'across-the-pavement' robberies were not sure whether money was being delivered or collected and hence were uncertain when best to attack. Some operators undertake dummy runs to confuse robbers and there is much merit in this.

Second, and in a different sense, a few robbers were deceived into receiving something other than money; one robber was given shredded paper. Keeping such a supply available can prevent the loss of money and may have other advantages in that robbers will have less incentive to return to the scene or to provide information to others wishing to do so. Given the levels of repeat victimisation reported in the last chapter these considerations are important.

A third aim of the robber is to escape. It was suggested in the last chapter that much could be done to deter robbers by measures to impede escape. Putting obstacles in the robbers' way represent important elements of crime prevention strategies. Fourth, robbers must avoid capture. Most robbers wear disguises (which includes clothing) to avoid being identified, although technology is being designed which may overcome some of the protection disguises afford. Robbers must also avoid the police and this subject is covered in the next chapter.

[NOTES]

[1] It will be recalled from the previous chapter that some robbers only conducted raids when they were sure that no customers were present and others saw advantages in security screens in that these physically isolated them from their biggest danger, people.

[2] Morrison and O'Donnell (1994) found that 69% of robberies were successful. The robbers may therefore have been exaggerating, or been too embarrassed to admit failure. It may have been that the robbers chose to speak about their last successful robbery rather than their last robbery. These possibilities need to be borne in mind. See also, Batterton (1997).

[3] Actually, 40 post office robbers had a gun, but one respondent did not specify whether the gun was real or imitation. For the purposes of this summary that response is classified as 'Missing.'

[4] Fifty-five commercial premises robbers had a gun, but one respondent did not specify whether the gun was real or imitation. For the purposes of this summary, that response is classified as 'Missing.'

[5] However, this was a sensitive issue and given that some robbers were discussing an offence for which they had not been convicted, there was a high non-response to some of the questions.

[6] One robber claimed that he did not need to carry a weapon because he was an expert at martial arts.

[7] Thus legal controls of legitimate guns which ensure they are kept secure may help stem the flow of guns onto the black market and reduce the opportunity to facilitate a crime.

[8] There is clearly no way of checking this, but if robbers are correct then some reputable companies have been involved in what amounts to insurance fraud.

[9] Robbery is by definition a violent offence, and many victims suffer emotional injury. But physical harm is less common and the aim here is to examine the circumstances in which it occurred.

[10] Injuries involving guns were most commonly caused by robbers using them as a blunt instrument, 'pistol-whipping' their victims.

[11] For example, if they fired a shot it would make a noise, attract unwelcome attention and leave evidence (a bullet) at the scene.

Chapter 4
Robbers: The Police, the Sentence and Imprisonment

Crime prevention can result from an effective criminal justice process. In theory the existence of the police, courts, community sentences and prisons may serve as a deterrent to those contemplating offending. They make crime less attractive for those rational offenders who weigh up the risk of being caught and punished against the possible benefits from a crime. Thus the more effective the criminal justice process is, or the more effective it is perceived to be, the less likely it is that a crime will be committed. Of course, this is not the only way of judging its effectiveness: sentences can rehabilitate, prisons can incapacitate. These points will be addressed. However, the main aims of this chapter are to offer an insight into robbers' perspectives on the risks posed by the criminal justice process, and their views on its potential to reduce the frequency and seriousness of offences or to stop robberies altogether. During the interviews questions were asked about the potential of the police and the courts (via sentencing and prison) to impact upon offenders' behaviour. It may perhaps be helpful to first consider briefly how these agencies might have an influence.

The role of the police has, since its inception, been the prevention of crime and the maintenance of public tranquillity (Ascoli, 1979; Reiner, 1985) and more generally to deter offenders. In recent times a diverse range of strategies have been developed and debate has focused on whether the police should be reactive or proactive in their approach to crime (Audit Commission, 1993) and the extent to which they should target serious and repeat offenders (Audit Commission, 1993; 1996). While there is a wealth of evidence which suggests that increased levels of policing have a minimal impact on crime levels targeted police operations have shown evidence of success (see Hopkins-Burke, 1998). During the interviews robbers were asked what they considered to be the chances of being caught before and after their last robbery and to give reasons. They were then asked a more general question about their views on the effectiveness of the police at apprehending and prosecuting robbers. They were also asked if they had ever considered the threat posed by the police Rapid Response Units and whether they had ever monitored police activity in any way and to give reasons.

There is similarly much debate about the proper function of sentencing and prisons, not least about whether the priority should be to deter, incapacitate, rehabilitate or punish (for reviews see Ashworth, 1994,1994a; Morgan 1998; Walker and Padfield, 1996). Clearly, the robbers who were interviewed in prison and who admitted their guilt[1] have not been deterred; and most of those in the sample had been in prison before, although not always for robbery. Given that robbery carries a maximum sentence of life imprisonment it is interesting to explore why robbers were not deterred by this threat.

Deterrence requires that potential offenders are aware of the penalties they will face if they offend and are caught (Beyleveld, 1979; Zimring and Hawkins, 1973).[2] In order to find out more about this issue a number of questions were included in interviews to ascertain robbers' views of their sentence and the impact on them of their period in prison. Since sentences could be deemed to be less effective as deterrents if robbers underestimated the seriousness of their offence or, more specifically, if they underestimated the sentence they were likely to receive, interviewees were asked to compare the sentence they received with what they expected.[3] In order to determine the deterrent potential of prisons, robbers were asked whether they would have committed the robbery had they known that, if caught, they would serve a sentence of five years in prison. And in order to gain an insight into the impact of prison they were asked whether they felt that they would commit a robbery or other offences on release. Robbers were invited to give reasons for their answers to all these questions.

It should be stressed that the data here is limited in its implications. It does not provide offenders' evaluations of the criminal justice process; but this was never intended to be the case. Rather the aim was to evaluate the extent to which the criminal justice process can deter robbers, judging by the experiences of some of those who have committed robbery. At the same time it was hoped that the analysis would help show the sort of reasoning that was carried out by robbers at the scene. Given that the rational offender will weigh up the risks and may consider risks beyond those presented by the immediate situation, a consideration of these issues is important.

ROBBERS' VIEWS ON POLICE AND ON THE PROSPECTS OF BEING CAUGHT

During the interviews robbers were asked about the ways the police had an impact upon how they planned and carried out the offence. Table 4.1 shows that before their last robbery very few robbers considered it likely that they would be caught (see Feeney, 1986). The majority of the sample had either considered the threat of the police and considered it to be very low, or had not given the matter any thought at all.

Table 4.1   Robbers' perceptions of the likelihood of being caught prior to their last robbery

	Bank		BS		PO		CIT		CP	
	No.	%	No.	%	No.	%	No.	%	No.	%
V. High	1	1.3	5	5.0	1	1.6	1	2.1	6	4.0
High	1	1.3	–	–	–	–	–	–	6	4.0
Average	4	5.3	6	5.9	7	11.1	2	4.3	10	6.7
Low	4	5.3	3	3.0	8	12.7	2	4.3	4	2.7
V. Low	47	61.8	53	52.5	37	58.7	29	61.7	60	40.3
Didn't Think	13	17.1	23	22.8	9	14.3	4	8.5	47	31.5
Not Sure	2	2.6	3	3.0	–	–	2	4.3	7	4.7
No Reply	4	5.3	8	7.9	1	1.6	7	14.9	9	6.0
Total	76	100.0	101	100.0	63	100.0	47	100.0	149	100.0

The less organised and more amateurish robbers were much more likely to say they had not considered the possibility of being caught. This was especially true where the offence was in some way linked to drugs or alcohol. Some respondents were committing robberies on such a regular basis that they viewed capture sooner or later as inevitable. A few interviewees said that they had wanted to be caught or were resigned to it while some were in no state to consider the consequences. In these circumstances imprisonment was sometimes seen as a way out of a life inundated with personal problems. While the rewards might not objectively be judged to be high, they were easy to obtain. Some typical comments include:

'The state I was in on the drugs, all I was thinking about was the money.'

'Drugs and drink — I didn't give a monkeys.'

'Inside of me I was wishing to be caught so the whole affair would end, it was the only way. The police asked why didn't I go to them, but they were threatening and not idle threats either and also intimidation. I am quite a submissive person who is totally dispensable. There is a lot of this with drug-related organisations, especially in London.'

'My attitude was if I got caught I got caught. I didn't really give a damn.'

However, the relatively well-organised professional robbers were more likely to state that they had calculated the threat from the police and considered it to be 'very low'. There were several reasons for this. Many interviewees believed that with good planning and a well-constructed raid there was little risk. They pointed out that they would disguise their appearance and not leave evidence at the scene and there was no reason why they should be suspected, let alone prosecuted and convicted. Some argued that robbery was a fairly easy offence to commit and only lasted a short while and that capture was usually due to bad luck:

'If everybody does what they're supposed to, and it goes to plan, there is no way you should get caught.'

'We knew it was nil or else we wouldn't do it. We believed in ourselves 100% we'd get away with it. If it was 99% we wouldn't do it.'

'I spent a couple of days thinking about it, but by the time the police found out we should be 5 minutes away, and then they'd have no description, no fingerprints, so I thought we'd be OK.'

'I'd planned it well enough, but you never know. I knew if the police were called I'd be caught. I suppose I was confident.'

'The only chance (of being caught) is if you don't give a damn and go hair-raising about, or if the police happen to be there.'

Some robbers said that they blocked the thought of capture from their mind or at least relegated it to the deepest recesses. This is not uncommon amongst offenders (Bennett and Wright, 1984). To do otherwise was tantamount to 'negative thinking' and they felt this could affect their confidence:[4]

'It didn't even enter my head. If you go in there with preconceptions of being caught you'll balls it up. I am very careful.'

'That's negative thinking. If I thought about getting caught I wouldn't do it.'

'If you think you'll get caught, you will.'

'If I thought about it I'd panic.'

A few respondents believed that their determination to avoid capture was so strong that if necessary they would have become violent:

'I wouldn't have got caught. I was armed, I would have shot my way out. That is how I felt at the time.'

'I was prepared to shoot it out with the police if necessary.'

As will be shown later, many did not feel that the police were effective and therefore offered a serious threat. But what about after the raid, how did robbers view their chances then? The responses are shown in Table 4.2.

Table 4.2   Robbers' perceptions of the likelihood of being caught after their last robbery

	Bank		BS		PO		CIT		CP	
	No.	%	No.	%	No.	%	No.	%	No.	%
V. High	6	7.9	7	8.9	6	9.5	1	2.1	15	10.1
High	1	1.3	6	6.9	11	17.5	1	2.1	15	10.1
Average	2	2.6	4	4.0	2	3.2	2	4.3	4	2.7
Low	1	1.3	4	4.0	2	3.2	1	2.1	6	4.0
V. Low	43	56.6	57	56.4	33	52.4	28	59.6	65	43.6
Not Sure	1	1.3	3	3.0	1	1.6	1	2.1	6	4.0
Didn't Think	5	6.6	5	5.0	3	4.8	–	–	12	8.1
Caught in the act	9	11.8	6	5.9	4	6.3	5	10.6	19	12.8
Missing	8	10.5	9	8.9	1	1.6	8	17.0	7	4.7
Total	76	100.0	101	100.0	63	100.0	47	100.0	149	100.0

After the robbery most had given the possibility of capture some thought, although the majority felt that the chances of being convicted were negligible. This was less true of robbers of building societies, post offices and commercial premises. Bank robbers, and in particular cash-in-transit robbers, were the least likely to claim that they thought they would be caught, assuming that since no evidence had been left behind there was nothing to connect them to the raid.

When robbers were asked how they were caught nearly half of those responding claimed specifically that they were 'grassed'; and others included this as a possibility. It seems probable that the likelihood of this was overstated. It is much easier to serve a sentence for robbery believing that one was unfortunate enough to be grassed up than it is to put it down to personal error or to the competence of what some consider to be the enemy, the police. In reality many robbers were not certain why they were caught; and those who thought that they had been unlucky will have been largely unaware of the contribution of good police work to their fate. Certainly, robbers did not have a very positive view of police competence (especially the more organised robbers). When asked whether they thought the police were effective in catching and prosecuting robbers 60.3% answered in the negative. There were principally two reasons.

First, and echoing the point made above, robbers believed that without 'grasses' (and to a lesser extent information from the public) the police would catch very few robbers. Several reasoned that if they avoided making errors, and did not put themselves in a position where they could be informed on, then they could not be caught by the police. In other words, they believed their fate to be entirely in their own hands:

'Unless you are grassed up or caught in the act it is impossible to be caught.'

'99% are down to grasses.'

'If it wasn't for informers they wouldn't get anybody.'

'If you're stupid the police will catch you but if you use your head you won't get caught.'

Second, some interviewees believed police officers obtained results by adopting illegal and oppressive tactics. At least two interviewees claimed that they were serving sentences for robberies they did not carry out, although they admitted carrying out other robberies for which they had not been convicted. Others pointed to the fact that they had committed many robberies and never been caught and/or knew of others who had carried out raids and never been convicted:

'If they were that good, they would have caught me on the other 9 jobs.'

'I know no end of people who've done it and never been caught.'

In fact, prison folklore is rife with stories of police incompetence. The following is one example:

'Well, I come out of the Post Office, when the alarm bell was ringing, and I'd walked across the road, put me foot on the kerb on the opposite side of the road, and just something told me to turn round. So I looked and . . . a Maestro come round the corner, and then I seen a blue light on top. Anyway I carries on walking up the road, and then this copper had come round the corner and he just looked straight at me, straight in the eyes. I could see the guy looking at me, and he looked down at the gun, looked back at me in the face, and went straight past me, straight past the Post Office, and straight up the hill.'

It was reasoned that either the officer had not noticed the gun or had decided that it would be wiser, for reasons of personal safety, to ignore the threat.

Of those offenders who said that the police were good at catching and convicting robbers, many were reflecting on their own experience:

'Quite impressed with the police. They caught the driver so quickly. Someone took his number plate and as the driver got to his house the police boxed him in.'

'They had helicopters out within minutes. They were very efficient.'

Others had formed more general impressions:

'I remember saying to my friend "Yeah, we need them" [the police] and he said I was wrong, the old bill are this, the old bill are that and I said to him, "Just picture this, you walk in your kitchen, your mother's on the floor and there's a big carving knife sticking out of her neck. She's got one of her stockings round her throat, and her skirt's hitched up to her waist. Are you going to catch him?" I think the police do a good job. There's bad police, there's good police.'

By and large the police were not seen as a serious threat. Partly in response to this some police areas have attempted to increase the risk factor for robbers by introducing Police Rapid Response Units. In all just over four in 10 robbers (41.2%) who expressed a view said they had at some point considered the threat from such a unit in preparing for a raid. Some robbers were not aware of these units, and even amongst those that were there was considerable scepticism about their effectiveness. In many ways the comments here mirror those made in response to the previous question: proper planning and positive thinking should ensure that they were not a threat. Some claimed that the bigger worry, because it was more likely, was encountering an ordinary police patrol:

'They're only a worry to people who don't plan things.'

'I don't really worry about them. The chances of them being there are remote.'

'I am aware of these but they don't represent a real threat. A single PC on the street could be more of a problem.'

That the police were not considered by robbers to pose a major risk was confirmed when just under three in 10 (29.2%) of those who answered the question said that they had never monitored police activity. Most felt that it was unnecessary, and even those that had done some monitoring rarely saw this as an integral part of planning:

'Scanners. I like one on when I'm driving around but I only pick up local units. But the flying squad and (special) units have their own bands. I had one nicked out of a police car. It cost me about £1,000 for that.'

'I sometimes find out who CID are and what they look like.'

'It's a common practice for thieves to know what time the police change shifts and when there's less police on the street.'

'After the robbery we monitored the police on the radio.'

Morrison and O'Donnell (1996) found that there was little appreciation by robbers that effective police work was responsible for their capture. The results of this study too show that robbers believed that the police were not very effective at all.

ROBBERS AND THEIR SENTENCE

When robbers felt they had been treated badly by the courts, when they felt the sentence was unduly harsh, this sometimes affected the way they viewed imprisonment. It will be recalled that in Chapter 2 some people were quoted as saying that they engaged in robbery because of a sense of injustice after harsh treatment by the criminal justice process. It is thus important to compare robbers' views of the sentence they expected and received. In theory, if it could be shown that robbers underestimated the sentence they would receive or that a more severe sentence would discourage some, then there would be a greater potential than is sometimes thought for sentencing policy to have an impact on preventing offences from taking place. The problem in practice is that most robbers do not think about getting caught and so they view the threat of prison as, at best, a remote one.

Respondents were asked how the sentence they received for their last conviction compared with that which they had expected and the findings are shown in Table 4.3.

Table 4.3   Sentence received by robbers and what they had expected to receive

Sentenced Received	SENTENCED EXPECTED		
	Up to 5 yrs (%)	6–10 yrs (%)	Over 10 yrs (%)
Up to 5 yrs	65.0	42.1	5.9
6–10 yrs	33.0	47.9	41.2
Over 10 yrs	1.9	10.0	52.9
Total	100.0	100.0	100.0

Overall, robbers are not very good at predicting their sentence; a lot get it wrong. When asked to account for the differences most referred to recognised mitigating factors (see, Ashworth, 1995; Walker and Padfield, 1996). Many of those respondents who received a shorter term than expected believed that the judges had taken a positive view of such factors as their guilty plea; their (not too serious) previous criminal record; other mitigating circumstances (such as mental illness); their age (and especially the fact that they were young) and the fact that they were helpful to the police. One robber felt that his letter to the judge had helped earn him a reduced sentence; and many admitted that their sentence had been a pleasant surprise:

'We was quite shocked. For 6 months I fastened my mind on 14 years, so when he said 6 I leapt up.'

'Chuffed to bits. I could've shook the judge's hand.'

A few robbers claimed that they had purchased a reduced sentence by paying for good legal representation. Some considered this unfair and symptomatic of a corrupt system which favours those with the means to pay.

Those robbers who received a longer sentence than they had expected offered a variety of explanations. Some felt that the judges had taken a more severe view than they had expected of particular circumstances such as the amount of violence used, previous convictions and/or crimes taken into consideration. Some felt that their legal representation had been poor and there was considerable antipathy towards what robbers believed were bad barristers. Many claimed they had encountered a harsh judge; comments such as 'mean bastard', and 'raving lunatic' typified comments on this issue. Some robbers also reflected on the injustice of being sentenced by someone who was old and out of touch with reality.

Several robbers believed that they had been unjustly treated by an unfair system. Some felt they had suffered from racial prejudice, and a few respondents were involved in trials where the jury had been granted protection. Robbers claimed that this immediately stacked the odds against them getting a fair trial because the jury were made conscious that they were dealing with serious offenders. It has been impossible to test the validity of this concern because records were not kept centrally; but it does merit further research. Another source of the irritation some robbers expressed about the courts, and more particularly the judiciary, concerned the use of replica firearms. The fact that the law in the UK fails to make a distinction between real and replica weapons was considered unfair and unjust:

'On the premises I used an imitation gun. I didn't want to hurt no-one, never hurt no-one. I just wanted to get the money, you know . . . I suppose they [the victims] believed it was real. As far as the judge is concerned he sentenced me for a real one, which I don't think is right, I have to admit.'

'If the person is carrying a replica gun now, the police are saying that you can get the same amount in prison as if you're carrying a real gun, and I think that's just craziness 'cos people are just going to say "Well to hell with the carrying the replica gun now, I'm going to get the same amount of jail, so I may as well carry a real gun."'

As the last quote suggests, sentencing led some robbers to the view that there was now little incentive to refrain from carrying a real gun, with the result that the potential dangers for victims are inevitably increased. Of course, such a view does not take account of the fact that where a weapon is not real it may be treated by the judge as a mitigating factor, or that where a real weapon is used it may count as aggravating the offence.[5] One career robber who was interviewed said that he intended to retire when he left prison. He argued that if he did commit another robbery he would not hesitate to shoot to kill if that was necessary. He reasoned that if he was caught again he would go to prison for life and that it would make little difference whether it was for robbery and firearms offences or murder. And by committing murder he could remove the risk both of a 'have-a-go hero' who could thwart the robbery, and a potential witness.[6] Fortunately this was not a commonly expressed view; but it is an important one and serves to underline the importance of understanding offenders' perspectives.

ROBBERS AND THE IMPACT OF IMPRISONMENT

The issue of robbers' views on prison will be tackled by dividing the discussion into two main areas. Initially, how robbers view the threat of imprisonment prior to offending, and the extent to which these considerations impact upon their planning will be examined. Subsequently, the focus will move on to the question of how robbers regard prison having served part of a custodial sentence, and particular attention will be paid to the question of how their experiences as prisoners may affect the possibility of their re-offending upon release.

Prison aims to act as a deterrent but for this group of offenders it has failed. But the question remains of whether these robbers would have been deterred by a longer sentence. Thus, respondents were asked whether they would still have committed their last robbery had they known that they would have served at least five years in prison and just over four out of 10 (40.6%) of those expressing a view said that they would not. These were more commonly the less organised and amateurish robbers who in practice do not think much about the consequences until after they have been caught! This point emerged from the answers of those who claimed a severe sentence would not deter them; they had been so muddled at the time of the robbery that they had not considered the consequences of their actions. Others felt that thinking about prison was negative and bad practice. Some robbers had built the threat of prison into their life and accepted the risk but gave it very little thought:

> 'Because there's always the chance that you ain't gonna get caught, and if the prize is big enough, it's worth it.'

> 'You have to put it in context. When a person has eight kids and no job, you don't think about the sentence when you have to think about survival. 10 years won't make any difference, you have to live.'

'It's worth it. I'd do a 5 year stretch for £50,000. I'd do it for £10,000. I love money.'

'If the money is there. I mean what is 5 years if you're looking at £250,000? You can retire on that.'

'It's the £ signs that you count, not the number of years.'

'Because the money was stronger than the thought of coming to prison.'

More important was the fact, as noted earlier, that robbers believed the chances of capture to be low. Some robbers pointed out that the question was silly: if they knew they would be caught they would not commit the offence regardless of the length of sentence:

'I don't think deterrent sentences make any difference. If you thought you were going to get caught, you wouldn't do it.'

'You don't look at any sentence being a deterrent because you never believe you're going to get caught.'

It was the more organised and professional robbers who were the most likely to say that they would still have committed the offence even if they knew they would serve five years. Some of course would serve more time than this anyway, but for many it is unlikely that even if the question had specified 20 years the answers would have been very different. This group did not see the police as effective and did not see prison as a deterrent; they had calculated the risks to be low. This research adds to the body of literature which suggests that crime prevention activity needs to be focused on increasing the risk of being caught rather than increasing the severity of punishment. Current policy in the UK, and embodied in the Crime (Sentences) Act 1997, imposes an automatic life sentence (unless there are exceptional circumstances) on those convicted for a second time of robbery in possession of a firearm or imitation firearm. Seen as a measure to incapacitate, it may have some effect. But to the extent that it is intended to deter, there must be little optimism, given the robbers' views expressed here, that it will meet its objective.

But having been caught and imprisoned, how much ground was there for believing that these robbers would not commit further offences? In order to clarify this, robbers were asked whether they thought they would commit another robbery or other offence when they were released. The responses are shown in Table 4.4.

Table 4.4.   Whether robbers believed they would commit further offences on leaving prison

Response	Robbery		Another Crime	
	Frequency	Valid %	Frequency	Valid %
Yes	40	11.7	92	27.0
No	247	72.4	159	46.6
Not Sure	50	14.7	71	20.8
Refused/No Reply/N/A	4	1.2	19	5.6
Total	341	100.0	341	100.0

Only 11.7% thought they would rob again and 27% that they would commit another crime when released, while approaching a half (46.6%) of all respondents said that they would not commit another offence (see also Feeney, 1986). If these findings tell us anything it is that robbers are unrealistic and over-optimistic about their aspirations for a crime free life. The realities of post-prison life are somewhat different. It is worth recalling that nearly two-thirds (65.4%) of the sample had been in prison before and the experience of prison had not had the effect of deterring them at that stage. Moreover, those who were experiencing their first period of incarceration were more likely than those who had been imprisoned before to say that they would not commit another robbery when released ($x2 = 6.9$, $p < 0.01$), suggesting that some of the optimism was a reflection of inexperience.

Several explanations were offered as to why robbers believed they would not commit another robbery, reasons not unrelated to why offenders eventually give up crime (see Shover, 1985). For some the reason for offending had been removed and others felt they had developed as people:

'I've learned a lot about myself and my family, and I've realised I don't need to do it.'

'The reason for me doing armed robberies prior to this sentence was not having any patience; wanting everything yesterday. Now I have the patience of an oyster (sic). This sentence has taught me that.'

'I see myself as a young lad with plenty of time to rebuild my life. I've had help from a psychologist in prison and I'll continue on release.'

Many focused on the negative experience of prison both on themselves and their families:

'This has been a nightmare.'

'Because I've wasted the best years of my life.'

'I just can't be bothered, you know what I mean? I prefer my life. In here you haven't got a life. You're being told to do this, do that. I prefer going out, meeting people, all that sort of thing, you know, having a drink and that. No way I would do it again.'

'I'm not going to commit more crimes. I want to live a normal life. Life is too short to be in here.'

'Anyone who comes back again is a fool.'

'I'll never chance it again. It's a stupid game and the price is too high.'

'I don't ever want to do any more jail. Never. I have a daughter who is 6 years old, and I only started seeing her in August. I don't want to miss that.'

'I ain't having any more of this. It's made me mum ill and wrecked me girlfriend's life and mine.'

Some had made a commitment to achieve success by legitimate means, some knew that a job was waiting for them on release:

'The reasons why I started committing robberies have been resolved. I have a choice of jobs and my savings.'

'I have alternative plans — a writing career.'

'Definitely not. I have a good job to go out to.'

For others the decision to desist was a practical one; this included the belief of some that they were too old. Some of these robbers intended to commit other types of crime where the rewards were greater, the chances of capture were perceived to be lower, and the penalties less severe. A variety of offences were mentioned; some aimed to return to burglary, at which they had been successful in the past; but many saw drug-related crime and to a lesser extent fraud as more attractive. Many though referred to quite minor offences:

'No doubt. I don't think I've had tax on my car for years. Reformed-yes, angel-no.'

'Only things which get a little time — like driving while disqualified.'

'I may still smoke drugs, but I won't do anything heavily criminal.'

But what about those who were serving a sentence for robbery and claimed that they would commit more offences on release? These offered several reasons. First, robbery remained the easiest and quickest way to make money:

'I've tried burgling and shoplifting, and the money I've earned I could have got robbing in half the time.'

Second, there was a lack of knowledge of alternative ways of earning a living. Many believed that it would be very difficult for them to find employment after serving a prison sentence (see Gill, 1997):

'No-one will give me a chance. Not after 10 years in here.'

'If I can get a job I won't go back to robbery, but if I am broke, I will.'

'When I go out I'm willing to go straight, but I ain't gonna starve on the dole and play the goody goody, and sit and suffer. If the opportunity is there, I'll take it.'

'I'll have to. No job, no money. Robbery will put me back on my feet.'

Third, for some committing robberies was a way of life; they pointed out that they had no family and that there was no reason not to resume robbing:

'Definitely, because it's me only way of life. I ain't been offered any other opportunities. In fact I am more pushed towards it now than at any other time in my life.'

'I've been doing this since I was 13 years old, so the likelihood is quite strong.'

'I've only ever done robberies.'

'It won't stop me. (Prison) will never stop crime; it can't, because it doesn't do nothing to you except break your family up which makes you bitter, and once you've been here no-one will employ you so you have to do crime.'

'Without a doubt. It's in my nature now. I've been doing this for 19 years. I don't know anything else. To me, I look at robbery like you do going to work — I don't always wanna do it but I have to.'

Fourth, some claimed that the experience of prison had prepared them for future offences; prisons can often act as a 'school' for offenders. It provided an opportunity to discuss the mistakes of the past and strategies for the future. It is not that these offenders liked prison, very few did; it is merely that rather than take away the incentive to commit crime prison had provided inspiration and strengthened the feeling that there was little alternative to a life of crime.

A minority of robbers were not sure whether they would commit a robbery in the future. It depended on circumstances that they could not then imagine and also on the potential reward. Several robbers noted that it was easy for them to say that they would not re-offend while sitting in prison, being constantly reminded of the penalty for their law-breaking; but that on the outside, surrounded by temptation and an environment often conducive to getting involved in law-breaking activities, promises made to oneself in prison could be difficult to keep:

'Don't know. It just depends what happens when I get drunk.'

'I don't know. It's easy to say that you won't rob again when you're in here, but you can't say what you are going to do.'

'You see you soon forget a prison when you leave it. Three weeks after you're out and you've forgotten all about it; it doesn't exist in your mind anymore, except in the dark recesses.'

Certainly, for some robbers the imposition of a long custodial sentence merely exacerbated the problems which had led them to commit robberies in the first place. These include poor job prospects, weakened family ties (many respondents reported being left by their partners while in prison), a lack of money, an increased number of criminal acquaintances (as a result of being in prison for several years), and a deeper feeling of bitterness against 'the system'.

DISCUSSION

Robbery is seen as a relatively easy offence which reaps sufficient and immediate rewards; it can be conducted quickly and preparation can be minimal. Few robbers thought that there was a very high chance of being caught (and some of those that did mentioned that they would be better off in prison). But the data suggests there are two distinct groups. The less organised and more amateurish robbers who did not plan very much, and did not give any thought to being caught or to the consequences of their actions. Conversely the more organised and professional robbers thought about the chances of being caught and considered them to be low because they planned their offence to reduce the risk. They adopted a positive frame of mind which included thinking that the risk of capture was low. There did not appear to be much scope for the deterrent approach, not because robbers are irrational but because amateurs had more pressing concerns and professionals had planned to minimise the risk.

Robbers did not view the police as a serious threat. Even those who had monitored police activity were often not dedicated to the task. Only some had given thought to undercover operations and some viewed police patrols as a bigger danger than Rapid Response Units. The more organised professional robbers were more likely to say that they believed the police to be ineffective. From the robbers' perspective the police could claim successes only because they used grasses and informers and because they adopted unorthodox and illegal tactics. While police tactics and operations do result in the arrest and prosecution of robbers (Ball et al, 1978; Creedon, 1994; Jammers, 1995; Matthews, 1997), many offenders are not aware of this. It seems that robbers underestimate the effectiveness of the police and there may be scope for advertising their successes more widely, to make the rational robber think again about the wisdom of conducting a raid (see also Bowers, 1999: 144).

Once the robber is caught and prosecuted he/she will invariably be sent to prison and robbers know that. The sentence, which before the robbery had been a distant thought, becomes a reality. When robbers were asked to state what sentence they thought they would receive and compare it with what happened, it emerged that many had calculated incorrectly. This was principally because of judges taking a more severe or lenient view of the circumstances of the offence and the offender's record. Robbers who had underestimated their sentence pointed to a variety of factors, including bad barristers and unfair judges. According to some robbers, injustice also occurs because of race, jury protection, disproportionate sentences for robbery compared with other crimes, and because some defendants have the funds to pay for a better defence. The failure of the law to distinguish between real and imitation guns was criticised by some robbers on the grounds of both fairness and commonsense; but they failed to appreciate that distinctions are made at the sentencing stage and this point needs to be made more widely known. In a similar way it was noted that as sentences for robbery became more severe the incentive not to use violence was reduced; one robber felt that such was his criminal record if he were to offend again there would be little difference in his sentence even if he killed someone. This is a rational view also from the viewpoint that killing a victim can reduce resistance and thereby the risk of capture. Most offenders are rational and there are worrying signs that sentencing policies (and ignorance about the rules) may lead to more violence rather than less when a robbery is committed.

And a major limit on the value of deterrent sentences is that robbers do not expect to get caught. Amateur robbers were more likely than professionals to admit that had they believed they would serve at least five years in prison they would not have committed the robbery, but they did not think about getting caught. Professional robbers did not expect to be caught and so prison was not a relevant consideration. In any event, when asked to explain why they would commit further robberies they pointed to the easy opportunities, the fact that robbery was a way of life and the difficulty of earning money another way. Prison had merely compounded some people's problems and provided an environment in which to learn more about the techniques of illegal trades.

Yet while in prison most were optimistic that on release they would lead a crime-free life. The reasons for the offence had been removed, they had changed as people, prison had caused misery for themselves and their families, they had prospects for the future (see Cusson, 1986). Some aimed to commit other crimes, although these would be mostly less violent and often minor. Yet the realities are somewhat different. Indeed, for two-thirds of the sample this was not their first time in prison. Some of those who were unable to predict their future behaviour articulated quite well the pull on the one hand of a belief that there must be a better life than that offered by imprisonment, and on the other hand the realities of returning to the same communities and to the influences which had contributed to their previous offences. However well intentioned and genuine their aspirations, and this finding is important, the bitter experience is that many will not fulfil them.

It would be wrong to argue that prison is always wholly uncon-structive or without benefits of some kind and many have advocated longer sentences as an appropriate response to robbery (Home Office, 1986; Kapardis, 1988; Marsden, 1990), especially for those who cause physical harm to victims (Cooke, 1980). Prison does incapacitate; as Clarke and Field (1991) found, at least some reduction in the robbery of convenience stores was due to persistent robbers being imprisoned. Some robbers admitted that incarceration had given them a chance for reflection. Some had managed to restructure their lives although one has to be careful about interpreting this as a beneficial impact of prison. Some might have changed anyway and others changed despite being in prison rather than because of it. While it was not an aim of the study to fully evaluate the effectiveness of prison, according to robbers it does not work as a deterrent. Nor is there much scope for suggesting that, even if punishments were made much more severe, robbers would be more likely to be deterred. Some indeed use the threat of long sentences as a justification for violence in carrying out the raid. And while some may go on to lead better lives on release, others learn new tricks needed to commit crime.

As presently structured the criminal justice process does not deter robbers because it does not impact directly on their biggest and most immediate concern, that is the threat of being caught. Robbers want to avoid incarceration, but it is unlikely deterrent sentences can work because often robbers do not consider the possibility of being caught; or if they do, they take steps to minimise the risk of it happening. Thus while robbers do not appear good at predicting their likely sentence, they do know they will go to prison for some time; but robbery is easy and the chances of capture are small and this typifies robbers' thinking on this issue. Once they are in prison many are optimistic that they will not offend again, but this is probably a delusion. For some offending is all they know and the lack of alternatives forms a barrier between them and a crime-free life. Perhaps the biggest opportunity for the criminal justice process relates to the role of the police. Research has shown that effective police strategies can result in arrests; while the findings from this study suggest that robbers often underestimate the ability of the police to arrest and prosecute them. If robbers believed that there was a real chance of their being caught, if the risks could be shown to them to be serious, then some would desist. But, as the case studies in the next chapter show, it would not be easy to get the message across.

[NOTES]

[1] Robbers were only interviewed about offences that they admitted.

[2] Deterrence assumes that people will decide not to commit a crime because of the likely sentence. The questions here on their expected sentence were answered in the context that they had already been apprehended. Their view, had they been asked at the time of the offence might have been different. This point needs to be borne in mind.

[3] Some may have expected a lower sentence because they undertook some form of plea bargaining, although, as will be shown, the reasons given were different.

[4] Some robbers used the fear of getting caught as an incentive to prepare properly; thus rather than negative thinking, this was a positive way of ensuring they conducted an effective raid.

[5] See *R* v *Gould* (1983) 5 Cr App R (S) 72, a judgment given by the then Lord Chief Justice, Lord Lane.

[6] This point was made in a lecture given by Lord Taylor, at King's College, London, 6 March 1996.

Chapter 5
Case Studies of Robbers

This chapter is based on the accounts of four robbers who were interviewed, and then re-interviewed during the project. They have not been chosen because they are 'typical' or 'representative'. Indeed, it will be suggested in the next chapter that since robbers' styles vary so markedly one has to be cautious about classifying them in this way. Rather, they have been included here because they have a range of experiences which help to explain or highlight some issues associated with robbery.

For example, Billy was adopted while a baby by a middle-class family who sent him to a good school, and he won a place at university. Many of his crimes were committed in order to support or please his gay partners in one way or another. In contrast, Dennis spent his childhood in foster homes, and when he did manage to establish contact with his parents he found that his mother was a prostitute and his father an alcoholic. He was caught because he committed a robbery at a premises protected by racketeers.

John was an offender from a young age. He was clever and ruthless and was able to rise within the criminal hierarchy quite quickly and become the leader of a team of robbers. John subsequently co-operated with the police and claims that there is a contract out on him. Tom was also disaffected from a young age. He was made to feel inadequate and met someone who provided him with an opportunity to escape the limits of his environment. He proved good at what he did and made a lot of money from robbery. But reality has dawned and Tom feels that there may well be no life other than crime even after his long sentence.

The names of individuals mentioned in this chapter have been changed and so has any detail which might identify them; at least two of these robbers have received a considerable amount of media attention. They were chosen, at least in part, because they were candid about their circumstances and were able to articulate their views. Space will permit only a part of their experience to be discussed here, but it is hoped that, collectively, their accounts will provide an insight into why and how people commit robbery and will illustrate many points that have been raised in the first part of the book and which will be expanded on in Chapter 6.

BILLY

Billy was given away to an adoption service at the age of six weeks and was adopted almost immediately and raised by a relatively wealthy, but quite strict, Methodist family who had two daughters, one of whom was also adopted. He was brought up in a comfortable middle-class neighbourhood, attended a good school and won a place at university. However, he only stayed a few weeks. His life became dominated by crime, spurred on by the need for money to live the good life and to support his relationships with other men. It all culminated in robberies which led to his receiving a seven-year sentence, and another three years when he escaped and committed more offences. Billy now claims to be a reformed character. He has taken a degree, made contact with his family and established an almost paternal relationship with two boys he refers to as his sons. Billy was confident that his future would remain crime free.

Billy's childhood was almost idyllic. By the age of twelve he was a church organist, he swam for the county, and was a member of various school teams and took part in plays. His family went on two foreign holidays every year, and although his parents were strict about certain things such as being home on time, in many ways he was spoiled as a young man:

'I knew that if he [Billy's father] said ''no,'' first, within half an hour I could have persuaded him to change his mind. I used to use that skill and persuasiveness that I've got to get money out of people. From a very early age I had absolutely no idea of the value of money or saving money or anything, as I always knew that I could go back to my dad and get some more. So yes, I was very spoilt in that respect.'

Billy attended a grammar school, 'one of the best schools in the north of England', from the age of five to eighteen and received 'a very good education'. He felt he was brighter than average and was one of a group of six to eight boys whom he described as:

'All middle class, fathers had jobs, two car families, and four, five bedroom houses. That sort of environment. Kids of mill-owners, lawyers, and people whose fathers owned local businesses.'

Despite these advantages Billy remembered committing his first offence at the age of eight:

'We had a house [at school] for sports and things and . . . we used to have displays of quality coin collections and quality stamp collections. I collected coins and stamps and I used to take the coins and stamps from the displays.'

Billy recalled feeling no guilt at doing this:

'It was the most natural thing in the world. I didn't have that stamp and I needed that stamp . . . and I didn't have any conscience about it being wrong; I didn't think ''this is wrong.'' '

After that first episode, Billy began to steal things regularly:

'If I didn't have what I wanted I would take it . . . I made a pact with myself that I had to steal one object a day. This object had to be a piece of jewellery or bits of silver. These objects used to come from the houses of my friends, because you could go round to these big houses and play around, sneak into their parents' bedroom . . . and pick up the first bit of china thing I saw, and then that was put into a chess box. I stored up quite a little parcel; knives, forks, and trinkets. I was like Fagin, taking them out at night.'

His thefts were not discovered until he was ten and his parents made him return all the items. He recalls his friends' parents being quite understanding, and he felt little remorse:

'I felt I had this secret world of mine which was only just beginning to evolve. It became more important to me. I knew there was something there that I couldn't share with anyone else. I was very aware of what I was doing, I was aware that it was theft but I was totally unworried about the fact that it was wrong. I thought because it was me that was doing it, it was okay; it was all for the greater good of me. It was all totally egotistical.'

From the age of ten Billy's delinquency began to escalate. He started playing truant from school, mainly to avoid being punished for not completing homework and he continued to steal including possessions of staff at school. By the time he was thirteen Billy's days truanting were spent in Manchester and Liverpool:

'Manchester . . . was a very exciting place for me . . . with these big Victorian buildings, and I felt a sense of power. I loved this, being in the centre. I loved being in on the action, in the heat of things, right where it's happening . . . Big days out. I was the boss and I could do exactly what I wanted to do. I could tell anybody anything because they didn't know who I was. I was living in a little fantasy world . . . It was like going out of one life and into another. I've always been able to move between social worlds easily.'

Since these adventures were more fun if he had money Billy decided to steal from the most accessible source, his parents. He would sneak into his parents' room while they slept and take money from his father's wallet. Eventually they noticed that money was missing, but Billy always denied taking it:

'In the end it got to the stage where my parents put a lock on their bedroom door. They knew very well I was taking it, I knew very well that they knew I was taking it, but I continued to take it. Gradually this feeling of distrust came in the household and I became more and more an enemy within.'

As Billy became older he discovered another virtue of the big city, the availability of sex. From a young age he had known he was gay, and this became another feature of his 'secret world':

'I had a lot of sexual romps . . . when I went to Manchester. This would have been totally unacceptable to my parents. There was no way I could tell them that I used to fancy other boys.'

Billy's first sexual experience occurred at the age of eight and was with a Spanish sailor he met on a trip with his parents to the Canary Islands. However, Billy did not find the episode traumatic:

> 'I didn't find the experience in the slightest bit unpleasant; I enjoyed it. I didn't go and tell my parents. He knew my name, he said "you have sweet peaches," peaches being my balls. I got the feeling I'd know exactly what to do, and he gave me an erection straight away. So that was my first sexual encounter; I don't feel any revulsion now or anything.'

Billy kept his homosexuality secret until much later. He had had several 'encounters' with other boys at school including an affair with the headmaster's son, but when he was in the sixth form he 'came out' after falling in love with Wayne, a fifth form boy. Billy's parents found out about his homosexuality when they caught him in bed with his lover. Their response was to send Billy to a psychiatrist, to remove the telephone from his room, and to restrict his access to money:

> 'I had started throwing quite bad tantrums. My parents were frightened of me and my sisters were. I was drinking and drinking. It made me really unpleasantly arrogant; it had a really bad effect on me.'

At this stage, Billy had not anticipated embarking on a career in crime:

> 'I'd never even thought about prison . . . I had planned a glittering career for myself. I was thinking it would be rather nice to be Prime Minister. In all seriousness, such was my egotistical nature.'

However, Billy's first involvement with the legal system was to follow soon after. He went to university to study economics but lasted only six weeks. Problems arose because he had started gambling and would squander his allowance. He was drinking a lot too and this resulted in the ending of his relationship with Wayne:

> 'I would have done absolutely anything for Wayne, and it's been the pattern ever since. After Wayne it was someone else, and someone else . . . This was the whole business about building societies. I was robbing them because I was in love with someone who didn't have anything at all, and I would have done anything for them. There's been about six or seven of them.'

The Christmas after quitting university Billy was caught sneaking a bottle of gin into a pub, and when the landlord tried to throw him out Billy attacked him. The police were called and Billy assaulted several police officers while being arrested. He was charged by the police and resolved to change his ways. He was sentenced to 24 hours at an attendance centre and while his parents felt disgraced he believed that he had been lucky:

'At the time I got caught I really meant it, I wasn't going to do it again. Until I got away with it, and then everything was back to normal again.'

Billy's sentence consisted mainly of scrubbing floors at a police station. But it was here that he came into contact with other criminals for the first time. Before Billy had completed his attendance centre sentence, he was arrested again:

'I stole my father's (credit) card . . . I needed it to finance my days in the cities, my days of lust really. It was a very decadent time; there were days when I may have more than one sexual encounter and I was paying for it . . . I was spending a lot of money so . . . I signed my father's signature and went off to Manchester on a spree. I was caught the following day at some jewellers . . . I didn't know anything about credit card procedures . . . I was just sat there in the jewellers and the police came in and arrested me.'

Billy went to court again and was placed in a remand centre for ten days to await his sentence. Even after he had been at the attendance centre, it had never occurred to him that he might be sent to prison. But after this latest period of incarceration, he was determined to change his ways:

'When I was finally released I was determined never ever to get into trouble again. It was horrific. Imagine the upbringing I'd had. I mean it must be bad for someone who's been dragged up through institutions and children's homes and borstals . . . but for someone who'd been molly-coddled like I had; travelled around the world by this stage; always had the best of everything, bang, I was in the remand centre. It was dreadful. In the mini-bus travelling there I got talking to someone who asked me if it was my first time inside. I said "yes" it was and he said, "Get your self in the hospital." "Why?" "Because it's easy enough in there. The tellies are on all day, you're alright in there. Get yourself in the hospital." I said "How am I going to get in there?" "Act mad." So when I got to the reception procedures, ''Name?'' and I just went quiet and refused to answer the questions. They put me in a strip cell; an observation cell. Nothing allowed in. They took my clothes off and gave me one of those strange smock things that they make them wear in there. Anyhow, I soon came to my senses and as soon as the doctor came round I said ''There's obviously been a great mistake here There's nothing wrong with me at all''. ''I was a little confused as I came through and I'm fine thank you, and so would you mind letting me out of this place.'' So I missed out of going to the hospital, straight onto the wings and was locked up with a black guy for the first time. I'd never met a black guy before. I'd never really realised there was a black race. We had one black guy at school in about a thousand boys.'

When Billy went back to court he was given a two-year conditional discharge and went back to committing crimes. He started getting arrested for breaches of the peace, and took to stealing from the changing rooms in his tennis club and his father's golf club:

'I kept getting away with them, and this went on, and every time I went to court there was another excuse and another excuse, and they wore it, quite simply because of my background. I just needed more and more money to feed my lifestyle . . . It was all hedonistic; all going on boys, gambling . . . I had discovered gay clubs by this time, and a casino in Manchester.'

Billy's life took an interesting twist when he decided to travel further afield, and spend a some time acquainting himself with the gay scene in London. He stayed in The Park Lane Hilton, lost most of his money in a casino and with what he had left bought a ticket to Paris and joined the Foreign Legion. He did not find this to his liking and managed to extricate himself and found the gay scene in Paris more agreeable:

'Paris had a very good gay scene . . . there were lots of counts and barons . . . They were looking after me. I was allowing myself to be spoilt. They were pleasant enough company, and I was sleeping with them . . . I kept going back . . . I liked it. I did another trip down to the South of France and used a few contacts I'd made in Paris to get myself into a decent setting in St Tropez. At the time it was being funded by the gay scene, but it was also beginning to get funded by crime as well. I was picking people's pockets . . . I could always charm myself into any circle because I'm a good pianist. There was always a grand piano in these hotels and things, and if necessary I just used to sit down and play, and that was that

. . . My aim of doing this was to get into someone's confidence efficiently enough so that I could get drinking with them, get them drunk, somehow get back to their rooms, and then afterwards, in the middle of the night, I planned to take their wallets, credit cards, whatever took my fancy. If it involved sleeping with them I'd sleep with them, if they didn't want that, it didn't matter. If it was a woman, so what? I'd try it with whoever happened to come along. Again, it was the sense of adventure, the sense of going out and staying in the garret, going up the Champs Élysées.'

When Billy returned to England on a permanent basis, he immediately returned to crime, and appeared in court on many occasions:

'If they gave me bail I'd just fuck off and never be around again, and the next time there'd be that sanction added on to that, and then maybe I'd be able to con bail again. It was a big con trick every time . . . I was a really good actor.'

At the time Billy was unconcerned about the prospect of being sent back to prison and was soon back in custody. His father had secured him a job on a cattle farm in Scotland, and one of his tasks was to bank the weekly takings. On one occasion Billy took the money to London where he gambled it all away. When he returned to face the consequences the police were waiting, and he was held in custody. Billy's father deliberately blocked the bail process 'to teach him a lesson,' and Billy was sent to prison for six weeks. However, this experience did not make him resolve to change his ways:

'After the first week or so I began to adapt . . . I'm like a chameleon; I change to fit in with my surroundings . . . and of course the more criminals I began to talk to, the more I learnt about various robberies and the ways to perpetrate various crimes, and the more attractive the idea of becoming a criminal became . . . I became totally a horror . . . I would take anything, tell any lie, do anything as long as I had a bit of money in my pocket and I had something decent to get on my way again.'

At this stage, though, Billy was not committed to armed robbery. His only attempt, carried out while he had been living at home, had failed:

'I never got any money. I had just gone into this newsagent's shop with a stick and said "I'll have the money," and the guy pulled out a brush from behind the counter and started waving it around, and I went: "Alright then, cheerio.'' So it was just a complete and utter farce and I thought I'm not doing this again, it was bloody ridiculous.'

Before Billy did turn to robbery he served two twelve-month sentences, and a three-year and a four-year sentence for theft and deception. During this time he met Nigel, a man serving eight years for building society robbery, and began an affair with him. Nigel showed Billy photographs of himself committing armed robberies which made a strong impression on him. This relationship ended when Billy was moved to another prison where he started an affair with another robber, Dave; this was also to prove influential. Billy was released a short period before Dave and wanted to give his lover a warm welcome on release:

'I had to get some money from somewhere. I had £20 in my pocket. (In) East London, Stratford, there's a shopping arcade, a pub, and I went in there and ordered a large whiskey, right opposite the (name) Building Society. So eventually after another couple of whiskeys, I thought: "Okay, this is what I'll do, I'll go and rob that building society." I was dressed in shorts and a track-suit. I went into the shopping centre, bought a pad, a pencil, and a baseball cap. I put on the baseball cap and wrote out a note which said: "Hand over all the £20s and £50s over the counter to me and you'll not get hurt. No alarms, no delays, and no fucking me about. Do it now." I went in, handed over the note and she just gave me the money. Very easy; much easier than cashing cheques, and you get a lot more.'

Billy committed another nine armed robberies in the following three months, mainly in an attempt to raise enough money to impress Dave and persuade him to 'come out' and leave his wife. But when Dave's wife realised what was occurring, she informed the police. Billy went on the run, and carried out two more robberies, but the Flying Squad eventually caught up with him in Scotland:

'By now I'd done . . . quite a long list of robberies without getting caught and in a short period of time. They knew it was the same person because it was always the same demand note I was using. It worked and so I just kept using it. They put my photograph around all the hotels . . . I was staying in a hotel . . . and they burst in first thing in the morning and I was just about to go and rob a building society that morning. I'd written the demand note out and everything and I'd put it in my pocket and they came in, so I was bang to rights.'

Billy was sentenced to seven years imprisonment. However, he escaped after seven months and made contact with Dave who arranged for him to live with a woman and her two sons while he sorted things out. The children became a major influence in his life and in time he became almost a surrogate father to the boys. His relationship with the children was so close that he stayed in London despite Dave's wish for them to go away together. However, Billy was still very much involved in crime:

'I was getting my money from various credit cards and cheque books which I was picking up along the way, so I was able to buy food for the house. I just used to go to supermarkets and spend £50 to £100 a time, stick it on a credit card or cheque book. I was living in a criminal environment outside [of prison] for the first time in my life, knowing people who could get cheques for me and I didn't actually have to go and steal myself; I'd just go out and buy a cheque book.'

Soon afterwards however, though, Billy was arrested by the police again, and made to serve his original seven-year sentence and an additional three years. He used this time to take a degree and develop professional interests which were covered widely in the media; and he has retained a relationship with the two boys whom he refers to as his sons. He has re-established a relationship with his parents but they do not acknowledge his homosexuality, and he is keen not to cause them any more distress. Billy is committed to a very different life in the future and one that is free from crime.

DENNIS

Dennis was 20 years old at the time of the interview. He was taken into care as a young child, along with his sister, and started committing offences when he was very young. While principally motivated by the need for money he found that crime was a way of showing that he was 'macho'. He graduated to robberies because he found that he was not very good at other types of offence and because they offered greater rewards, although less than he had expected. Dennis was serving a six-year sentence; he was caught after robbing a shop that was covered by a protection racket, the gang involved tortured him and then took him to the police. Prison held no fears for Dennis; if anything it enhanced his reputation, at least in his own mind. While he did not wish to return to crime on release, he felt that there was no obvious alternative way of earning money.

Dennis was taken into care at the age of five and in the ensuing years he and his sister were cared for, initially in a residential children's home and later by two sets of foster parents. Dennis first became involved in criminal activity at the age of seven while at the home:

> 'I was robbing off the nurses and staff; robbing them of the money out of their purses. They had like a staff room and no-one was allowed in there except the staff, but because we were such young kids . . . no-one thought of us . . . I used to do it with my sister . . . We would go from one block to another. The security was supposed to be quite good, but because we were quite young, everything was open to us.'

Dennis was clear about why he was stealing:

> 'I needed money and I didn't have any money to buy anything. I'd see the social workers go to the shop and buy anything they wanted, and I'd want money to buy sweets and things.'

Dennis considered this behaviour normal; many of the other boys in the home were involved in similar activities. However, from the age of ten Dennis became violent:

> '[I was] kicking and fighting a lot. [I] smashed a door [at school] so I had punishment every dinner-time when I had to stand outside the head-master's door. I smashed a few windows and got some scars, and had some more fights.'

At school he began to bully other children. He went out of his way to make friends with the 'hardest' boy in school who had the added advantage of being quite big. Together they used to demand other pupils' dinner money:

> 'We used to go up to people and say "Give us your dinner-money," and if they said "no," then I'd bring my mate in.'

Dennis found that he could not hide behind his friend all of the time and would become embroiled in fights when he was on his own:

'No-one would say anything to me when I was going around with my big mate, but when I was on my own they used to have a go all the time. So I had to have a go at them. Sometimes I lost and sometimes I won.

Most or all of Dennis's antisocial behaviour took place at school, partly, it seems, because it was the one place where his misbehaviour would not result in strong disciplinary action. Dennis explained why his behaviour improved when he was at home:

'My foster parents would give me a good hiding if I did anything wrong; they'd just give me a good hiding to sort me out.'

Between the ages of eleven and fourteen, Dennis was suspended from school five times. On one occasion he was caught stealing from the school tuck-shop. The police were called and he was arrested; although no further action was taken Dennis admitted to being frightened. At about this time a row with his foster father led to him leaving:

'He [Dennis's foster father] was a big bloke and he pushed me on the bed and I just snapped. I threw him on the floor and I was really surprised that a little kid like me could do that to him. I realised that I was going to get absolutely hammered for this, and so I went into my room and got the money from my paper round and decided to head off to London.'

Dennis's attempt to run away to London lasted only a few hours, but his foster parents sought advice from a social worker about how best to care for him:

'When I went to the meeting with the social worker, they [Dennis's parents] had all the excuses ready . . . I kept saying that anything I do, they hit me, and they keep slapping me, and they just go well over board. I was just trying to get back into care. I didn't want to live there any more. Then they turned around and said they could give me anything I wanted like computers and bikes, which was true; anything I wanted for Christmas I got. They couldn't understand why if I could have computers and bikes and stuff, why? I said I was living in constant fear.'

Dennis was placed in an assessment centre for four weeks and at the end of this period it was decided that he should stay in care. Dennis pleaded not to be sent back to his foster parents; perhaps fortunately for him, they were tired of the trouble he caused and did

not want him back. So he was moved to a new residential home, an
arrangement that seemed to suit everyone and especially Dennis:

> 'The best time of my life . . . At weekends they used to take us out in the
> van to Chester and Wales; ice-skating, swimming, hill-walking . . . There
> were lads and girls there, and some psychos and weird kids . . . I knew I
> could rule it from day one.'

Social services were now helping Dennis and as a consequence he
was reunited with his natural father who ran a scrap-metal business.
Dennis would work there some days, then go drinking with his father,
who was an alcoholic, in the evening:

> 'Most days we were earning sixty or seventy pounds, and so I was earning
> £30 a day. With him drinking, I thought I'd be a big man and go and have
> a drink with him . . . there was no way I'd take it [the money] back [to
> the home] because the cash would just be taken off me . . . so I had to
> spend it. I used to drink it all.'

Dennis's natural parents were now separated, but lived at opposite
ends of the same housing estate. While working for his father, Dennis
was also reunited with his mother. She was not as he remembered her:

> 'I was very shocked when I saw her. She just didn't look like my mum. I
> remembered her from when I was five, and she had straight black hair, and
> she was very gentle. When I went round to see her, this woman opened
> the door and she still had black hair, but she was fat and ugly and scarred,
> and she had a cheap can of lager in her hand, and this was about eight
> o'clock in the morning.'

Dennis found out that his mother was working as a prostitute, and
although he still kept in touch ('she gave me the odd fiver') he was
keen to put some distance between himself and her. And he had to
stop working with his father and return to school. But this return to
normality was short-lived. Dennis began to sell drugs to his fellow
pupils and within a few months was in trouble again:

> 'Someone's older brother found out his brother was doing drugs, and
> found out that he'd got them from me at school. One day I was going
> home from school to my mum's . . . and this other lad turned round and
> asked me if I knew that a bloke called Noddy was after me with a knife.
> I just laughed it off. I was trying to be hard, but I was really scared.'

Dennis's involvement in drug dealing resulted in his leaving school, and this time he never returned. He went back to working for his father on an occasional basis and became more and more inclined towards criminality:

> 'I flitted around the criminal fraternity to see what I was best at. I tried shoplifting — no good; I tried burglaries — no good . . . I feel really bad when I do them because I don't like going into people's houses as you never know if someone's going to come downstairs with a baseball bat and clobber you one . . . I tried robbing cars; not actually robbing the vehicle, but breaking into the car and robbing a leather jacket, or whatever was in there.'

Dennis also participated in a form of street robbery:

> 'I got money from people in the street . . . I'd pick young people; I wouldn't pick a big twenty-four year old who could turn on me. I'd pick people who were standing outside shops and stuff, and go up to them, put my arm around them and squeeze and squeeze until they said they'd give me the money.'

At the time, Dennis gave no serious thought to the possibility that he might be caught and punished for his activities:

> 'To be perfectly honest with you, I never thought I'd be caught for what I was doing. I thought I was too young, and jail didn't enter my head ... I didn't really know about borstal. You know, I was in care and I'd met other kids who were into crime and were sent into care, so I thought if I'm in care already, what can they do to me?'

Dennis was still aged 14 when he was caught for a variety of offences including being drunk and disorderly, carrying offensive weapons, 'robbing the milkman' and a serious assault:

> 'This lad was a nonce; abusing kids and that, and he was only about the same age as me, and he lived in the same place, and so it was doing me a favour as I could take my aggression out on someone, and also be doing the staff a favour. They didn't really want anyone to hurt him; they just wanted someone to give him a backhander . . . We broke his nose and his ribs and fractured his skull. Hurt him on his face and chest, that's what you do to nonces. I just carried on and carried on to see how far I could go.'

Even after being caught for such an attack, Dennis did not expect to go to jail:

'When I went to court I didn't really know what I was expecting. I asked for bail and they said "no". We went to Crown Court and my brief said I'd get two and a half years. So I thought: "Two and a half years in care. That'd be alright." He didn't tell me that when he said two and a half years he meant in prison detention . . . When he [the judge] said four years, I thought: "Ah well, at least in four years time I'll be eighteen," and my Probation Officer and IT worker are jumping up and crying. I didn't really understand and the court officers got hold of me and . . . they even handcuffed me. I don't know why they did it, but I was thinking: "This is great. I just got really big-headed about it; that I'd got four years, at my age.'

It was not until one of the bailiffs informed Dennis that he had been sentenced to four years' custody that he became worried:

'I'd heard about lads who'd gone to borstal for a couple of weeks or months and absolutely shitted themselves, and there I was with four years there. It was a bit like a life sentence really.'

In fact Dennis started his sentence at a secure unit, which he found preferable to borstal. However, he was not able to 'rule the roost' as he had been able to do in the residential home:

'I didn't really like them [the other people in the secure unit] because even though I thought I was Jack the Lad and I'd been around, it was obvious that they'd all been around more than me. They were going on about how they'd done this burglary, robbed this car, robbed this house . . . they were obviously a lot more wiser than me. It meant I couldn't really intimidate them as I'd get my head kicked in.'

Just as Dennis settled into life in the unit, and began to receive regular visits from his father, it was decided that he would be moved to a youth custody centre after all. Dennis reacted badly to this news:

'I kicked off . . . I was just trying to take my aggression out on something . . . I just wanted to draw attention to myself, so I smashed up my room and set all my posters and everything on fire. They came in and took everything out and they stripped me naked . . . I didn't like that. They used to feed me through a window; they wouldn't open a door in case I did someone in. I quite liked this though, because I liked all the attention I was getting . . . One day, two busies came and opened the door . . . they put the handcuffs on me and took me out to the car. I was really impressed because it took two busies, and another one who was the driver, and I just felt like I was really bad . . . I felt infamous.'

Dennis found himself in a nearby adult prison, where he claimed that he was amongst murderers and rapists. For the first few hours he was terrified:

> 'There was loads of really bad blokes in there . . . If you think about it, it's obvious that at 15 I was going to be one of the youngest in there, and it was obvious I was going to be raped. That's what I kept thinking: "I'm going to get raped or battered or done in." I was shitting myself.'

But it wasn't long before he began to enjoy life in the prison, and particularly the prestige associated with being one of the youngest inmates:

> 'I felt really impressed saying that I was fifteen, in jail for four years on my own, and telling people what I was in here for.'

Dennis's enjoyment was short-lived. He spent only one month in prison before he was moved on to a long-term Young Offenders Institution where he served the remainder of his sentence.

When he was released and just before his eighteenth birthday, he moved in with a girl who lived next door to his mother. He soon discovered that she was a heroin addict and strongly disapproved. To show her how easy he considered it to be to break the habit he decided that he would become addicted to heroin and then stop. Unfortunately, once he had become hooked Dennis found that quitting the drug was harder than he had anticipated, and in order to fund his continued heroin use he turned to crime.

Initially, Dennis raised money to buy drugs by shoplifting with his live-in girlfriend and her brother, but he quickly made the transition to robbing commercial premises, and eventually banks:

> 'I didn't really get into the bank thing until I'd robbed a shop. Then I found out that I'd get a couple of hundred pounds and that didn't used to last me very long . . . I could spend it all going out and drinking on a night-time . . . I realised that I was robbing a little shop to get some pocket money. I'd wake up in the morning without any money, so I'd go to a shop, wait until there were no passers by and then steam in . . . rob the money and leave. If I got eighty or a hundred pounds it was good, because I was only robbing little, tiny shops.'

Dennis began to consider more lucrative targets:

'No-one advised me to do it. I just read in the papers about it, saw it on TV, and talked to people about it in the pub. I sussed on that if you go into a bank, they're instructed by the managers that if someone comes in to rob the bank, don't press no buttons or anything because he'll hurt you, just give them what they want and let them get the fuck out of the bank and then press the buzzer. So I thought: "Fucking great!" I knew I could rob and I knew that they weren't going to press the buzzer on me.'

Before long, Dennis was planning bank robberies:

'This is the way I got into armed robbery: I did a couple of shops first and . . . I kept hold of the money and bought a car . . . bought a couple of wigs because if you're doing a robbery and you wear a ginger wig, the first question they'll ask is: "What did he look like?" And if they say: "He's got ginger hair," that cuts me right out. I'm not thinking about forensics or anything like that; none of that even enters my mind. All I thought was that if I disguise myself with a long ginger wig then I'm laughing . . . If I was wearing a wig, I'd wear glasses as well, and put cotton wool in my mouth to make myself look fat. And I'd wear baggy clothes to make myself look bigger . . . I'd do anything to change my appearance . . . I could be stocky or I could be thin. I made sure all the clothes I was wearing were dirty and cheap so I could throw them away at the end of the day.'

Dennis carried out most of the bank robberies with one or two associates, although occasionally he would carry out a raid alone. He used a getaway driver whom he would pay just ten pounds, despite the fact that a 'wheelman' is liable to receive the same sentence as others involved in the raid. Dennis explained his reasoning:

'[If we got caught] I'd turn round to the police and tell them that he [the wheelman] didn't do anything, and I'd just told him to drive up to the bank and wait for me.'

Dennis was disappointed by what he would make from bank raids:

'The most money you'd get is a couple of grand. It's not as much as I expected, it's not tens of thousands or anything.'

On some occasions, Dennis obtained no money at all:

'I've been to garages and shops before, and they've told me to "fuck off", and jumped behind the counter, or they've stood there blatantly and said: "No." I showed them my gun, but it was only an imitation.'

Dennis never used a real gun, and was, to an extent, scared of them. However he believed that having a real, loaded gun would have been advantageous:

> 'If you fired it, and it went "bang," and all the smoke'd come out, everyone'd shit themselves. If I had a gun I would have robbed the till . . . and then tried robbing the people on the floor; nicking their wallets . . . I would have said: "Look, you've just seen me rob a till, fire a gun off, you can see the smoke, so just lie there nice and quiet.'

Dennis's robberies were closely linked to his dependence on drugs. He became desperate and began taking diamorphine and temazepam and he became less particular about the premises he targeted. On one occasion he raided a relative's shop, but big trouble came when he robbed an apparently insignificant convenience store on his estate:

> 'I was on drugs . . . and I just needed the money now for drugs, and so I just went into this little '8 to 8' shop and I showed my gun and said: "All I want is the change," and she [the shop owner] looked at me and said: "You must be fucking joking. Do you know who I am?" I had to go across to the till . . . and she gave me some money. I got fifty pounds out of that robbery, but the daft bitch put it down as seventy pounds, so she must have pocketed twenty for herself.'

It turned out that the shop owner had links with some of the 'heavies' on the estate. In his desperation for money Dennis had inadvertently robbed a premises that was protected by an organised gang, and was in effect part of a protection racket:

> 'They used to sit outside the bookies all day and protect a row of shops . . . It's not a sort of regular thing where you give them £100 a week; it's more they could go into the shop and their missus wants this and that, and they mark that down to stolen goods . . . The shop I robbed was further down . . . but they were still sort of protecting that as well and no-one had ever robbed that shop. It had been burgled, but no-one had ever robbed it before, and . . . [they] had to set an example. What it comes down to . . . is that they're the heavies on the estate and I made a mistake with robbing the shop, and robbing my (relative's) shop . . . They weren't pleased that I'd robbed off my own. They classed what I had done as a serious offence; I'd broken the rules of the criminal class. You don't rob off your own; you treat each other with respect.'

Dennis had been recognised (despite his disguise) during the robbery and word soon circulated that he had been responsible:

'The heavies on the estate didn't like it . . . They found out that I was a drug addict . . . They weren't arsed about criminals because they were criminals themselves; they were just different types of criminals. But they didn't like smack heads.'

On the same night of the robbery Dennis was visited by the local 'heavies':

'They bundled me into their van . . . and my legs were rammed right by the gear box. One of the fellas turned round and put the shotgun between my legs . . . and then they threw me down on the floor and started spitting at me and punching me and kicking me. They threw cushions on my legs and started using a baseball bat on my legs . . . It wasn't actually hurting but I was in fear . . . I was shitting myself here. I had a shotgun pointed at my balls, I didn't know whether it was loaded or unloaded, and in the last couple of years I'd really built up my reputation, but I just started crying. As soon as I started crying he fired the shotgun . . . but it was unloaded, and as he fired it I jumped backwards and he just burst out laughing. That's when they put cushions on my head and started hitting me with a baseball bat.'

Eventually Dennis's tormentors took him to the police station where he was charged with robbery and sentenced to six years' imprisonment. Even after receiving this punishment, Dennis appeared to be enjoying the attention that his criminal activities brought him:

'When the judge said his little speech . . . all eyes were on him and very few were looking at me, but when the judge passes sentence, all eyes were on me in the court. So I puffed my chest out and just calmly walked out of the court to show I wasn't arsed . . . I was walking out of the courtroom buzzing.'

Dennis's future is uncertain. Prison does not frighten him; he settled into his present sentence with relative ease. There is no family that he can rely on for support and advice and if he were to give up crime he does not have any idea what he would like to do to finance a legitimate life. He could offer no guarantees that he would not be back in prison some day:

'. . . (prison) didn't really affect me. Some other people have got families, got wives, got kids, got money. I had nothing. The social worker came up about my review in front of the board the other day and she said she couldn't believe how easily I'd adapted to it.'

JOHN

John was 28 years' old at the time of the interview. His early school years were spent in a northern city where he lived in a two-roomed bed-sit with five brothers, and his mother and stepfather. He was a disruptive child and he received his first conviction at the age of ten when he was taken into care. He committed a whole range of crimes before graduating to robbery because it was more lucrative. He organised and planned his robberies in considerable detail, and indeed led a team which specialised in cash-in-transit robberies. However, he co-operated with the police when he was caught and claimed that his life was under threat as a consequence. Despite being very critical of those who traffick in hard drugs he admitted dealing in soft drugs. At the time of the interview he was serving eight years for robbery and felt that his appeals for help had been ignored by the system. He thought it very likely that he would be returning to robbery when he was released.

John's father left his mother to look after six sons, all aged eight or under. The family were very poor:

'. . . we had two beds; one for my mum and one for the six lads who slept three at the bottom and three at the top in a double bed.'

John's parents were never reconciled and when he was still very young his mother met a man who became his stepfather. This man stayed for about ten years; he helped raise the family and left only after an argument resulted in him being stabbed by one of John's brothers. John met his natural father again at the age of sixteen and, although he had seen him a couple of times since then, they did not have an ongoing relationship.

Although he was told by his mother that he had started stealing as a two year old, and that at a slightly later age had attempted arson on houses, John recollected first committing a form of crime at the age of six:

'It was when we were living in the bed-sit with around twelve other families (in the building). I came down the stairs and saw the bottom floor flat open and went in there. I knew I was doing wrong, so I'd obviously been stealing little bits here and there before this, but this was the first

major thing I remember. I looked around for something to steal but there
was nothing there . . . these people were like us; didn't have much. On the
way out I noticed these big brown bottles and thought they were sweets,
so I started eating them, moving on from bottle to bottle. They were
actually tranquillisers . . . and I went upstairs and was sick. A few years
later my mum said they found me wandering around a park, naked, crying
for her.'

John remembers stealing from purses soon afterwards; he stole
from a teacher and took £5 from his mother which he used to buy toys
for his brothers. When his mother found out she punished him and
made him take the toys back to the shop. He was forced to admit that
he had stolen the money to pay for them. John recalled feeling
embarrassed about this, and sad about upsetting his mother, but
because he did not really understand his behaviour he did not feel
guilty about it. Nevertheless, he did not steal more than small amounts
from his mother again, mainly because of her financial difficulties. For
similar reasons, John never stole from his brothers: 'They were in the
same predicament as me in that they had no money either.' Indeed,
John claimed that his early offending was usually for the benefit of
others:

'When I stole up until the age of sixteen, it was always to give to other
people. It just made me feel good to do this; I think I felt like kind of a
father figure. If I stole £1, I'd spend 10p on sweets for myself, and 90p
on my brothers and friends.'

At the age of ten, and after years of being a known trouble-maker,
John was expelled from his school on the grounds that he was a bad
influence on the other children; he was never to settle in school again.
Petty offending progressed to more serious crimes including burglary
and after receiving several formal cautions John ended up in court: 'I
had no remorse for what I had done. As far as I knew, what I had
done was completely normal'. When he was told that he was going
to be taken into care he decided that he would make the most of his
freedom and 'went on a spree', committing several burglaries.

John was sent to a home but never settled: he absconded several
times and the burglaries continued. Eventually he was transferred to
a privately run home for boys in Wales but continued to steal. He was
allowed to go home at weekends and would steal then. After a while,

and because he was seen as a bad influence on the younger boys, he was moved to a different house with older boys; but the stealing continued and after further moves from one home to another he ended up in a detention centre:

'A group of us left and went on an adventure, and broke into and robbed a posh house in the country, and we found out the owners were away, so we adopted it for the night and made it our house. The next day the police came to the house, so we hid, waited until they went and then left and robbed another house. When we got back to the home they went mad at us because no-one had ever done what we had done before. The police came and charged us. I was thirteen at the time, so they kept adjourning the case until I was fourteen, then they could put me in a detention centre. They wanted me to be punished for what I had done so they put me in there.'

John found the regime in the detention centre little to his liking:

'They were really sadistic in there. A lot of ex-army geezers who liked to bully people and beat them up. They treated you like scum. It made me a lot worse than what I was, it showed me how to make people fear me, which I didn't have before . . . they were slapping me around because I was a very stubborn person. To stop this, in the end I reformed so then I only had to serve six weeks out of a three month sentence. The first thing I did when I got out of there was rob a kiosk at the train station, a chocolate egg or something like that.'

Upon his release, John found that he had few options:

'No home and no school wanted me. I was a fourteen year old with nowhere to go, because if you go to a detention centre then they don't want anything to do with you. I was really aggrieved at the way I'd been treated. I was on the streets and going to live back with my mum.'

A local police officer tried and failed to get John into a school and so he started to commit burglaries again. Soon he found himself serving another sentence in a different detention centre. He was told that this would provide him with an opportunity to acquire an education, but the reality appears to have been very different:

'When I came out of the detention centre six weeks later I was just the same except that I had been treated like shit. You see these American films with American GIs screaming at you, soldiers committing suicide. That's exactly the same thing, the only difference is that we were fourteen years old, not nineteen or twenty. You see people committing suicide and that does affect you, but it doesn't affect you to the extent that you want to die, it affects you to the extent that you get harder and harder.'

On release, John once again was unable to find a school that would accept him, and once again he started committing burglaries, now more persistently:

'I started to do more and more burglaries, and I never seemed to get caught . . . I only got caught for one in every six or seven hundred. I just did so many I couldn't count [them] up. It was day in and day out; burglaries three, four, five times a day, six, seven or eight houses. I remember one when I was fifteen or sixteen, I went into these flats, there was about twelve flats in a block. We knocked on some doors and there seemed to be no-one in. I did the whole lot, the whole twelve. That was just one day's work, and I did that every day.'

John was finding that crime was lucrative; he sold his stolen goods on the informal economy and this brought him into contact with other offenders. He started to become involved in more violent crimes:

'I had been hanging around in gangs and was becoming more used to violence . . . There was no crime that was beneath me. Not so much robbery, but muggings. If we needed a jacket that someone else had, we would take it. If we needed to beat someone up, we would do it.'

When John was fifteen he appeared in court again charged with burglary. He was told that because no educational institution would have him he must go to Borstal in order to receive some schooling. Although John did 'get a bit of an education' while serving this sentence, his time in Borstal did not have any rehabilitating effect:

'The detention centre was a million times harder than Borstal . . . I had been brutalised in a detention centre and I go to the Borstal, and I expect to be totally brutalised but it is the total opposite. It's like it messes your brain up. In the detention centre you get continuously harsh treatment because they want you to know that you are scum and that's why you're there. Then you go to the Borstal as an older more vicious person and yet it's easy. So you think to yourself well, what's going on? One minute I'm getting brutalised, then I'm getting treated like this. Then I start thinking well, what am I getting worried about being caught for. You lose all sense of reality. It's very hard to explain. Then you start to realise that they do brutalise you in this place, but they also try to manipulate your brain. That is when you become a clever criminal.'

Although John claimed not to have learned much from his fellow prisoners (he already knew a lot anyway), the Borstal experience appeared to reaffirm in his own mind his status as a criminal:

'They [the other inmates] had all been through the same system; they could not tell me something I didn't already know. You picked up odd things, but you would have picked them up anyway. You don't pick up like a college experience, you just realise that being a criminal is your occupation. At this time I wasn't sure what I was going to be . . . Most people who have been to Borstal then decide to become criminals for the rest of their lives. That is the only way they know; they have come to a part where they are leaving school, they have no qualifications; they have nothing, so as far as they are concerned, this is where they make the break.'

When John was released from Borstal he was soon drawn back into crime. He was older and now no longer obliged to attend school but, although he had learned to read in Borstal, he had no qualifications, and immediately encountered difficulties in finding employment:

'When I came out of Borstal I was sixteen and it now came to the time that I should get a job, but there was no jobs and I had nowhere to start. I knew nothing about jobs. All my mates were on the dole, and the only thing there was was the DHSS. I went and signed on . . . then all of a sudden this new thing came out about having to go on training schemes. They gave me one of these jobs and it lasted for two days or so because they were asking me to do all sorts of work for £25 a week. You work the same job as the person who is sat in the room with you, but he is getting £100 a week because he works for the company, and you are getting £25 a week because you work for the government. You can only take that for so long. Then I went out one day and did a couple of burglaries and made a few hundred pound, and I thought to myself: "What am I doing this job for if I can work for a few minutes and make a few hundred pounds?" I sacked that job and I have never worked since.'

John appeared to believe that the only way that he could achieve any sort of success was through illegitimate means:

'We get shown all this stuff that we can't afford and then they wonder why we go out and rob. I'd watch Dallas and see all these beautiful people with all these beautiful things and you think to yourself why can't I have these things? You can't get a job so you can't buy them; you can't be a high-powered solicitor or psychologist . . . because you haven't got the capabilities. The only way we can get to the top is through crime, so we do armed robberies because we know that's where the money is for us guys and not the white-collared guys.'

John continued to commit burglaries until he was seventeen, when he was caught again and put in prison. While serving this sentence John made the decision to move into armed robbery:

'It [the decision] just came to me naturally. I don't think I saw anything on TV and thought that I would have some of that. I think I was intelligent enough to know that this was the best thing to get into. It's like when you have been in a job so long you get a bit pissed off with it and you look for other work . . . I thought I might as well go on to bigger things.'

When John was released he purchased several guns, and 'put the word out' that he was looking to move into armed robbery. Soon a friend with whom John had committed burglaries found a security guard who was willing to help them organise a robbery. John was initially sceptical but only because he felt that what he was hearing was too good to be true:

'He went on about the money he had carried in vans, and the deliveries he had done, and I thought this geezer is talking shit. All of what he was saying to me was unexpected. I expected police to be in the back of vans . . . I didn't believe him because it sounded too easy . . . It totally played into our hands. The geezer said you could have hundreds of thousands of pounds in the back of a van, and in these vans, nine out of ten times the radio doesn't work, and . . . the only thing that it had got on it that was armoured was the mesh over the windows. He also said that the insurance company tells them that if one of the guards is in danger, the other guard should hand over the money.'

The guard told John and his associate about a van that delivered wages totalling £45,000 to a nearby school; but, still doubting what the informer was telling them, John delayed and the van was robbed by another gang. When this crime was reported in the news, the guard's story that it had been delivering nearly £50,000 was confirmed. So John became more eager to get involved in this kind of crime.

John's associate found another guard who was willing to be part of an 'inside job' and this time John went ahead. Using two getaway cars and a safe house, he successfully carried out the robbery of a van delivering wages to a works depot. The only negative aspect of the job, as John saw it, was a bad feeling about threatening the guards with a shotgun:

> 'With the second guard, when I shoved the shotgun underneath his jaw-bone and walked with him to the office, his legs started to go . . . his bottle had gone . . . There was no cartridges in the gun; I was just there to get the money. I didn't realise that the geezer didn't know that there was no cartridges in the shot-gun. I then realised how terrified he was and I started to feel uncomfortable . . . so I pulled the gun away. That was the only part of the job that stuck in my mind because afterwards I felt really bad about what I had done.'

John soon found himself leading a gang of armed robbers. He arranged for members of his team to drive around looking for vans that presented an easy target, especially those delivering to schools and works departments. His robberies were always carefully planned; the van would be followed several times. John always took part in the raids, but with different associates, in order to give the impression that they were the work of different gangs. John invested some of his takings in soft drugs; indeed he used the £10,000 he made from his first armed robbery to finance a cannabis deal that doubled his money. However, when it came to hard drugs John's views were very different, as illustrated by his treatment of a known heroin dealer:

> 'There is one thing I have hated all my life . . . I can't stand heroin and people who deal with it. They are worse than pimps the way they destroy the addict's family. I picked this up from my younger brother being an addict and what it did to my mother. I couldn't handle anyone doing that near me, and if I could stop them I'd do it. I knew this dealer who was giving heroin to kids of 15–16 years old, so we broke into his house and beat the hell out of him with baseball bats. [We] held him down and took an iron from the closet and plugged it in, turning it to full blast . . . we stripped his chest and told him to tell us where the heroin was. He was screaming but he wouldn't tell us where it was. I think he knew that if I'd have found it I would have killed him . . . By this time the iron was halfway through the geezer's chest, bubbling over, sort of thing, but he still wouldn't say, so I pulled the iron off him . . . I smacked him on the corner of the eye with the iron, and ripped his eye open. I felt nothing for

him . . . because of what he was I just wanted to kill the bastard. I felt he
was just scum, and I knew what sort of damage he could do in the area
. . . selling it to kids, not caring where the heroin was going, they used to
go around and beat up the mother if a kid couldn't pay. I just tortured him
and tortured him, but in the end he still wouldn't tell us where it was so
we just left. More than likely he hadn't any heroin left.'

John was twenty-four when he was next charged. He was well
known by the police at this stage and was arrested regularly. On one
occasion he was arrested for assault, and the police also found him to
be in possession of a small amount of cannabis. Feeling sure that he
was 'going down,' and anxious to carry out a robbery that had already
been prepared, John went on the run. He rented a safe house and used
it as a base for the robbery of a security van. Shortly afterwards he
was arrested again after a fight in a nightclub, and he was charged
with causing grievous bodily harm and absconding. The safe house
was raided by the police who found several guns and balaclavas left
over from the last robbery and he was charged.

When questioned John co-operated with the police and gave them
information they sought about other offenders. He 'grassed' principally because he felt that his ex-associates had let him down; he had
asked for help and they had not delivered despite promises. His old
acquaintances were aggrieved and threats were made against his life:
'I've a few friends who said if you go back, you're dead, and so on.'

John is still a young man but after a life of crime so far he is not
optimistic that he will be able to avoid crime in the future. He feels
that he has been let down, and while any future criminal activity
would not be motivated by feelings of revenge against the system,
they would be a consequence, as he sees it, of his failing to receive
help when he needed it:

'When you go to certain areas and that's the fad in your area, robbers and
all that, you follow the mainstream. Some people say you could have got
a job here or there but that's bollocks. It's easy for them to say that
because they are not in that situation. They think you must get a job
because they believe that's what they'd do. But their mind has been
developed and processed somewhere else. My mind doesn't come up with
the request to get a job, my mind comes up with 'lets go and *do* a job.'
It's the total opposite. No matter how hard I try to change that I can't. I've
been in this [violent crime] for 20 years and they don't think that I need
de-programming . . . they don't know what to do with me. I know I need

help but I'm just not getting it. I sit down and talk to people and they ask me what my problem is. They say I'm an intelligent person and if I channel all my abilities into something else I will be able to do it. But... I need to be programmed to do that. When I go outside, the only thing I know is how to do armed robberies . . . I'll take 50% of the blame for it, but I'm not going to take all of the blame. I've tried to seek help while I've been in prison and I'm not getting it, so how can I be completely to blame?'

TOM

Tom was 36 years old, married with three children although he had severed his ties with his family because of the long sentence he was serving. He is by any criterion a career robber. He graduated from theft, vehicle offences and burglary to commit his first robbery at the age of 22. He has committed lots of robberies, possibly 'hundreds', although he specialised in robbing building societies. He was attracted by the lure of easy money which robbery provided. He stopped for a while but was arrested for an offence that he had not committed, which exasperated him and led him to conclude that he was destined for a life of crime. Tom was half way through a fourteen year sentence when the interview took place, having just been recaptured after absconding while on compassionate release.

Tom was born in Ireland and raised by his parents, but his earliest memories are dominated by the animosity that existed between himself and his mother:

'There was only three of us [children] — I'm the eldest. My brother was born deaf in one ear . . . he had to have operations every eight or ten months . . . consequently he was pampered . . . he had to be taken care of . . . Then my sister was born, ''ah, the little baby girl,'' no problems with her, so everything sort of came back on me . . . I didn't feel I was put aside or anything, but when my mother had a problem she would take it out on me . . . The woman was evil; she had a malicious, vicious streak through her. She was just a bad person.'

While Tom considered his mother uncaring, he felt that his father, a manager in a factory, was neglectful in a different way:

'My dad never laid a hand on me in all his life . . . He was a nice alcoholic; he wasn't the sort that would come in and scream and holler and all that kind of thing. He was a very pleasant and gentle man. I think he drank to get away from my mother . . . We very seldom saw him, because when he'd finish work, he'd go to the pub, simply because I don't think he wanted to come home.'

Tom's first exposure to crime occurred when he was about five years' old. He became involved with a gang of local children which was led by a boy, Bob, aged 16, who had already served a borstal sentence and was later to become a significant influence in Tom's life. The gang was involved in delinquency and Tom viewed its antics as fairly normal:

'I've only done the same things as the other kids in the street . . . There was just a little gang of us, daring each other to go further and further... You'd stand in front of a house and put a brick through the window, and go down to the supermarkets . . . and it was a challenge to see who could steal the most.'

A main motivation behind Tom's wrongdoing was a desire to 'get even' with his mother. On one occasion he stole some money his mother was keeping to pay for tickets for the whole family to fly to England for an uncle's wedding:

'I was retaliating against my mother. I knew the only thing . . . [she] has ever cared about was money . . . The only way I could really upset her was to steal her money. So, I stole her purse out of her handbag . . . found this money . . . and to get rid of it, I burned it . . . I was pleased I done it, especially when I thought of the reaction I'd caused. I mean every time she looked at me after that, for about three weeks, she kicked the shit out of me.'

Tom continued to steal and when he reached seven his parents concluded that they needed to take drastic action; they decided to send him to boarding school. Although he disliked the school he felt it was 'better than home'. The school was to be his home for the next seven years. He would return home for a day each month, and for three weeks each summer. He claimed that during this period he was 'a model student.' He passed all of his exams and became an accomplished musician, performing regularly in the school band. During his time at boarding school Tom avoided crime completely.

When he was in his teens the school closed and Tom returned to live with his parents. Once again he had to confront the treatment that had led to his criminal behaviour as a very young child. He found a job in a bakery but his mother claimed nearly all of his earnings, leaving him with very little:

'The clothes I was wearing were shit . . . and I mean insultingly cheap . . . trousers up around your ankles, plastic shoes, that kind of thing . . . I remember always feeling inferior to everybody else.'

Soon after his fourteenth birthday Tom joined an army school of music and began a three-year training course. Despite the fact that he lived in the army barracks his mother demanded two-thirds of his wages. Initially Tom refused, but his parents contacted officers at the barracks and because Tom was still just 14, they enforced his parent's wishes, again leaving Tom with little money to live on. Although he was bitter he was not involved in any criminal activity while at the school of music. However, the pressure mounted and just before the end of the course, and to 'get even' with the officers at the barracks who had sided with his parents, Tom left without taking his final exams and joined the regular army:

'I was just letting them know I wasn't happy with all that they'd done (to) me. When they had gone to all the expense of training me to be a competent clarinet and saxophone player, I jacked it in . . . became a proper soldier, which really fucked them off, no doubt about it.'

Tom was rebelling against what he saw as unfair treatment by his mother and the army:

'At seventeen I just went ape-shit. I couldn't save anything . . . and I mean nothing. I was having to borrow clothes, that's how bad I was . . . I started going back to the estate where I knew all my pals, started drinking in the basements, taking pills. I just found I was struggling with things and never having anything . . . I couldn't figure out why I was going round dressed like a fucking scarecrow.'

At about this time Tom bumped into his old friend Bob, and was immediately drawn into criminal activity. Bob, now in his late twenties, had a burglary of commercial premises planned and invited Tom to take part. Tom, while nervous, was also excited at the idea.

The job was a success and both men obtained nearly a thousand pounds. This was a major turning point for Tom:

> 'After that I lost interest in the army; I lost interest in any kind of work at all. This was easy money for me, all of a sudden I can get all the things I want, and I can get them now . . . I didn't have to wait six or eight months for a new pair of shoes . . . I actually bought my first motorbike . . . That's basically how I started . . . I couldn't give a shit about the consequences.

Over the following months Tom committed a burglary nearly every night, initially with Bob, but later, after becoming irritated by Bob taking the lion's share, on his own. This spate of burglaries was carried out in such a frenzy that Tom did not discriminate with regard to target or to what he stole: 'Houses, shops, anything . . . I didn't give a fuck. If it was nailed down, I'd pry it loose.'

Tom's run of luck ended after six months when he was caught and sentenced to six months imprisonment. Tom claimed that he was barely able to believe what was happening to him:

> 'This was completely new to me; this was my first time to get nicked . . . I didn't understand what was happening, I was totally naive.'

Tom served four and a half months of his sentence in a 'filthy, dirty . . . stinking cell'. However, this period in custody did not persuade him to change his ways:

> 'That's the strange thing. About five or six hours after I was released I was on the back of a stolen motorcycle.'

The army had given Tom a dishonourable discharge, so upon his release he went home to live with his parents. He made an effort to find work, mainly to placate his mother, but after trying a string of jobs, all of which lasted no more than a few days, Tom found companionship with his friends on the estate. He became involved in shoplifting and for a while got by on the proceeds of these activities. He learned to pick pockets, and practised at big race meetings in the city but discovered that he wasn't suited to this type of activity:

> 'I lost my nerve. It happens to a lot of dippers [pick-pockets], unless you're going to make it a sort of vocation in life . . . I think it was just a stage I was going through; it was like serving an apprenticeship.'

Unable to find a suitable job, Tom rejoined the army. At this time, the army's register had not been computerised, so Tom was able to join up at a different barracks, just a year and a half after receiving a dishonourable discharge:

'[I wanted] a stable surrounding. I was fed up with living in people's flats and moving in with women . . . having all this pressure . . . "Where are you going? What are you doing?" You didn't want that shit, did you? I just wanted to get away from everybody; I wanted to be on my own again.'

This time Tom stayed in the army for several years, but a few months after rejoining he committed his first armed robbery. He was having a drink with an old friend of his, Pat, in a pub that was known as a meeting place for those involved in minor crime:

'It was about half four in the afternoon. He [Pat] was waiting for somebody to turn up and they were going to go out in a car and do a robbery. The guy never showed and he asked me would I drive? I said: "Yeah, alright."'

Tom helped Pat to steal a car (he already had experience of this) and the pair drove to the building society Pat had selected. Tom entered the premises first to check that everything looked okay, then Pat came in and carried out the robbery:

'He jumped up on a shelf that hung down from the wall . . . run down it, leapt up, grabbed the top of the bandit screen, vaulted over it, and he was behind the counter . . . I was amazed that he had so much courage to do this . . . this was just way out of my league. And he was just emptying this drawer which was full of money . . . into his pockets, down his shirt. He came back over and off we went. I got about two grand out of that; split it right down the middle. I thought: "This is for me." I could buy my own suit, I could buy my own car . . . It gave me self-respect . . . and I just cracked on from there.'

So, just as Bob had introduced Tom to burglary, so Pat showed him how he could make money through commercial robbery. Tom considered himself fortunate to have been able to learn from a good teacher; they carried out close to twenty robberies together. But when Pat became involved with heroin Tom decided to branch out on his own. Initially he used a toy gun which he had painted black, but later, on account of his belief that the police were being armed, he began carrying a real gun for self defence:

'It was only in case of policemen . . . I mean I wouldn't even dream of shooting a bank teller. Not a civilian. Unless they jumped on me, and only Christ knows what would happen then . . . Just probably smash them over the head.'

Tom would drive around looking for suitable targets, then simply get out of the car and commit the robbery. He would carry out at least one robbery a week and on only one occasion did he fail to get any money. His reaction on that occasion had been simply to drive to another building society a mile away and rob that:

'It was so easy . . . You just sort of went into remote control, sort of automatic pilot; everything just happened for you . . . I never consciously thought about what I was doing . . . I've always found that as soon as I put my hand on the handle of the door; once I've made that final decision, that's it. I start and I don't stop.'

Tom believed that in a sense, he became addicted to committing robberies:

'It's a buzz. I think that's the biggest problem with it. I suppose it can be compared with any drug you want to think of . . . I think I became an adrenaline addict, over a period of maybe a year . . . You'd do it [the robbery], you'd be right as rain. You leave, and when you get home, that's when the adrenaline stops flowing, and that's when you're sick, you sort of shake. [It was like that] every time I did a robbery.'

Tom began to enjoy the money his robberies provided; he bought clothes, a new car every three months, and a house for himself and his new wife. He remained in the army, but took pains not to draw attention to, and raise suspicions about, his additional income. His relationship with his parents was still strained. He was giving them money and he felt they suspected that he was involved in some sort of crime. Tom's wife knew about the robberies; he allowed several members of her family to accompany him on raids to help them get out of financial difficulties. This practice of 'taking people under his wing', as Pat had once done for him, was one of the factors which led to Tom eventually being caught.

During a police crackdown on armed robbery, Tom decided to get himself 'off the streets' for a while, and took an evening job with his wife's brother on a building site. He reasoned that the job would also help him to account for the extra money he had. By now, Tom had left the army:

'They slung me out. I started to get sloppy; staying three days without going into the barracks, things like that. Basically I lost interest in it. I had my own home now; they had nothing to offer me. It was only about ninety-five quid a week; that was nothing compared to what I was doing myself. It was a place that was taking up my time during the day when I could have been doing other things with my wife and daughter. I became very negative . . . and we had a parting of ways.'

However, while working on the site, Tom met Mick, a man who had serious financial problems. Tom felt sympathy for Mick, and tried to help him by involving him in his robberies:

'This guy sort of got into my head. I could certainly associate with what he was feeling because I'd spent years and years myself being without anything, and I was watching him and he was working hard but he wasn't getting anywhere . . . I just felt sorry for the guy, stupid of me, but that's what happened. I took him out with me, done a robbery, and his end was about two grand.'

Despite the fact that Tom did not consider Mick to be a good robber, he did eighteen jobs with him over the following eight weeks. However, on the day of what would have been the nineteenth robbery, Tom had a bad feeling and told Mick that he was putting off the robbery until the next day. Mick went to his local pub, got drunk, then went out and robbed a building society before returning to the same pub and buying everyone a drink. Someone in the pub phoned the police and Mick was arrested two hours later. He confessed to all eighteen armed robberies, implicating Tom in the process. Although there was little evidence to connect Tom with the offences, he was charged by the police, but was given bail. He wasted no time in arranging for all of his possessions, including his house, to be sold and took off to England with his wife and baby daughter. Tom resolved to start a new life in England without resorting to crime. However, things did not go well in the period immediately following the move and almost inevitably Tom was tempted back to robbery:

'We got half a house in . . . [London] and it was abysmal, mice everywhere, just filthy dirty . . . (the landlord) wouldn't let me paint it;

wouldn't let me wallpaper . . . I got myself two jobs. I was working as a painter and decorator during the day and a security attendant for a nightclub at night . . . So we was doing okay, but neither of us were happy with the situation we were in . . . The Christmas of '81, money was a bit tight, and I was thinking . . . then my wife went back to Dublin for two weeks in February, and she was out of the country a day and I started again.'

By the time Tom's wife returned from Ireland he had carried out another two robberies. Then Tom's tendency to involve in robberies others whom he considered to be in difficulty proved to be his downfall again. Peter, one of the men Tom worked with at the nightclub, was being evicted from his flat, and after consulting his wife, Tom allowed him to move into their home until he found somewhere else. However, once he had settled in, Peter showed no sign of looking for a place of his own, so Tom decided to help him on his way:

'I got so frustrated with him that I decided to take him out with me, and that way he'd have his own money, get his own place, and we'd have our family back again.'

Tom was not being entirely naive. Peter was aware of his robberies and Tom felt that he would be more secure if Peter became involved:

'It was just like I wanted him to be implicated so he could never say anything about me . . . that would make him a guilty party as well. So it was like insurance.'

Tom took Peter with him on two robberies but instead of using the money he made to find himself a place to live Peter bought himself a car and a new wardrobe of clothes. Tom was exasperated:

'I said: "Right, we're going out Monday, you're getting your dough, you're going . . ." He's going, "Yeah, alright." That was on a Friday .. I'd already told him that I had one [a building society] and where it was . . . He vanished over the weekend, didn't know where he went or what he done. He came home Sunday morning . . . We went out on the Monday.'

Tom described the events of the following day:

'[We] got down there and there were police everywhere . . . all around this particular building society . . . So I went to another one. There was police outside that one as well . . . He [Peter] was with me. I said: "They're police." He was going, "No, they're students . . ." We went back to the car and waited about an hour and a half. Come back, they weren't there . . . I've gone in, robbed the place . . . I come out, and there was an armed response unit outside waiting for me. I knew they couldn't shoot at me because there was pedestrians . . . I ducked down behind a car and ran. They chased me, then about a hundred yards down the road they took two shots at me and missed, so I took a hostage . . . [Peter] is supposed to be the getaway driver, but he's not actually in the car. He's standing across the road from the building society watching everything that's happening . . . So I've taken this hostage, I've got four or five armed policemen around me, I've got a gun at the back of this guy's head, but it's only a replica . . . I've got a car, a taxi that has stopped . . . I'm trying to figure out a way to get this guy in the car, me in the car as well, without taking the gun away from his head, because I knew that as soon as the gun was away from this bloke they were going to shoot me. And while I was trying to figure it out, I was run over by a policeman in a Panda vehicle. We were on a hill, and he just switched off his engine, free-wheeled down the road and just drove over the two of us.'

Tom was arrested, charged, and sentenced to seven years' imprisonment. During this period his father died and his wife left him. Peter, who had informed the police about the planned robbery, received two years. Tom recalled his feelings:

'I was pretty pissed with this guy. I mean he totally fucked my whole life up. All I felt for him was contempt . . . once my wife had left me, once my dad had died, I started to feel quite bitter towards him again.'

Perhaps because he had heard about the death of Tom's father, and suspected that Tom would come looking for him after his release, Peter went to visit Tom as he approached the end of his sentence. Peter offered Tom a job as manager of the successful breaker's yard business which he had set up. Tom accepted and when he saw just how well Peter had done for himself, he decided that he would do his best to get even. He went all out to ruin Peter:

'I started work on the Saturday. We took about six or seven hundred . . . I nicked about four hundred of that . . . he never said anything. Opened up Sunday for half a day, kept more of the money. A couple of days later, I sold the Rover he gave me, took another car, and this went on for about eight weeks. I just fleeced this guy. He knew what was going down but he was too afraid to say anything. In the end . . . I had taken him for everything he had.'

Peter went out of business and Tom found another job with a large vehicle repair and tyre company. He got a mortgage, built up a steady relationship with a new partner and, despite the fact that he was not earning a vast amount of money, he refrained from robbery. Then, after more than two years of law abiding life, Tom was arrested for a robbery which he had not carried out and was remanded in custody. Tom claimed he had six witnesses who were willing to testify that he was in a particular pub at the time of the robbery. The only evidence offered by the prosecution was that one of three shop assistants in the premises which had been robbed picked Tom out in an identity parade. After he had spent three months in prison awaiting trial, a mix-up occurred and Tom was told that the trial would be postponed for another two months. His frustration provided the impetus to escape:

'I'm really pissed off about the whole thing . . . They're taking me back down to the cells . . . for another eight weeks, and I'm seething. And I've got this copper taking the piss out of me . . . showing off in front of his work pals, so I told him I wanted to go to the toilets . . . When I came back, I walked towards him and I kicked him in the bollocks. I just flipped. He's gone down, so I dragged him into the cell and I kicked the shit out of him. I sort of blacked out for a second. I was so frustrated, I just smashed him to fuck . . . I took his keys off him . . . popped him in the cell, opened the other cells. I asked everyone if they wanted to fuck off. Some of them did, some of them didn't . . . Then they went one way, I slipped off the other way.'

Tom's escape received extensive press coverage. His photograph appeared on the front page of local newspapers with the warning that he was suspected of being armed and was dangerous. Tom felt that he had no option but to return to crime:

'I thought to myself: "What's the fucking point?" I stayed out of trouble for nearly three years, got myself a flat and everything as legal as possible, and then here they were nicking me for something I didn't even do. Had I been at it, I would have accepted it, but I hadn't done anything and I was still going to jail . . . [Being arrested] finished any chance I had of continuing in the tyre game . . . so I thought: "Fuck it," went out and saw a friend, bought a gun, and went back at it. I committed three robberies.'

He was caught just a week later and sentenced to fourteen years in prison. Reflecting on his life Tom believed that his upbringing and environment had contributed to his repeated lapses into criminality;

but he also acknowledged that he bore some responsibility for his actions:

'When they're sending me to jail for fourteen years . . . they don't try to find out why all this has happened. It doesn't matter to them that they've created this monster . . . They put you in these filthy homes . . . you see atrocities getting committed all day long, and that kind of thing rubs off on you . . . You just want to be the same as everyone else. Unfortunately, the people I was around were all crooks and scallywags and little bastards, and I just wanted to be like them . . . I didn't feel that I was doing anything wrong . . . Had I lived on another estate where everybody owned their own houses and we all went to schools and wore uniforms and that, who knows? . . . but a lot of it is down to me as well . . . Nobody can make the final decision but yourself. I found it easier to steal it and have the pleasure now, as opposed to grafting the next thirty years and having it all when I'm sixty-five.'

With regard to the future, Tom had already decided to sever most of his existing family ties in order to spare his relatives further anguish:

'It's not fair on them to sort of walk into their lives again after nine years. It's not possible, you can't do that.'

Tom did not know whether he would return to crime. In many ways his spirit appeared to have been broken:

'I've got no goals anymore, you know? It seems like my life has just stopped . . . I've lost my way . . . I don't know what's going to happen in the future. At the moment I don't really care.'

Chapter 6
Rethinking Situational Prevention:
Where Do We Go From Here?

This chapter has two main purposes; to suggest how the techniques of situational prevention might be revised, and to examine the extent to which the rational choice perspective explains the behaviour of robbers. It argues the case for a typology of robbers which takes account of their rationality. The techniques of situational prevention as presented by Clarke (1997) — and discussed in Chapter 1 are then evaluated in a crime risk management context. Changes are suggested and a new *Crime Risk Management Process* is presented which builds on Clarke's work but adjusts the terminology, revises the categorisation of techniques, and locates them within a broader frame of reference. While situational crime prevention has a lot to contribute to crime risk management, it is argued that this needs to take account of management and organisational practices. While the research lends support to the key elements of the (revised) situational approach, it is clear that situational measures have their limits and can even work in the interests of offenders. Moreover, what is good practice in terms of containing and reducing crime is not necessarily good practice in terms of marketing, public relations or other commercial priorities (Beck and Willis, 1998), and ways have to be found of reconciling these objectives.

TOWARDS A TYPOLOGY OF ROBBERS

Since as a legal category robbery includes a wide variety of behaviours, patterns are not easy to identify (CBA/MUC, 1987). This complicates attempts to evolve a typology. Early attempts at classification were based on identifying the circumstances in which victims were attacked (McClintock and Gibson, 1961). Conklin (1972) presented a typology which identified four types of robber (including the mugger) on the basis of the level of 'professionalism' shown by the robber in carrying out the offence. The 'professional robber' was distinguished by a long-term commitment to crime which showed itself in the planning and organising of the offence. The 'opportunist robber' committed unplanned (and usually unarmed) street robbery for small amounts of cash. Conklin's 'addict robbers' are in a category between opportunists and professionals; they use the proceeds of fairly well-planned attacks to feed their opiate addiction, but, notwithstanding their planning efforts, they are not committed to robbery. 'Alcoholic' robbers form the final category: their robberies are generally an afterthought following an unplanned assault (often on another alcoholic).

Later, Haran and Martin (1984) evaluated the commitment of 500 New York bank robbers to the offence and identified four sub-typologies. 'Heavy career robbers', defined as those with four or more previous robbery convictions, made up 29 percent of the sample; 'compulsive' robbers (addicts) accounted for a further 24 percent, 'casuals' (two or three convictions) 25 percent and 'amateurs' (with one or no previous convictions) 22 percent. The problem with this classification, if applied to the findings from the study discussed in this volume, is that some robbers who had committed only a few robberies showed the high levels of organisation associated with the professional robber, while casuals could be either professional or amateur in terms of how they approached the offence.

Marsden (1990) evolved a typology based broadly on the number of robbers involved, but taking into account the amount of planning and violence used. The study was conducted in Australia where half of the robberies were drug related and carried out by lone robbers. The typology that evolved showed a close link between lone robbers and a lack of planning and more than one robber and a degree of planning. Walsh (1986) too adopted a typology based on numbers of robbers involved and the degree of planning. He identified big 'firms' who assemble teams; small teams of two or three; solo men; desperate men (linked with drink and drugs); the casual mugger; and the mugger.

These classifications evolved for different purposes and with different foci although they each make a contribution to an understanding of robbery. However, in this study the aim was to think about crime prevention and from this viewpoint typologies which take account of the style of the robber (including the amount and type of planning undertaken, the choice of weapon, attitudes to violence, aspirations and so on) are likely to be the most helpful. As will be shown, it is much easier to identify clear categories at the extremes; there are certain characteristics that clearly typify the professional robbers and the amateur robbers. Indeed, as 'ideal types' professionals and amateurs are relatively easy to identify.

Professional robbers typically planned their last robbery for more than one day, undertook activities such as visiting the targeted premises and keeping it under surveillance, considered the possibility of being caught, and wore disguises and special clothes to counteract the threat. Further, they considered the threat of the police and often monitored police activity; and they considered the police to be ineffective. They were more determined in that they would not have given up on the idea of robbery if somehow they had been prevented from committing their last robbery; and they would still have committed their last robbery had they known they would receive a sentence of at least five years' imprisonment. They were more inclined to the use of weapons and in particular firearms, and of violence in the sense that they were prepared to do whatever was necessary in order to get the money (see also Harding, 1993).[1] They obtained bigger rewards from the robbery (often over £5,000), and, perhaps as a consequence of all this, expected and received longer terms of imprisonment when caught.

Amateur robbers typically prepared for less than one day, and often not at all, did not undertake preparatory activities such as visiting targeted premises and keeping them under surveillance, and wearing disguises and special clothes. They did not consider the threat from police Rapid Response Units, and did not monitor police activity; but they considered the police to be effective at catching and prosecuting robbers. They were less determined in that they were more likely to say they would have given up on the idea of robbery if they had somehow been prevented from committing their last raid, and less likely to say they would still have committed their last robbery had they known they would receive a sentence of at least five years' imprisonment. They were less likely to use weapons (and in particular firearms) and violence, were less likely to have gained over £5,000 from their last robbery, and less likely to have expected and received a sentence of more than five years if caught.

So at the extremes, and in theory, it is possible to identify two clear groups, the professionals and the amateurs. In this study the weight of evidence would characterise robbers of cash-in-transit vans and bank robbers as typically 'professionals', and robbers of commercial premises as amateurs. The problem is that in practice the picture is less clear cut. The accounts of robbers, as illustrated by the case studies in the last chapter, show that while professionals sometimes carry out what may appear very amateurish raids (although often using a wealth of experience), often amateurish robbers carry out quite organised raids. Although it is possible to identify variables which differentiate amateurs from professionals, large numbers of robbers (although invariably a minority) fail to meet the criteria of the 'ideal type'. Thus preventative strategies built on ideal types may fail. Indeed, all the categories which focus on offenders and are mentioned above were represented within the study; there were casual robbers who could be amateur or professional, a few first-time robbers, and there were addict robbers, who were often desperate individuals. But it is also not clear how these categories can be helpful for crime prevention. For example, not all 'addict' robbers linked their addiction to their last offence; about half of those who took illegal drugs and drank heavily claimed this was unrelated to their last offence; and drug-taking and alcohol consumption were frequently characteristics of a lifestyle that included a lack of a job and was on the borders of criminal activity.

The usefulness of a typology for (situational) crime prevention purposes depends on its being based on the type of issues that robbers consider and reason over as they plan and carry out a raid. If robbers make a decision at some point, then at that point there are opportunities to intervene with situational measures. If they say that at some point they took the time to weigh up, at least to some extent, the merits of pursuing the robbery, then there is the possibility of changing the circumstances in which that decision is taken in order to encourage the robber to refrain from pursuing the robbery. This is the premise on which situational crime prevention is based. Previous attempts at evolving typologies have, as shown, had a somewhat different aim.

ARE ROBBERS RATIONAL?

It is important to be clear what is meant by the term 'rational' or 'reasoning' offender (for a full discussion see Cornish and Clarke, 1986; also, Elster, 1986). It is not realistic to suppose that robbers will always attempt to develop a sound knowledge of all the facts relevant to the crime and think through each one prior to committing it. The question is rather whether robbers show some form of 'limited' or 'bounded' rationality. As Hirschi (1986: 115) notes, 'Accepting a choice model does not require that we assume planning or foresight beyond the bare minimum necessary for the act to occur.' Since choice is subjective (Elster, 1986), what deters some offenders will not deter others (Fattah, 1993) and the aim must be to find out what types of issues robbers consider when they plan and carry out the offence. This will then give clues as to appropriate response measures. Even where an offender is pre-determined to commit a robbery, situational measures may make the raid less likely, although the consequence may be to deflect the crime elsewhere; there is then the possibility that the time taken to search for a target will expose the offender to greater risk.

Other studies which have considered the rationality of robbers have generally reported that robbers do, at least to a limited extent, behave in a rational way (Bellamy, 1996; Feeney, 1986; Morrison and O'Donnell, 1996; Walsh, 1986). The present study points to the same conclusion. For example, at least one of the distinctions between professionals and amateurs is the way in which and the extent to which they prepare for the robbery; the professional is more thorough and thoughtful, the amateur more casual and reckless, but they both make a range of decisions. While the research was not geared to examining this issue specifically, it was possible to identify 15 questions which were included in the interviews, an affirmative answer to which may indicate a degree of reasoning. For example, those who visited and/or kept watch on the target before the robbery, changed their clothing or wore a disguise, or chose the day or time of the robbery, specifically did so because they felt it would bring them an advantage. Knowing this, and understanding the logic behind their actions provides clues for prevention and this is the essence of the situational approach. These 15 questions, presented as 'indicators of rationality', are listed below.

Indicators of rationality

1. Did you visit the target before the robbery?
2. Did you keep the target under surveillance before the robbery?
3. Did you wear a disguise?
4. Did you wear special clothing?
5. Did you choose the day specifically?
6. Did you choose the time specifically?
7. Was the fact of whether the target was on the corner relevant in its selection?
8. Was the fact of whether the target was on a main road relevant in its selection?
9. Was the fact of whether the target was on a pedestrian street relevant in its selection?
10. Was the fact of whether the target had been robbed before relevant in its selection?
11. Did the fact of whether the target had CCTV affect the way you carried out the robbery?
12. Did the fact of whether the target had security screens affect the way you carried out the robbery?
13. Did the number of teller units affect the way you carried out the robbery?
14. Did the fact of whether the target had a time delay safe affect the robbery?
15. Did the fact of whether the target could be seen from the street affect the robbery?

The 15 questions could easily be added to. For example, questions on weapon choice were not included, principally because there was no question to establish whether they routinely carried weapons. And questions about whether they had monitored police activity were general questions which did not refer to the last offence. Moreover, the robber is bound to reason about the way the offence is being carried out as particular measures are confronted, even if preparatory reasoning has not taken place. Future studies could incorporate questions along these lines. There are other limits too. A negative answer to some of the above variables would not necessarily mean a lack of rationality; people may not keep watch because they do not want to risk being seen and this is just as rational (although this is not the reason most commonly offered for not keeping watch). These questions were included because they serve to identify specific actions or decisions made by robbers in preparing for their last robbery. Thus, while the 15 questions are being used as 'rationality indicators', other research focusing on this aspect could ask more and better directed questions. The interpretation should be treated with caution, as indicative and perhaps best justified by the lack of previous research.

Table 6.1 shows that most robbers made at least one decision when committing their last robbery (although no-one made all 15 decisions), and so most robbers carried out some form of reasoning.

Table 6.1 The extent to which robbers displayed rationality indicators, by target

Number of rationality indicators displayed	Bank No.	%	BS No.	%	PO No.	%	CIT* No.	%	CP No.	%
None	6	7.9	5	5.0	2	3.2	3	6.4	10	6.7
1 or more	70	92.1	96	95.0	61	96.8	44	93.6	139	93.3
2 or more	65	85.5	87	86.1	58	92.1	42	89.4	121	81.2
3 or more	61	80.3	77	76.2	51	80.9	35	74.5	96	64.4
4 or more	50	65.8	66	65.3	43	68.2	25	53.2	66	44.3
5 or more	38	50.0	46	45.5	33	52.4	14	29.8	45	30.2
6 or more	30	39.5	34	33.7	23	36.5	7	14.9	27	18.1
7 or more	21	27.6	21	20.8	11	17.5	–	–	13	8.7
8 or more	12	15.8	12	11.9	6	9.5	–	–	7	4.7
9 or more	3	3.9	6	5.9	3	4.8	–	–	1	1.0
10 or more	2	2.6	4	4.0	0	0.0	–	–	0	0.0
11 or more	0	0.0	2	2.0	0	0.0	–	–	0	0.0
12 or more	0	0.0	0	0.0	0	0.0	–	–	0	0.0
Total	76	100.0	101	100.0	63	100.0	47	100.0	149	100.0

*Note: Only six rationality indicators were applicable to CIT robbers.

What fails to emerge from this is any indication that cash-in-transit and bank robbers are more rational than robbers of building societies and commercial premises. However, it is important not to confuse rationality as defined here with professionalism. Even amateurs can be influenced by the location and the amount of security at a target (which bodes well for situational measures). Professionalism also reflects a level of organisation and planning which may be indicated by the first six of the rationality indicators (used in the text to differentiate between professionals and amateurs). And, of course cash-in-transit represents a different type of target and fewer of the indicators of rationality were applicable. Indeed, it may be that certain types of robbery create a greater need for rational planning. Table 6.2 offers an analysis of just the first six indicators by target. Even on this calculation most robbers can be considered to be reasoning offenders, although there is a marked difference between the highly reasoning (and professional) cash-in-transit robber and the typically more amateurish and less reasoning robbers of commercial premises.

Table 6.2. The extent to which robbers displayed selected rationality indicators, by target

Number of rationality indicators displayed	Bank No.	%	BS No.	%	PO No.	%	CIT No.	%	CP No.	%
None	7	9.2	16	15.8	7	11.1	3	6.4	31	20.8
1 or more	69	90.8	85	84.2	56	88.9	44	93.6	118	79.2
2 or more	60	78.9	69	68.3	51	80.9	42	89.4	89	59.7
3 or more	51	67.1	52	51.5	36	57.1	35	74.5	56	37.6
4 or more	38	50.0	28	27.7	29	46.0	25	53.2	30	20.1
5 or more	21	27.6	9	8.9	14	22.2	14	29.8	13	8.7
6 or more	7	9.2	3	3.0	4	6.3	7	14.9	3	2.0
Total	76	100.0	101	100.0	63	100.0	47	100.0	149	100.0

This somewhat cursory analysis shows most robbers to be rational. A future study could helpfully look more closely at the type of decisions made by offenders as they contemplate and commit the offence and evolve better formulated and more ambitious indicators of rationality. A classification of robbers (or for that matter any other group of offenders) based on such research will offer important clues for prevention. In the meantime, the rather less meaningful distinction between professionals and amateurs is used. While it is far too general to be of practical use, different types of questions need to be asked in order to develop meaningful typologies and this must be the focus of another project. It is likely, however, that the data gathered will have some value for crime prevention. Given that the findings support the rational choice perspective, they invite attention to situational techniques and ways of improving them.

RETHINKING SITUATIONAL PREVENTION: THE CRIME RISK MANAGEMENT PROCESS

The situational classification advocated by Clarke merits more evaluation (see Gill, 2000). It has evolved with reference to the crime prevention literature and ignores the literature on security management almost entirely. This is not so much a criticism of those working in the world of crime prevention; they (and Ron Clarke in particular) have helped develop a very useful set of techniques. Rather it is the weakness of those of us who have been working in security education and have failed to take on the task of synthesis. What follows is an attempt to merge the wisdom of the situational approach with the lessons that can be gleaned from texts on security management (particularly those parts concerned with crime management). The result is a *process* — illustrated in Figure 1 — that moves beyond a classification of opportunity reduction techniques, to an approach based on identifying the key action points and issues that merit consideration in tackling crime. It is presented as a tool to be of use to the person(s) responsible for crime prevention in an organisation; this will often be the security or crime risk manager. At the same time it is hoped the process will provide a more comprehensive framework for understanding situational crime prevention.

   An attempt is made to provide more structured distinctions between the techniques. It has to be stressed that the emphasis has shifted somewhat from the area of interest to Clarke and this needs to be borne in mind. The *Crime Risk Management Process* is applied to organisations[2] and the new techniques are discussed with reference to the foregoing work on robberies of commercial premises, although based on a broad review of the literature. It is hoped that the *process* will have a wide relevance.

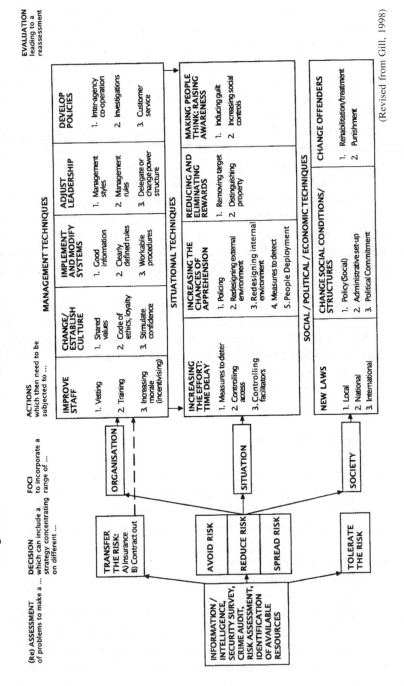

Figure 1: The crime risk management process in the context of the workplace

(Revised from Gill, 1998)

Initially, a situation has to be *assessed*. This will call for the collection of relevant information (see Ekblom, 1988; Burrows, 1991), intelligence, previous research and evaluations and will include a risk assessment or a crime audit and the identification of the resources available to tackle the problem. Once the situation is assessed there are five types of *decision* that can be made. A decision may be made to do nothing, that is to *tolerate* the risk. This is not necessarily a negative approach, the risk may be too small or the cost of dealing with it may outweigh any impact an incident(s) could make. Or a decision may be made to *transfer* the risk. This could involve taking out insurance or contracting out services.[3] And there are three other possible ways of managing the risk, and these are of particular interest here because they involve taking actions that directly impact in changing the situational context. This involves taking steps to *avoid* the risk (for example, by eliminating it; if there is no cash at the counter, no cash can be stolen from the counter), to *reduce* the risk, or to *spread* the risk.

There are at least three possible *foci* of that response. The focus could be on the organisation, on the situation and/or on society. Each *focus* will involve a different set of *techniques*: management techniques, situational techniques, or social/economic/political techniques. Each of these foci are discussed in the remainder of this book although, given its focus, only situational techniques are considered in depth.

Management Techniques

It is important to understand that the techniques of situational prevention discussed in this book are applied within an organisational framework. Clearly, the role of security and the role of managers will vary between and within organisations (Nalla and Newman, 1990), but there is a range of management techniques that can be used to make the situational response better. While there is not the space to discuss these techniques in depth, some general comments are merited.

Some thefts take place because staff collude with 'customers' (Bamfield, 1998); and this study has shown that employees are sometimes bribed by robbers. Whether this is because they are not properly vetted or poorly trained, or because of a low morale was beyond the scope of this study, but each of these can be a contributory factor. In any event, properly trained and motivated (and supervised) staff are essential for any initiative to be effective; and all staff can play a part in helping to prevent crime (Rodger, 1996). Indeed, Calder and Bauer (1992) found that convenience stores with two staff rather than one was a significant issue in rendering a target less attractive to robbers. Similarly, it has long been recognised that crime is bred by a poor organisational culture (Ditton, 1977) and the objective 'to change/establish culture' has therefore been included. And just as the starting point for a security strategy is the assessment of the problem, so the quality of information available will be dependent on the effectiveness of 'systems' (and staff) in delivering it. The lack of effective procedures for a whole range of functions, and not least cash handling, provides robbers with opportunities.

Effective management depends on good leadership, and managers have to be clear about their role and mission and trained to fulfil their potential. Another management technique is to 'develop policies' or launch special initiatives. This could easily be considered a catch-all category but this would be a mistake. Managers do need to launch special or specific initiatives, to carry out investigations and to develop a joint response with other agencies and this can form a vital part of the overall strategy.

If management techniques are not recognised as important and if these techniques are not applied effectively then situational techniques are unlikely to have the desired impact and may fail altogether. Indeed, implementation failure is a common problem. Hence the importance of locating situational prevention within a broad management framework. Indeed, there would be some merit in identifying the type of management support that would be needed for each situational technique, although this is not possible here.

Situational Techniques

A strategy contains a number of elements, and there is a range of guides (e.g. Wyllie, 2000) and security manuals (e.g. Klewers, 1999) that articulate these rather well. What is clear is that techniques need to be related to specific circumstances, and while it is always the case that good policy will be dependent on a good audit — a proper risk analysis taking account of the likelihood and impact of various events taking place — it is never the case that one blanket set of procedures or measures will account for all eventualities. And there ought to be a recognised set of principles that guide practice. In the security world there is reference to 'defence in depth', where the aim is to deter, delay, detect, deny and detain. Hamilton (1979) evolved a set of 'principles of defence' which provide a useful starting point and include: security should be commensurate with the threat; it should have a good image; no single measure gives security but the sum of several; security is as strong as the weakest link; quality is more important than quantity; security can be increased by co-operation with others; security must defer to the principles of human freedom. Elsewhere I have suggested that there may be others, such as a criterion for 'success' (see Gill, 1998). These principles are important because they provide a framework for guiding action but this needs more research and is beyond the scope of this book.

While Clarke's (1997) situational techniques have been very helpful in developing the *process*, they have undergone a revision and have been located within a broader context. This merits further comment.

Much of what is involved in Clarke's (1997) objective of 'increasing the effort' actually increases the risk. Indeed, all four of Clarke's classifications can lead to increasing the risk; hence the change of title of the second objective to 'increasing the chances of apprehension'. Similarly, Clarke's (1997) technique of 'target hardening' is a general term to describe a range of measures including some which increase the effort and others which increase the risk; for example, locks increase the effort and silent alarms the risk and this needs to be made more clear.[4] Hence I believe that it may be helpful to distinguish between measures that deter (increase the effort) with measures that detect (increases the risk). In fact increasing the effort is more commonly associated with a key component of security, namely 'time delay', that is using security and space[5] to increase the amount of time it takes to penetrate a target. There are essentially three aspects to increasing the effort: physical barriers, access controls (including what Clarke refers to as screening), and a reduction in the availability or usefulness of tools needed to commit a crime or to make it easier. And much of what Clarke calls 'deflecting offenders' is really access control (e.g. street closures), environmental design (e.g. tavern location) or people deployment (e.g. crowd control).

Action to increase the risk for offenders is important; even if offenders are not rational the increase in risk may result in them failing and getting caught. But there are problems with Clarke's categories when used for the purpose of classifying the key areas of action if they are to be of use to practitioners. There is more to increasing the risk (and to increasing the chance of apprehension) than different types of surveillance. And while there is much to commend the use of a range of surveillance techniques, a bigger danger for robbers arises when there is personal contact and when a victim resists. This can lead to robbers being injured, and not getting the money or being caught. Thus making space visible is one thing (as suggested by 'surveillance'), but increasing the risk by bringing about contact with people is another stage and part of the process. Therefore, 'people deployment' has been included.

I have chosen to classify the various points Clarke makes under the three surveillance headings separately. I have replaced 'formal surveillance' with 'policing' which would include a range of groups who carry out policing functions, including neighbourhood watch. And 'environmental design' is more encompassing than 'natural surveillance' and includes a range of techniques which can be used to increase risks for offenders, as Clarke has acknowledged.

What is missing from Clarke's classification is any explicit recognition that the interior design and layout of the premises can be manipulated to increase the effort, and the risk, for robbers. Research on shop theft has shown how the design and layout of a retail premises can reduce opportunities for theft (Beck and Willis, 1998; see also Farrington, 1999). During the interviews discussed above robbers noted how L-shaped banking halls could affect their vision and made clear their dislike of long distances between the doors and the counter and impediments in between such as queuing rails. Robbers who ventured a view about the teller position they preferred to rob favoured the one nearest the door. In a raid robbers need to take control and internal design can affect this. In banks and other premises there are sometimes doors which open onto the banking hall, and are seen by robbers as a danger because they never know who is behind them. There is clearly much more that can be done to apply some of the lessons of defensible space to interior design. 'Measures to deter' and 'measures to detect' replace 'target hardening', reflecting the aims of different types of measures.

The objective of the third set of techniques has a new definition, 'eliminating and reducing rewards'. Given that one of the techniques is to remove the target, for example, by means of cashless tills, it is important to recognise that the reward may be eliminated and not just reduced. While 'removing the target' remains a separate classification, Clarke's other three classifications (which overlap considerably) have been combined into 'distinguishing property'.

The fourth set of techniques entitled 'removing excuses' is a recent and very helpful addition and is mainly concerned with opportunities for crime that can be found in everyday life. It is possible that in due course this will generate thinking on how situational techniques can reduce the motivation to commit crime. Wortley (1997) has suggested that this set of techniques might usefully be divided into two objectives, one concerned with 'inducing guilt' the other with 'increasing social controls'. This suggestion has been adopted in part, but as two sets of techniques under a revised objective of 'making people think: raising awareness'. 'Rule setting' is a very important technique, although it is a more general management activity. Hence, it has been placed under the management *focus* in the diagram as 'workable procedures'.

What follows is an adaptation of Clarke's classification, based on the research on robberies of commercial premises discussed above but taking account of other studies in the area of crime prevention and security and crime risk management.

Increasing the Effort: Time Delay
Increasing the effort involves making the target harder to get at, in effect making it less accessible, ideally just to offenders. The security world frequently works on the principle of introducing measures to cause maximum delay combined with the earliest warning that something is amiss so as to generate a quick response. In practice things are rarely that simple. Increasing the effort involves at least three types of techniques: measures to deter; controlling access, this may mean screening baggage or people as they require access to the departure lounges at airports, or otherwise checking people as they request entry to a premises; and controlling the supply and availability of tools that are needed in committing offences or make them easier to carry out. Tools includes intelligence and not just physical items such as weapons and cars. Each of these is considered below as they apply to robbery of commercial premises.

Measures to Deter

Security screens are common in many financial institutions and other premises such as betting offices, effectively imposing a barrier between the robber and the cash. Most studies which have evaluated the potential of security screens in preventing robbery have generally reached favourable conclusions. Indeed, Austin (1988) concluded from her study of building societies robberies that bullet-proof screens were the main feature differentiating between failed and successful robberies. Similarly, the CBA/MUC (1987) found that banks where screens had been installed were less likely to be robbed.

Two of the potential problem of screens, as with any other physical barrier, is that they may displace crime and they may increase the amount of violence that is needed by robbers to complete the robbery (see Normandeau, 1983; Poyner et al, 1988). However, Grandjean (1990) found that bullet-proof screens did not increase the amount of violence used in robberies of banks in Switzerland but that there was displacement to less protected banks. Interestingly, Grandjean advances the argument that because there were still unscreened banks where the haul would be sufficient for most contemplating robbery, there was no displacement to less protected (and less lucrative) targets. Marsden (1990) in Australia found that following the installation of screens in some banks, robberies were displaced to banks without screens. But he expressed concern that one of the effects of screens would be to force robbers to gain access to the area behind the counter and so increase the trauma for staff.

The findings from the present study of robbers offer an interesting perspective. It has to be underlined that some robbers would not attack a premises that had screens[6] — they were better avoided when there were sufficient targets that were unscreened — so there is clearly some displacement effect. Screens frustrated some robberies; staff, who had faith in the screen, refused to give the money, leaving the robber with little alternative but to leave empty-handed. Austin (1988) found that robberies were more likely to be unsuccessful when the building society was empty, because staff with faith in bullet-proof screens felt confident in refusing the robbers' demands to hand over cash.

But in most raids on banks, building societies and post offices robbers knew there would be screens or thought they were inevitable. This was not a serious problem for most, however, because robberies frequently involved demanding money at the counter; and even if the aim was to get behind the counter they could trick (or threaten) someone into opening the safety door, which would permit them access. Some (in particular post office) robbers who had smashed the screen had been surprised at how easily it had cracked; some had assumed that it was unbreakable and were surprised to be able to gain access to the area behind the counter.

Some robbers were more aggressive because they were confronted by screens. Care needs to be taken in the interpretation of this finding. It has to be remembered that most robbers were not intent on causing injury and so the presence of the screen enabled them to show aggression without the risk of injuring someone. From the victims' perspective a screen being smashed in temper is perhaps marginally better than being confronted by a robber jumping across the counter. Thus robbers' claims that they use more aggression because of screens do not necessarily represent a negative feature of that measure when weighed against the drawbacks of alternative strategies that may be adopted. More research is needed on this issue.

Some robbers claimed that there were advantages for them in screens. They had never considered the possibility of getting behind the counter and they were concerned about the risk of being attacked by staff. So a big advantage of screens was that they reduced what they saw as one of the main threats to them: eager staff prepared to tackle them. Essentially, screens reduced the unpredictability of the raid.

At the time of the research 'rising' or 'pop up' screens were being installed. These are screens that are activated when a raid is taking place. The screen rises quickly, preventing robbers from getting behind the counter and therefore to the money. The noise made by the rising screens had shocked some robbers. One thought a partner had discharged a gun and this added to his worries, particularly since he was behind the counter when the screen was activated. This was clearly alarming for him but it can hardly have been comforting for staff. Some commentators have been impressed by the extent to which screens reduce robbery (Batterton, 1997). During conversation robbers expressed confidence that this measure would be overcome in time; some pointed out that it might result in more robberies being conducted with more violence. Indeed, Rodger (1996) has reported that robbers are overcoming screens by 'steaming' — several crossing the barrier in one go before staff have had a chance to activate the screen.

Clearly, there are many advantages to physical barriers such as screens. Some robbers stated categorically that they would not raid premises with screens; but they also present problems which have received scant attention in the literature. Still, there is considerable optimism that screens can be an effective deterrent albeit that for others they provide the ideal solution to their biggest fear — protection from members of staff acting as 'have-a-go heroes'. As new measures emerge, so robbers will adjust their tactics; the effectiveness of rising screens is already being tested by robbers. Hence the need for ongoing research, not least that which incorporates offenders' perspectives.

Controlling Access

Stopping robbers from entering premises is clearly an effective way of preventing a robbery. Robbers need to access the premises at speed, demand and obtain the money and exit the premises as quickly as possible. Anything that can frustrate the easy movement in and out of the premises will complicate the robbery. It may result in a target being less attractive and may make money less easy to obtain; interior design is a part of this process (discussed later) and access control is another.

At least one robber mentioned the difficulty posed by revolving doors; and double doors have been used successfully in Puerto Rico (Rodriguez, 1995). They make access and exit much slower and from the robbers' perspective there is always the danger that an automatic device may trap them. There have been a few instances in the UK, some caught on camera, where a robber has rushed to the door after a robbery, tried to push it open and been unable to do so. They presumably leap to the conclusion that an automatic lock has been activated because of the robbery. In fact the door could only be opened by pulling, not pushing. There are two episodes which are often shown on British television as comical clips. In one the robber smashes the door down even though it could be pulled open; in the other he sits to await for the arrival of the police only for a customer to walk through the door, enabling him to realise his error and make good his escape.

Slowing down access and exit is all very well; but trapping robbers inside the premises is fraught with dangers. Some robbers are determined not to get caught whatever the cost, even if this means shooting someone. While staff can be safe behind certain types of protective screens (at least against weapons presently used in robbery), there would need to be some way of ensuring that customers[7] could not be trapped and taken hostage or otherwise victimised. That aside, access (and exit) controls offer important means of frustrating robberies.

Clarke (1995) has argued that entry screening is undertaken not so much to exclude potential offenders (which is access control) as to increase the chances of detecting those who do not meet entry requirements. In practice they are part of the same thing and this is complicated in the case of robbery because often there is little that distinguishes the robber from the honest customer. However, during the interviews one robber said that he wore a crash helmet as a disguise; when he arrived at the counter he pointed a gun at the clerk, demanded money and walked out; and he could not easily be identified. Had the premises had a rule that no-one wearing a crash helmet would be given access (as some businesses now do) it is possible the robbery could have been avoided. Disguises such as balaclavas and scarves, quite common in British winters, are slightly more problematic since it may not be good business or practical to refuse access to people wearing these garments. However, making staff aware of the dangers and encouraging them to look for suspicious individuals may halt robberies in the early stages. In short, access controls can make an important contribution to tackling robberies.

Controlling Facilitators
There are several things that facilitate a robbery. Some of the robbers stole cars for their last raid; had it not been possible to steal cars then some of the robberies might not have taken place. Two common facilitators for robbers were knowledge of a target and the possession of a weapon (or something that looked like a weapon). Those planning raids with a view to obtaining lucrative rewards sought knowledge about their target. Some overheard staff carelessly talking about cash levels or cash-handling procedures and some cash-in-transit robbers bribed security staff. It could be argued that the low standards of the security world create opportunities for robbers. Indeed, this has been used as a reason to justify regulation (Button and George, 1996;

George and Button, 2000). Where a robber can leave prison one day and set up quite legally as a security expert the next, the facilitators of crime are endemic to the system. Ensuring that appropriate staff are vetted and trained prior to involvement in protecting and using assets (a management focus) is an important step in preventing robbery. This is especially true when someone is motivated by revenge against an ex-employer.

Weapons were used by the majority of robbers and this sometimes involved a real gun. In the UK official reaction to gun crime has been to tighten the law regulating gun ownership. This has been seen as a positive step in tackling armed robberies in Australia (Marsden, 1990), although alternative evidence offers less scope for optimism. For example, Skogan (1978) has argued that if guns are banned it could lead to attacks on more vulnerable targets such as women and the elderly, while Wright and Rossi (1986) suggest that restricting the availability of guns may make it more difficult to commit robberies for large sums and that this could lead offenders to commit more crimes. They argue too that banning handguns will encourage some to give up and others to move to more lethal weapons. For their part Harding and Blake (1989) claim that the link between the availability of guns and their use is a matter of culture rather than supply and that therefore to restrict the numbers is to miss the key issue in gun control.

The real problem with attempts to control the legal supply of guns as a robbery prevention measure is that robbers generally obtain them on the black market. Some weapons are stolen in burglaries and so target-hardening procedures may help stem the slippage onto the black market. Periodically, authorities declare amnesties, not just of guns but of a range of weapons and these may help in reducing the supply. However, this is a major battle. Some robbers in the survey pointed out that the supply of guns had increased with the break-up of the armies in Eastern Europe, and few robbers who wanted guns found them difficult to get hold of. While restricting the illegal gun supply would make robbery less easy for some people, it has to be said that the impact on the supply would have to be immense if it was to have a serious effect. Wright and Rossi (1986) found that many felons routinely carry guns and this was true for some of the robbers interviewed in this study. Hence, policies aimed at reducing street crime or the offence of carrying a weapon may have an indirect impact on robbery. Finally, some robbers carried guns because they believed the police would have them and herein lies the danger of an armed police response.

Increasing the Chances of Apprehension

At present amateur robbers do not give much thought to being caught, while professional robbers give more thought to the risk of being caught and take steps to minimise the risk of capture. There are a range of techniques which can increase the chances of offenders being caught.

Policing

'Policing', rather than 'police', denotes a range of activities by a variety of personnel, whether they be a part of the statutory sector (the police), the private sector (security guards), the voluntary sector (special constables), or the informal sector (business watch). An important finding from the present research is that robbers conduct a raid because they believe the risk of apprehension to be low. However, some robbers had underestimated the effectiveness of police work and there may be scope for advertising police successes more widely.

Some robbers spoke to others about their offences, and some were caught as a consequence, which perhaps argues for increased support for initiatives which encourage the flow of information from the public to the police (see van Dijk, 1997), for example, informants and information hot-lines (CBA/MUC, 1987). Some businesses are offering rewards for information leading to the prosecution of robbers, and some banks and building societies have said this has worked effectively. Television programmes[8] which reconstruct offences, including robbery, expose clues to viewers. While these have been successful in detecting some robbers they have encouraged some people to think about committing robbery. There is a need for more research on the type of measures which can increase the risk of offenders being caught by the police at the scene and subsequently.

The use of private security guards is another measure, and they are regularly deployed when cash is being delivered. The main limit to their wider deployment is that they are expensive; and there is a lack of evidence to suggest that they are effective (see George and Button,

2000). While Beck and Willis (1995) reported favourably on the work of security guards in shopping centres, and Hannah (1982) in banks, the CBA/MUC (1987) warn that armed guards may increase the levels of violence robbers use and do provide a supply of guns to the underworld; some victims worry that armed guards increase the potential for a shoot-out (Normandeau, 1983).

A pointer to possible ways of improving police detection is the finding that robbers frequently visit and carry out surveillance on the scene before the robbery (and those that plan may do this at the time of the robbery on the day or a week before). Moreover, many robbers return to the scene of a previous raid while others rob premises they know have been robbed before. There may be opportunities here for an alert business watch scheme. Policing has much potential to impact on robbery and not least because robbers underestimate it.

Redesigning the External Environment

Clarke (1995) has summarised the way in which environmental criminology has contributed to the development of rational choice theory. He has shown that various schemes such as 'Secured by Design' in Britain, and CEPTED in the USA have promoted the principles of designing-out crime, incorporating many of the concepts of defensible space. The theoretical underpinning of the Secured by Design concept have been evaluated and it was found to be soundly based (Pascoe and Topping, 1997).

During the interviews for this study robbers were asked some questions, the answers to which give indications of how to benefit from and improve environmental design, although any future study should include more focused questions. On a general level what emerged is that escape is a priority for the robber, and so premises located near main roads (if escaping in a car) and alleyways and tube stations (if escaping on foot) are favoured. One-third of robbers who robbed a premises located on a main road claimed that this was relevant to their choice of that target; and it was an added advantage if there were side roads. Indeed, Duffala (1976) found that convenience stores were more vulnerable to robbery when located on a main road. Although as Bellamy (1996) found, the advantages of busy streets can be offset by busy traffic flow. Also, it was viewed as a disadvantage if the main road was a one-way street (another form of access control).

For those who thought pedestrian streets were an advantage the main reason was that it facilitated a quick getaway on foot. The location of the building on a corner was generally not viewed as an important issue for robbers (and sometimes was seen as a disadvantage), although half of those who robbed building societies claimed that a corner location was relevant. There are, of course, many other considerations related to location that go far beyond the scope of this study. For example, Hunter and Jeffery (1994) found that convenience stores located in areas with evening commercial activities were at less risk than others.

The design of the environment has an important contribution to make to robbery prevention, as even the few findings discussed here suggest. Environmental features which frustrate robbers' escape are particularly important.

Redesigning the Internal Environment

This technique was given little emphasis in Clarke's classification, but is an important aspect. A few comments by the robbers interviewed provided some helpful insights. In the context of robbery a number of writers have noted the benefits for crime prevention if store owners keep their windows as uncluttered as possible, thereby underlining the importance of natural surveillance (see Hunter and Jeffery, 1992; Macdonald, 1975). Similarly, Gabor et al (1987) advocate making cash registers visible from the street.

Yet only a minority of robbers interviewed in this study considered visibility to be an important issue, even though in the majority of cases the inside of the premises robbed were visible from the street. However, a number of robberies only take place because robbers walk by and see an opportunity. Those seeing benefit in visibility from the outside pointed to the advantages of being able to check the premises — in particular the number of customers and staff — prior to conducting the raid. Those taking the opposite view pointed to the fact that it reduced the chances of a passer-by noticing what was happening and raising the alarm.

The Home Office (1986) considered that full or partial open-plan offices were proving a deterrent to robbery but this has yet to be subjected to rigorous research (see Rodger, 1996). Robbers reported that they did not like anything that interfered with the escape and that queuing rails and other impediments posed a problem for them. And robbers need to exercise control, so one response might be to include an element of surprise in the protection of targets. Where an office door leads in to, say, a banking hall, it presents a danger for the robber because they cannot be sure whether someone is behind it. Similarly, where a premises is L-shaped, or there are blind spots for other reasons, this can affect their ability to exercise control. And the danger is greater the further the counter (or the location of the money) is from the exit. Indeed, the type of measures that can be introduced will be affected by the amount of space available (Batterton, 1997).

Locating money in central teller units has been shown to be helpful in reducing the number of raids. The CBA/MUC study (1987) found that while 35.5% of banks with screens had been robbed, 48.4% of banks without screens had been; but where there were screens and a central teller unit then only 3.5% of branches had been raided. The problem is that when a central teller unit is raided the losses are much higher. Thus while a central teller unit can be an important impediment to robbery, it will need different and appropriate security.

One robber claimed that if music was playing it would affect his concentration. Perhaps others feel the same way? Once again it has to be concluded that more research is needed. But all in all the contribution which interior design can make to protecting premises should not be underestimated.

Measures to Detect

There are a whole range of measures that are available to increase the chances of an offender being apprehended. Robbers were questioned about just some of these and the answers were instructive. Where alarms have been sounded in some types of robberies, and post offices are a case in point, it seems that most have been aborted (Ekblom, 1987; Home Office, 1986). Although there are general problems with alarms in terms of false activations (Buck and Hakim, 1990), this has not been shown to be the case in the context of commercial robbery. A bigger problem has been victims forgetting to activate the alarm (Macdonald, 1975) or being scared to do so (Normandeau, 1983); there appears to have been confusion as to whether the alarm should be activated during the raid or immediately afterwards (CBA/MUC, 1987). Certainly, some UK businesses advise staff not to sound the alarm until the robbers have left the premises.

Robbers' accounts in the course of the present research suggest that alarms are of (limited) benefit. True, some admitted that they would abort the robbery if they heard an alarm and some had done so and as a consequence have left empty-handed. However, many had psyched themselves up not to be shocked by an alarm being sounded; in any event they could never be sure that a silent alarm had not been activated and so they always acted with haste. In reality robberies do not take long and the police take much longer to arrive. A few robbers suggested that an alarm might add to the urgency of the robbery. While it is too much of a jump, on this evidence, to suggest that when alarms are sounded there is a greater risk of force or injury, that possibility exists and merits further research.

Austin (1988) reported that building society staff believed that cameras, like alarms, are more relevant as an aid to detection than as a deterrent. There is certainly much in robbers' accounts that supports this assertion. A minority of the robbers in the present study noted that they would not raid a premises that had cameras, so these do deflect some robbers onto other targets. Some robbers were caught on camera (see also Morrison and O'Donnell, 1994) and as a consequence were identified and prosecuted. However, one study of building society robberies found that disguises did not cover the whole face and cameras were activated in most robberies, but that managers did not want the pictures released to the media to help in identification for fear of compromising security (Batterton, 1997).

There were a few robbers who claimed that cameras were an advantage because they added to the risk and sense of adventure that a robbery provided, and another, perhaps more seriously, felt that cameras lulled staff into a false sense of security. So while cameras have advantages in that they deter some and are a major factor in the capture of a few, most are prepared for cameras and adjust their styles accordingly. Indeed, most robbers were aware that cameras would be installed in the places they raided alongside other measures but this was not sufficient to stop them carrying out the raid (see also Wright and Decker, 1997). There is evidence that cameras can affect the amount of violence used; a few robbers sought to destroy cameras and this included firing shots at them. As camera technology improves and is more widely used the value of pictures will increase both in identifying individuals and in enabling police to compare styles (Home Office, 1986). Whether this will increase the numbers wearing disguises, or the levels of violence used, or will lull staff into a greater sense of insecurity are matters that need to be monitored.

Whether a safe is a temptation for robbery in the same way that it has been shown to be for burglary (Wiersma, 1996) is beyond the scope of this enquiry but merits further research. Clarke and McGrath (1990) found that safes with time locks had proved effective in Australian betting shops, although the effects were less clear when the locks were installed in convenience stores. Few robbers in the present study were concerned about gaining access to the safe, not least because sufficient money was available at the counter and it was much easier to seize.

People Deployment
Given that robbers frequently visit the scene of the robbery before-hand and/or keep the target under surveillance there is much to be gained by having alert and enthusiastic staff (see Hemingway, 1989). Robbers claimed they sometimes 'checked' their potential victims — just by looking at them — to gain an idea as to whether they are likely to be 'have-a-go-heroes'. Some robbers check premises directly before a raid. This may amount to nothing more than looking through a window but the point is that because there are robbers at the scene and because they may be behaving suspiciously, it might be possible for alert staff, just as for business watch, to realise what is going on.

It was interesting to note that some robbers admitted that they had robbed a premises which had been robbed before. This is not unusual; there is a growing amount of evidence that certain commercial premises are victims of repeat offences including robberies (Gill, 1998b). For example, Conklin (1972) found that a quarter of victims were revictimised within two and a half years and Gabor et al (1987) found that three-quarters of people interviewed were the victims of more than one armed robbery during their period with a company (a median of 2.5 years), and that one-fifth had been held up seven or more times. Hindelang (1974) in a study of burglary and robbery reported that three in 10 of those victimised were victimised more than once. There is some evidence that repeat victimisation occurs quite quickly; Formolli (1998) found in a small study of betting shops that over half were revictimised within a month of the original offence. The findings here suggest that the adoption of procedures and measures soon after a first robbery would be wise.

Identifying robbers is not easy. There will often be nothing suspicious about disguises; most robbers wore 'ordinary' clothes, chosen usually so that they did not distinguish themselves. Many robbers considered that victims and witnesses were very poor at identifying them. Others concur with this view. Bellamy (1996) founds clerks' descriptions to be unreliable and McClintock and Gibson (1961) found that a main reason why robberies remained undetected was the vagueness of the victim/witness descriptions. Yet for detection a description is of paramount importance (Conklin, 1972).

It has already been noted that the potential intervention of staff was one of robbers' most pressing concerns. Employees could resist with the result that the robbers were injured, or caught, or did not get their haul or got only a reduced haul. So where surveillance includes direct contact there may be greater risks to the staff but to the robber too. At least one bank robber favoured the deployment of staff in the banking hall because, he claimed, it would enable him to take hostages. There is some evidence that the vulnerability of a target is linked to the number of staff employed (Bellamy, 1986; Hunter and Jeffery, 1994). On the issue of gender, the few robbers who expressed a preference claimed that they would prefer victims to be women. Thus extra precautions may be needed when women are working with money alone.

Reducing and Eliminating Rewards

Removing the Target
Robbers are motivated by the desire or need for money and a range of studies have highlighted the advantages of improved cash-handling procedures (Clarke and McGrath, 1990; Griffith, undated; Hunter and Jeffery, 1994; Marsden, 1990). Macdonald (1975) advocates drop safes, while CBA/MUC (1987) underline the importance of minimum cash levels. Meanwhile, Wright and Decker (1997) note that the elimination of cash from the economy by means of cards and electronic systems would stop commercial robberies.

While reducing the potential haul for robbers has much to commend it, it should be stressed that many robbers have very modest aims and are prepared to raid for comparatively small amounts. Thus even effective financial procedures are unlikely to stop raids altogether, although they may well reduce the attractiveness of the targets for the more professional robbers. A few robbers who had demanded that cashiers put money in a bag later found that they had obtained shredded paper and not cash. One of these could see the funny side and was not deterred from committing another robbery soon after.

Thus there may be scope for experimenting with fake money, but unless this occurs on a wide scale it is unlikely to have anything other than a marginal effect. And if such a measure was applied on a wide scale then robbers would soon hear of it and adjust their tactics, which may not necessarily be a gain. There is also the problem of ensuring that fake money is available to give to robbers at the point of a raid, and the need to ensure that the supply of fake money does not leak on to the black market.

Distinguishing Property
Only a few robbers were concerned that they might have taken identifiable bank notes during the raid, and these more professional robbers claimed that they were able to have the money 'cleaned'. A number noted that they did not have the money long enough to know whether it was identifiable. Macdonald (1975) reported that there had been successes with exploding money packages, although this technique can be dangerous (Normandeau, 1983).

Of course robbery is not just about money. Sometimes goods are stolen; and one robber recalled how he had been involved in a robbery linked to an insurance fraud. The owner of a clothes company arranged for the robbery to take place, the robbers kept the clothes and the owner claimed money for the 'losses' from the insurance company. Some products could carry a unique identification number to reduce their second-hand value; if they did, that would militate against this sort of offence.

Making People Think: Raising Awareness

This objective was formulated after the completion of the research work, but some of the findings do lend support to its inclusion.

Inducing Guilt
There was certainly some evidence that robbers portrayed their offence as much less serious than it was. Some robbers not only lacked sympathy for victims but a few felt they had helped their

victims by giving them something to remember in an otherwise dull life. Others had pointed guns not capable of firing a lethal shot at victims but failed to appreciate that they would not have known this, and would have been very distressed as a consequence. Other saw businesses as legitimate targets and seemed unaware that businesses contain people (Gill, 1994). Indeed, when robbers were asked whether they had ever been convicted of street robbery (mugging) some went to great pains to differentiate themselves and their offence (against business) from those who had victimised individuals; this was viewed as far more sinister and unacceptable.

Thus, the technique of inducing guilt — raising awareness of the impact of crime and making robbers think — has potential. There is some evidence that re-offending may be prevented by working with robbers to ensure that they understand the implications of their behaviour, and not least the impact on victims.

Increasing Social Controls
The process of increasing social condemnation and reducing social approval offers a possible technique for reducing robbery. During the research some robbers admitted that they had looked up to known robbers in their area when they were young, and that this had influenced them in choosing to commit robberies. Certainly times have changed; robbers are no longer the cream of the underworld and they are much more likely to be desperate people who risk long terms in prison for relatively low rewards. Some of the more experienced robbers took the view that robbery was no longer viable as a career and considered that other offences carried less risk, attracted lower punishments and were more lucrative. In other words robbers have lost much of their status as elite offenders and the offence reaps fewer rewards these days. There is a need to raise awareness of this and to make people think about the wisdom of embarking on robbery.

In a different way robbers learn and gain ideas about robbery by watching television and, ironically, particularly programmes that are focused on catching offenders because these reconstruct offences and, in the process, offer useful lessons. Some robbers claimed that they gained notoriety in criminal circles from having their offences covered by television. There is no doubt that the UK programme Crimewatch has helped solve crimes, but at the same time it gives people ideas and some claimed that they first picked up the idea of robbery from watching the programme. Reducing copycat crimes is a proper aim of crime prevention and the advantages of programmes like Crimewatch need to be carefully weighed. Certainly, there is potential for increasing social controls to have an impact on robbery, although more research and thinking is needed about the best way forward.

SOCIAL/POLITICAL/ECONOMIC TECHNIQUES

This focus covers social, economic and political as well as legislative techniques. It includes but moves beyond what might traditionally be called social crime prevention. In essence it includes techniques which are not directly related to the management and structure of any particular organisation or situation. These will be wide ranging and merit a chapter (perhaps even a book) in their own right. The comments below cannot do justice to the range of possibilities in this area, which, indeed, fall outside the scope of this study of robbers.

Legislation is an important weapon in the prevention of crime. In this study changes in law relating to gun control and the length of prison sentences have been briefly discussed. Jammers (1995) drew attention to a law in the Netherlands which required petrol stations to have a range of security measures installed if they wished to remain open overnight. Making security measures a legal requirement may in some circumstances reduce the number of easy targets and protect staff; but much depends on proper installation.

If robbery is going to be significantly reduced, there will have to be changes in social conditions. Robbers frequently came from poor backgrounds where they came under bad influences from a young age. Most progress to robbery having carried out other types of offences. Stories of broken homes, addictions and unemployment are common. Despite the fact that the emphasis of this book is on the situational response, the evidence is quite clear that if robbery is to be prevented or reduced, changes in social policy, or the impact of social policy, are required. This may itself require changes in social structures at different levels; an emphasis on collaboration (and the present emphasis on community safety is showing encouraging results); and a political lead and commitment to tackling problems such as the structure of illegal markets and the disruption of resources needed for offending.

Changes in the attitude of offenders may be brought about through contact with the criminal justice process, although judging by the accounts of those who were interviewed in this study there is not much scope for optimism. While many robbers were hopeful that they would change when released their optimism, experience suggests, is misplaced. Robbers need help to change. Many claimed that this was their only hope but responding is fraught with practical as well as political difficulties. Nevertheless, there is potential here to stop future robberies and its importance must not be underestimated.

CONCLUDING COMMENTS

Conducting interviews with robbers provides some useful insights into the way robberies are planned and carried out. The focus has been very much on generating information which can be used as a basis for preventing robbery and for improving the techniques of situational crime prevention. In so doing an attempt has been made to assess the rationality of robbers, and to suggest ways to study the reasoning offender as source of ideas for refining the techniques of situational prevention. Present typologies of robbers were not developed with crime prevention purposes in mind, and while the development of rationality indicators may help, this will require another more focused study. The book has presented ideas and principles common in the subject area of security management which has been largely ignored by criminologists. And from the information generated Clarke's (1997) situational classification has been adopted, and revised for the purpose of developing a *Crime Risk Management Process* which can be used as a guide to policy for those working in organisations and with a responsibility for tackling crime.

It seems that robbers are rational; they carry out a degree of reasoning at the scene, be they amateurs or professionals. To a greater or lesser extent robbers (normally) weigh up the possibility of getting money and avoiding capture. Not all were able to articulate what made a target attractive, but well-directed questions may be able to determine more precisely what types of robbers saw what features of the location and the target as making the crime 'look easy'. The fact that robbers carry out some form of even rudimentary reasoning at the scene suggests that there is potential for appropriately applied measures to make a robbery less likely. Most robbers think they will not be caught, many give no thought to the possibility, and in the normal course of events they are probably right. The challenge for research is to identify the types of decision made, and the logic or reasoning process behind them, and to suggest responses which can alter the thinking of the robber. Surprisingly little research has attempted this.

Future studies may benefit from taking offenders back to the scene. Inviting them to discuss their thoughts about the different decisions they made, and the reasons they made them, would provide a better way of understanding the offenders' perspective on situational influences. This is not a new idea and is not without problems of its own (see Cromwell et al, 1991),[9] but interviews with robbers in prison cannot yield profound insights into the types of decisions made at the scene and this is essential if crime prevention is to be improved. A second best is to take robbers to some other location or to simulate crime scenes as Bennett and Wright (1984) did with domestic burglars. Nevertheless, there is much that can be gained from incorporating offenders' perspectives, especially when situational measures are being evaluated.

This is in part a reflection of the lack of interest in business crime, security management, private policing, and evaluation work although new ideas and interest are beginning to emerge (see Ekblom and Pease, 1995; Pawson and Tilley, 1997; Tilley, 1997). There is certainly value in looking to other disciplines, such as security management, to supplement work that is being done in criminology. Indeed, the *Crime Risk Management Process* combines the lessons of security management and situational crime prevention and provides a means of linking the initial assessment of the problem through to the response; and the importance of management issues is reflected in its formulation. Where situational techniques are applied within organisations — the normal environment of most security managers — it is important to appreciate the influence of the organisation, and the range of management techniques that can be used to supplement and guide the situational ones. Indeed, the effectiveness of situational techniques will be greatly influenced by features of the organisation and the skill with which management techniques are applied. In the past this has been largely overlooked, especially by proponents of situational crime prevention.

It is hoped that the *Crime Risk Management Process* will provide a basis for thinking about the total response to crime and generate interest in improving it; certainly it is in need of improvement. It helps very little with techniques for social crime prevention. Yet, interviews with robbers showed that they had in their lives encountered a range of problems that present a challenge to the best social policies. Social and situational responses have sometimes been portrayed as ideological alternatives but they are both important techniques in tackling crime. And better ways have to be found to use policing so that it increases the risk, or appears to increase the risk, for offenders. And much more emphasis needs to be placed on improving situational techniques. As new ideas, policies and technologies emerge and are implemented it is important that they are subjected to proper independent evaluation. In this study it was possible to identify at least five general sets of problems associated with situational measures, on which it is worth commenting briefly in conclusion.

First, situational measures can lead to displacement. There is nothing new in this finding but it is an important nonetheless. Some robbers would not raid premises with screens, and others premises with cameras. These were viewed as unnecessary risks when there was an abundant supply of alternatives without these impediments. Clearly, organisations which cannot afford or for other reasons do not install screens and cameras are at greater risk of robbery from these types of robbers.

Second, situational measures can increase the amount of violence robbers feel they need to use in carrying out the raid. It has to be emphasised that robbery is, by legal definition, a violent act; and it is not easy to distinguish the extent to which situational measures were responsible for violent incidents. Yet some violence was directed at security measures: cameras were destroyed and screens smashed. Had they not been there perhaps robbers would have shown their aggression by attacking people? Perhaps the consequences of removing some measures would be more severe? These remain important but unanswered questions. Certainly though, screens provided the opportunity for robbers to show that they meant business, by being aggressive without hurting people. A slightly different but related point is that one of the major impacts of CCTV was to force robbers to wear disguises and, as some pointed out, this made them more menacing to victims and certainly made them more difficult to recognise.

Third, some measures appeared not to work or were absent altogether. Robbers gave examples of camera pictures which were of a poor quality, or screens that could be smashed with relative ease (to the surprise of robbers), or money that was left unguarded, 'inviting' robbery. In a different way some robbers were helped in their preparations for robbery because staff spoke carelessly about security arrangements or the availability of cash, or because security guards were bribed. And there were many other examples. A part of the problem here may be that measures were poorly conceived, a reflection, in the UK at least, of an unregulated security industry. But it is also a consequence of poor risk analysis, lack of guidance and procedures, the careless behaviour of staff, and a failure to evaluate the measures that were put in place. Robbers rarely encountered difficulties in circumventing the measures adopted to stop them.

Fourth, some situational measures can work in the interest of robbers. This conclusion merits careful interpretation since no measure was found to be wholly bad, and most had beneficial effects which outweighed the negative impact. Yet, some robbers were helped by security measures. This includes those who said they would only rob premises that had security screens since they were protected from their biggest threat, determined staff who could not jump the counter and attack them. A few thought CCTV lulled staff into a false sense of security, which has independent support (Beck and Willis, 1994).

Fifth, a real problem of situational measures is that just as they deter the robber, so they can deter the honest customer too. Screens have been removed in favour of open-plan offices for this reason, and double doors are an irritant to both the robber and the customer. A key principle of security is that it should be sensitive to the environment to which it relates. Thus situational measures are not just about stopping robbers, they are about stopping robbers but not customers and about making people, customers and staff, feel and be safer. It has been suggested that there is a need to think about the key principles of good security as a basis for guiding policy.

Thus there has been confirmation that there are costs and benefits to the situational approach. As more measures are discovered and they become more complex, especially technical measures, there is a need for more research to inform theory and policy. There is a need to develop new ideas and frameworks that can inform practice. This study is one small contribution to the enormous amount of work that needs to be done.

[NOTES]

[1] Although Gunn and Gristwood (1976) found professionals to be less violent.

[2] It may have a somewhat different look if applied to communities or countries just as it would if it were applied to safety rather than security.

[3] In practice, it is often the case that only a part of the risk is shifted.

[4] Although it could be argued that by increasing the risk, more effort is needed to control that risk. Clearly, more research is needed here. I am grateful to Paul Ekblom for this observation.

[5] Herein lies an overlap with environmental design.

[6] The question did not request details about the type of screen, for example, whether it was bullet-proof or not. This is an important issue which further studies may want to research further.

[7] And for that matter contractors and others working on the premises.

[8] Crimewatch UK claims that a quarter of the crimes it covers in its programme are eventually solved. Clearly, this needs to be balanced against those who are inspired to commit offences because of ideas this programme and others like it generate.

[9] In the case of robbery there is an additional problem in that robbers often spend long spells in prison and so crime scenes will change.

Bibilography

Ascoli, D., *The Queen's Peace: The Origins and Development of the Metropolitan Police 1829–1979*, London: Hamish Hamilton, 1979.

Ashworth, A., *Criminal Justice Process: an Evaluative Study*, Oxford: Oxford University Press, 1994.

Ashworth, A., 'Sentencing', *Oxford Handbook of Criminology*, Oxford: Oxford University Press, 1994.

Ashworth, A., *Sentencing and Criminal Justice*, London: Butterworths, 1995.

Ashton, J., Brown, I., Senior, B. and Pease, K., 'Repeat Victimisation: Offender Accounts', *International Journal of Risk, Security and Crime Prevention*, 1998, vol. 3, no. 2, pp. 269–280.

Audit Commission, *Helping With Enquiries: Tackling Crime Effectively*, London: Audit Commission, 1993.

Audit Commission, *Tackling Crime Effectively, Volume 2*, London: Audit Commission, 1996.

Austin, C., 'The Prevention of Robbery at Building Society Branches', *Home Office Crime Prevention Unit Paper 14*, 1988.

Ball, J., Chester, L., Perrott, R., *Cops and Robbers*, London: André Deutsch, 1978.

Bamfield, J., 'A Breach of Trust: Employee Collusion and Theft from Major Retailers', *Crime at Work: Increasing the Risk for Offenders Volume 2*, Leicester: Perpetuity Press, 1998.

Banton, M., *Investigating Robbery*, Aldershot: Gower, 1985.

Barr, R. and Pease, K., 'Crime Placement, Displacement and Deflection', *Crime and Justice: A Review of Research*, 1990, vol. 12.

Batterton, I. P., 'Camera Surveillance Systems: a Valid Crime Prevention Measure for Robbery in Building Society Branches', *Unpublished MSc Thesis*, Scarman Centre, University of Leicester, 1997.

Beck, A. and Willis, A., 'Customer and Staff Perceptions of the Role of Closed Circuit Television in Retail Security', *Crime at Work: Studies in Security and Crime Prevention Volume 1*, Leicester: Perpetuity Press, 1994.

Beck, A. and Willis, A., *Crime and Security: Managing the Risk to Safe Shopping*, Leicester: Perpetuity Press, 1995.

Beck, A. and Willis, A., 'Sales and Security: Striking the Balance', *Crime at Work: Studies in Security and Crime Prevention Volume 1*, Leicester, Perpetuity Press, 1998.

Bellamy, L., 'Situational Crime Prevention and Convenience Store Robbery', *Security Journal*, 1996, vol. 7, pp. 41–52.

Bennett, T. and Wright, R., *Burglars on Burglary*, Aldershot: Cromer, 1994.

Beyleveld, D., 'Deterrence Research as a Basis for Deterrence Policies', *Howard Journal*, 1979, 18, 3, pp. 135–149.

Birbeck, C., *Theft, Robbery and Conning in Cali, Columbia: Some Implications for Policy*, Centre for Development Studies, University College of Swansea, University of Wales, Monograph no. viii, 1980.

Bowers, K., 'Crimes Against Non-residential Properties: Patterns of Victimisation, Impact Upon Urban Areas and Crime Prevention Strategies', *PhD Thesis*, University of Liverpool, 1999.

Brantingham, P. and Faust, F., 'A Conceptual Model of Crime Prevention', *Crime and Delinquency*, 1976, vol. 22, pp. 130–146.

Broadbent, P., 'There has been a Change in the Trend of Armed Robberies at Commercial Premises Together with a Shift in Status of Offenders', *Unpublished MSc Thesis*, Scarman Centre, University of Leicester, 1999.

Broadhurst, K. and Benyon, J., 'Gun Law: The Continuing Debate about the Control of Firearms in Britain', *Scarman Centre Occasional Paper Series*, 2000, vol. 16.

Bright, J., 'Crime Prevention: The British Experience', *The Politics of Crime Control*, London: Sage, 1991.

Buck, A.J. & Hakin, S., 'Burglar Alarms: What do we know about them?', *Security Journal*, 1990, vol. 1, no. 2, pp. 101–108.

Button, M. and George, B., 'The Case for Regulation', *International Journal of Risk, Security and Crime Prevention*, 1996, vol. 1, no. 1, pp. 53–57.

Burrows, J., 'Making Crime Prevention Pay: Initiatives from Business', *Crime Prevention Series Paper no. 27*, London: Home Office, 1991.

Burrows, J., 'Criminology and Business Crime: Building the Bridge', *Business and Crime Prevention*, New York: Criminal Justice Press, 1997.

Bury, M. R. & Katz, B. C., 'Rape, Robbery and Burglary: Responses to Actual and Feared Criminal Victimisation with Special Focus on Women and the Elderly', *Victimology*, 1985, vol. 10, pp. 325–358.

Butler, G., 'Commercial Burglary: What Offenders Say', *Crime at Work: Studies in Security and Crime Prevention Volume 1*, Leicester: Perpetuity Press, 1994.

Cahalane, M., 'Security isn't the Word for It', *International Journal of Risk, Security and Crime Prevention*, 1998, vol. 3, no. 3, pp. 235–238.

Calder, J. and Bauer, J., 'Convenience Store Robberies: Security Measures and Store Robbery Incidents', *Journal of Criminal Justice*, 1992, vol. 20, pp. 553–566.

Canadian Bankers' Association/Montreal Urban Community, 'Bank Robbers in the Montreal Urban Community', *Unpublished report*, 1987.

Challinger, D., *Armed Robbery*, Australian Institute of Criminology, Canberra, 1988, ACT.

Clarke, R.V.G., 'Situational Crime Prevention: Theory and Practice', *British Journal of Criminology*, 1980, vol. 20, no. 2, pp. 136–147.

Clarke, R.V.G., 'Introduction', *Situational Crime Prevention: Successful Case Studies*, New York: Harrow, 1992.

Clarke, R.V.G., 'Situational Crime Prevention', *Building a Safer Society: Crime and Justice a Review of Research Volume 19*, Chicago: University of Chicago Press, 1995.

Clarke, R.V.G., *Situational Crime Prevention: Successful Case Studies*, 2nd edn, New York: Harrow and Heston, 1997.

Clarke, R.V.G. and Homel, R., 'A Revised Classification of Situational Crime Prevention Techniques', *Crime Prevention at a
Crossroads*, Cincinnati, OH: Anderson, 1997.

Clarke, R.V. & Field, S., 'Target Hardening of Banks in Australia and
Displacement of Robberies', *Security Journal*, 1991, vol. 2.2,
pp. 84–90.

Clarke, R. V. & Felson, M., *Routine Activity and Rational Choice*,
New York: Transaction Publishers, 1993.

Clarke, R. & McGrath, G., 'Cash Reduction and Robbery Prevention
in Australian Betting Shops', *Security Journal*, 1990, vol. 1, no. 3,
pp. 160–163.

Clarke, R.V. and McGrath, G., 'Newspaper Reports of Bank Robberies and the Copycat Phenomenon', *Australian and New Zealand
Journal of Criminology*, 1992, 25, 1, pp. 83–8.

Cole, B., 'Armed Robbers: A Detective's View', *Armed Robbery,
Australian Institute of Criminology*, 1988, ACT.

Conklin, J., *Robbery and the Offender Justice System*, Philadelphia:
Lippincott, 1972.

Cook, P. J., 'A Strategic Choice Analysis of Robbery', *Sample Surveys
of the Victims of Crime*, Cambridge, Massachusetts: Ballinger,
1976.

Cook, P. J., 'Reducing Injury and Death Rates in Robbery', *Policy
Analysis*, 1979.

Cornish, D. and Clarke, R., *The Reasoning Criminal: Rational Choice
Perspectives on Offending*, New York: Springer-Verlag, 1986.

Crawford, A., *Crime Prevention and Community Safety: Politics,
Policies and Practices*, London: Longman, 1998.

Cromwell, P. F., Olson, J.N. & Avary, D.W., 'How Residential
Burglars Choose Targets: An Ethnographic Analysis', *Security
Journal*, 1991, vol. 2.4, pp. 195–199.

Creedon, M., 'Armed Robbery in Leicestershire and Northampton-
shire: An Analysis of Patterns and Trends in Crime and the
Response of the Police', *Unpublished MA thesis*, University of
Leicester, 1994.

Currie, E., *Confronting Crime: An American Challenge*, New York:
Pantheun Books, 1985.

Ditton, J., *Part-time Crime: an Ethnography of Fiddling and Pilfer-
age*, London: Macmillan Press, 1977.

Ditton, J. and Short, E., 'Evaluating Scotland's First Town Centre CCTV Scheme', *Surveillance, Closed Circuit Television and Social Control*, Aldershot: Ashgate, 1977.

Ditton, J. and Short, E., 'Yes, It Works, No, It Doesn't: Comparing the Effects of Open-Street CCTV in two Adjacent Scottish Town Centres', *Surveillance of Public Space: CCTV, Street Lighting and Crime Prevention, Crime Prevention Studies*, vol. 10, New York: Criminal Justice Press, 1999.

Duffala, D.,'Convenience Stores: Armed Robbery and Physical Environmental Features', *American Behavioural Scientist*, 1976, vol. 20, pp. 227–246.

Dujmovic, Z. and Miksaj-Todorovic, L., 'Criminological Characteristics of Offenders Guilty of Robbery', *Policing in Central and Eastern Europe: comparing first hand knowledge with experiences from the West*, Ljubljana, Slovenia: College of Police and Security Studies, 1996.

Eck, J. E., *Solving Crimes: The Investigation of Burglary and Robbery*, Washington: Police Executive Research Forum, 1983.

Einstadter, W. J., 'The Social Organisation of Armed Robbery', *Social Problems*, 1969, 17, pp. 64–82.

Ekblom, P., 'Preventing Robberies at Sub-Post Offices: An Evaluation of a Security Initiative', *Home Office Crime Prevention Unit Paper 9*, London: Home Office, 1987.

Ekblom, P., 'Getting the Best out of Crime Analysis', *Home Office Crime Prevention Unit Paper 10*, London: Home Office, 1988.

Ekblom, P., 'Proximal Circumstances: A Mechanism-based Classification of Crime Prevention', *Crime Prevention Studies*, vol. 2, New Jersey: Willow Tree Press, 1994.

Ekblom, P., 'Towards a Discipline of Crime Prevention: A Systematic Approach to its Nature, Range and Concepts', *Preventing Crime and Disorder: Targeting Strategies and Responsibilities*, Cambridge: Institute of Criminology, 1996.

Ekblom, P., 'Gearing up Against Crime: A Dynamic Framework to Help Designers Keep up with the Adaptive Criminal in a Changing World', *International Journal of Risk, Security and Crime Prevention*, 1997, vol. 2, no. 4, pp. 249–266.

Ekblom, P. & Pease, K., 'Building a Safer Society: Strategic Approaches to Crime Prevention', *Building a Safer Society: Crime and Justice: A Review of the Research*, vol. 19, Chicago: University of Chicago Press, 1995.

Ekpenyong, S., 'Social Inequalities, Collusion and Armed Robbery in Nigerian Cities', *British Journal of Criminology*, 1989, 29, 1. pp. 21–34.

Ellingworth, D., Hope, T., Osborn, D., Trickett, A. and Pease, K., 'Prior Victimisation and Crime Risk', *International Journal of Risk, Security and Crime Prevention*, 1997, vol. 2, no. 3, pp. 201–216.

Elster, J., *Rational Choice*, Oxford: Blackwell, 1986.

Fattah, E., 'The Rational Choice/Opportunity Perspective As A Vehicle for Integrating Criminological and Victimological Theories', *Routine Activities and Rational Choice*, New York: Transaction Press, 1993.

Farrington, D., 'Measuring, Explaining and Preventing Shoplifting: A Review of British Research', *Security Journal*, 1999, vol. 12, no. 1, pp. 9–28.

Feeney, F., 'Robbers as Decision Makers', *The Reasoning Criminal Rational Choice Perspectives on Offending*, New York: Springer-Verlag, 1986.

Felson, M., 'Routine Activites, Social Controls, Rational Decisions and Criminal Outcomes', *The Reasoning Criminal*, New York: Springer-Verlag, 1986.

Felson, M., *Crime and Everyday Life*, 2nd edn, Thousand Oaks, USA: Pine Forge Press, 1998.

Felson, M. and Clarke, R., *Business and Crime Prevention*, New York: Criminal Justice Press, 1997.

Ferreira, B., 'Situational Crime Prevention and Displacement: The Implications for Business, Industrial and Private Security Management', *Security Journal*, 1995, vol. 6, pp. 155–162.

Formolli, A., 'Robberies in Betting Offices: A Study of Situational Crime Prevention Measures Which May Reduce the Likelihood of Attack', *Unpublished MSc Thesis*, University of Leicester, 1998.

Gabor, T., 'Armed Robbery Overseas: Highlights of a Canadian Study', *Armed Robbery*, Australian Institute of Criminology, Canberra, 1988, ACT.

Gabor, T., 'Preventing Robbery', *Armed Robbery: Proceedings of a Seminar Held 22-24 March 1988*, Canberra: Australian Institute of Criminology, 1989.

Gabor, T., Baril, M., Cusson, M., Elie, D., Lebanc, M. and Normandeau, A., *Armed Robbery, Cops, Robbers and Victims*, Illinois: CC Thomas, 1987.

Garland, D., 'The Limits of the Sovereign State: Strategies for Crime Control in Contemporary Society', *British Journal of Criminology*, 1996, 36, 4, pp. 445–471.

Garofalo, J., 'Reassessing the Lifestyle Model of Personal Victimisation', *Positive Criminology*, London: Sage, 1987.

George, B. and Button, M., 'Why Some Organisations Prefer In-House to Contract Security Staff', *Crime at Work: Studies in Security and Crime Prevention*, Leicester: Perpetuity Press, 1994.

George, B. and Button, M., *Private Security*, Leicester: Perpetuity Press, 2000.

Gill, K., *Insurance Fraud: Causes, Patterns and Prevention*, Ph.D Thesis, University of Leicester, 2000.

Gill, M., *Crime at Work: Studies in Security and Crime Prevention*, Leicester: Perpetuity Press, 1994.

Gill, M., 'Risk, Security and Crime Prevention: a Forum for Developing Theory and Practice', *International Journal of Risk, Security and Crime Prevention*, 1996, 1,1, pp. 11–16.

Gill, M., 'Employing Ex-Offenders: A Risk or an Opportunity?' *Howard Journal*, 1997, 36, 4, pp. 337–351.

Gill, M., 'Crime at Work: Increasing the Risk for Offenders', *Crime at Work Series*, vol. 2, Leicester: Perpetuity Press, 1998.

Gill, M., 'The Victimisation of Business: Indicators of Risk and the Direction of Future Research', *International Review of Victimology*, 1998b, vol. 6, pp. 17–28.

Gill, M. & Matthews, R., 'Robbers on Robbery: Offenders' Perspectives', *Crime at Work: Studies in Security and Crime Prevention*, Leicester: Perpetuity Press, 1994.

Gill, M. and Pease, K., 'Repeat Robbers: Are they Different?', *Crime at Work: Increasing the Risk for Offenders*, vol. 2, Leicester: Perpetuity Press, 1998.

Gill, M. and Turbin, V., 'Evaluating "Realist Evaluation": Evidence From a Study of CCTV', *Surveillance, Closed Circuit Television and Social Control*, Aldershot: Ashgate, 1998.

Gill, M. and Turbin, V., 'CCTV and Shop Theft: Towards a Realistic Evaluation', *Surveillance of Public Space: CCTV, Street Lighting and Crime Prevention, Crime Prevention Studies*, vol. 10, New York: Criminal Justice Press, 1998.

Gilling, D., *Crime Prevention Theory, Policy and Politics*, London: UCL Press, 1997.

Grabosky, P., *Unintended Consequences of Crime Prevention*, New York: Willow Tree Press, 1997.

Graham, J. and Bennett, T., *Crime Prevention Strategies in Europe and North America*, Helsinki: European Institute for Crime Prevention and Control, 1995.

Grandjean, C., 'Bank Robberies and Physical Security in Switzerland: A Case Study of the Escalation and Displacement Phenomena', *Security Journal No. 1*, 1990, vol. 3, pp. 155–159.

Greenwood, C., *Firearms Control: A Study of Armed Crime and Firearms Control in England and Wales*, London: Routledge & Keegan Paul, 1972.

Griswold, D., 'Crime Prevention and Commercial Burglary', *Journal of Criminal Justice*, 1984, vol. 12, pp. 493–501.

Gunn, J. & Gristwood, J., 'Twenty Seven Robbers', *British Journal of Criminology*, 1976, vol. 16, pp. 56–62.

Hall, S., Critcher, C., Jefferson, T., Clarke, J. & Roberts, B., *Policing the Crisis, Mugging, the State, Law and Order, Critical Social Studies*, London: Macmillan, 1981.

Hamilton, P., *Espionage, Terrorism and Subversion in an Industrial Society: an Examination and Philosophy of Defence Management*, Leatherhead: Peter A Heims Ltd, 1979.

Handford, M., 'Electronic Tagging in Action: a Case Study in Retailing', *Crime at Work: Studies in Security and Crime Prevention*, vol. 1, Leicester: Perpetuity Press, 1994.

Hannan, T. H., 'Bank Robbers and Bank Security Precautions', *Journal of Legal Studies*, 1982, vol. 11, pp. 83–92.

Harding, R. and Blake, A., *Weapon Choice by Violent Offenders in Western Australia: a Pilot Study*, University of Western Australia, 1989.

Heal, K. and Laycock, G., *Situational Crime Prevention: From Theory into Practice*, London: HMSO, 1986.

Health and Safety Executive, *Prevention of Violence to Staff in Banks and Building Societies*, Sudbury: Health and Safety Executive, 1993.

Hemmingway, R., 'Environmental Design, Access Control and Surveillance as Deterrents to Thefts in Hospitals', *Security Journal*, 1989, vol. 1.1, pp. 47–57.

Hermann, L., *Street Robbery in Frankfurt: Growing Accustomed to a Crime?*, Frankfurt: Pozeiprasid, 1991.

Hindelang, M., *An Analysis of Victimisation Survey Results from the Eight Impact Cities: Summary Report*, Albany: Criminal Justice Research Center, 1974.

Hindelang, M., Gottfredson, M. and Garofalo, J., *Victims of Personal Crime: An Empirical Foundation for a Theory of Personal Victimisation*, Cambridge, Mass: Ballinger, 1978.

Hirschi, T., 'On the Compatibility of Rational Choice and Social Control Theories of Crime', *The Reasoning Criminal: Rational Choice Perspectives on Offending*, New York: Springer-Verlag, 1986.

Hoare, M., 'The Pattern of Experience in the Use of Firearms by Criminals and the Police Response', *unpublished MSc thesis*, University of Cranfield, 1980.

Home Office, *Standing Conference on Crime Prevention, Report of the Working Party on Commercial Robbery*, London: Home Office, 1986.

Home Office, *Prison Statistics England and Wales, 1995*, London: HMSO, 1996.

Home Office, *Criminal Statistics for England and Wales*, London: HMSO, 1998.

Hopkins-Burke, R., *Zero Tolerance Policing*, Leicester: Perpetuity Press, 1998.

Horne, C., 'The Case For: CCTV Should be Introduced', *International Journal of Risk, Security and Crime Prevention*, 1996, vol. 1, no. 4, pp. 317–326.

Hughes, G., *Understanding Crime Prevention: Social Control, Risk and Late Modernity*, Buckingham: Open University Press, 1998.

Hunter, R.D & Jeffery, C.R., 'Environmental Crime Prevention: An Analysis of Convenience Store Robberies', *Security Journal*, 1991, vol. 2.2, pp. 78–83.

Hunter, RD and Jeffery, CR., 'Preventing Convenience Store Robbery through Environmental Design', *Crime Prevention Studies*, vol. 2, New Jersey: Willow Tree Press, 1994.

Jacques, C., 'Ram Raiding: The History, Incidence and Scope for Prevention', *Crime at Work: Studies in Security and Crime Prevention*, Leicester: Perpetuity Press, 1994.

Jammers, I., 'Commercial Robberies: the Business Community as a Target in the Netherlands', *Security Journal*, 1995, vol. 6.1, pp. 13–20.

Jones, T. and Newburn, T., *Private Security and Public Policing*, Oxford: Clarendon Press, 1998.

Kapardis, A., 'One Hundred Armed Robbers in Melbourne: Myths and Reality', *Armed Robbery*, Australian Institute of Criminology, 1988, ACT.

Katz, J., 'The Motivation of the Persistent Robber', *Crime and Justice*, 1991, vol. 14, pp. 277–306.

Klewers Handbook of Security, London: Croners, 1999.

Kube, E., 'Preventing Bank Robbery: Lessons from Interviewing Robbers', *Journal of Security Administration*, 1988, vol. 11, pp. 78–83.

Kuhchorn, E. and Svensson, B., *Crime Prevention*, Stockholm: The National Swedish Council for Crime Prevention, 1982.

Lab, S., *Crime Prevention: Approaches, Practices and Evaluations*, 2nd edn, Cincinnati, Ohio: Anderson, 1992.

Laycock, G., 'Property Marking: a Deterrent to Domestic Burglary?', *Home Office Crime Prevention Unit Paper no. 3*, London: Home Office, 1995.

Lejenuce, R., 'The Management of Mugging', *Urban Life*, 6, 2, 1977, pp. 23–48.

Letkemann, P., *Crime as Work*, Englewood Cliffs, New Jersey: Prentice-Hall, 1973.

Levi, M., *The Phantom Capitalist*, London: Heinemann, 1981.

Levi, M., 'The Craft of the Long-Firm Fraudster: Criminal Skills and Commercial Responses', *Crime at Work: Increasing the Risk for Offenders*, vol. 2, Leicester: Perpetuity Press, 1998.

Leymann, H., 'Stress Reactions after Bank Robberies', *Work and Stress*, 1988, vol. 2, pp. 123–132.

Luckenbill, D., 'Generating Compliance: The Case of Robbery', *Urban Life*, 1981, vol. 10. pp. 25–46.

MacDonald, J., *Armed Robbery: Offenders and their Victims*, Springfield, Illinois: CC Thomas, 1975.

Maguire, M., *Burglary in a Dwelling: the Offence, the Offender and the Victim*, London: Heinemann, 1982.

Manunta, G., 'The Case Against: Security Management is Not a Profession', *International Journal of Risk, Security and Crime Prevention*, 1996, 1, 3, pp. 233–240.

Manunta, G., 'Towards a Security Science Through a Specific Theory and Methodology', *PhD Thesis*, Scarman Centre, University of Leicester, 1997.

Manunta, G., *Security: an Introduction*, Cranfield: Cranfield University Press, 1998.

Manunta, G., 'What is Security?', *Security Journal*, 1999, 12, 3, pp. 57–66.

Manunta, G., 'The Management of Security: How Robust is the Justification Process?', *Security Journal*, 2000, 13, 1, pp. 33–44.

Maree, A., 'Bank Robbery in South Africa: The Crime and The Criminal', *Security Journal*, 2000, vol. 12, no. 2, pp. 53–62.

Marsden, J., *Bank Robbery: Strategies for Reduction*, Australian Banking Association, 1990.

Martinson, R., 'What Works? Questions and Answers About Prison Reform', *Public Interest*, Spring 1974, 35, pp. 22–54.

Matthews, R., 'Armed Robbery: Two Police Responses', *Crime Detection and Prevention Series paper 78*, London: Police Research Group, 1997.

McClintock, F.H. and Gibson, E., *Robbers in London*, London: Macmillan, 1961.

McRoberts, J., 'Armed Robbery: Where does it Happen? How does it Happen? Who are the Offenders?', *A Research Study*, Edith Cowan University, Australia, 1992.

McVicar, J., *McVicar by Himself*, London: Arrow Books, 1974.

Morgan, R., 'Imprisonment: Current Concerns and a Brief History', *Oxford Handbook of Criminology*, 2nd edn, Oxford: Oxford University Press, 1998.

Morrison, S. and O'Donnell, I., *Armed Robbery: A Study in London Occasional Paper 15*, University of Oxford Centre for Criminological Research, 1994.

Morrison, S. and O'Donnell, I., 'An Analysis of the Decision Making Practices of Armed Robberies', *The Politics and Practice of Situational Crime Prevention, Crime Prevention Studies 5*, New York: Criminal Justice Press, 1996.

Nalla, M. and Newman, G., *A Primer in Private Security*, New York: Harrow and Heston, 1990.

Normandeau, A., Armed Robbery in Montreal, and its Victims', *Victimology: an International Journal*, 1983, vol. 6, pp. 306–317.

Norris, C., Moran, J. and Armstrong, G., *Surveillance, Closed Circuit Television and Social Control*, Aldershot: Ashgate, 1998.

O'Donnell, I. and Morrison, S., 'Armed and Dangerous? The Use of Firearms in Robbery', *The Howard Journal of Criminal Justice*, 1997, vol. 36, no. 3, pp. 305–320.

Pascoe, T. and Topping, P., 'Secured by Design: Assessing the Basis of the Scheme', *International Journal of Risk, Security and Crime Prevention*, 1997, 2, 3, pp. 187–200.

Painter, K, and Tilley, N., 'Surveillance of Public Space: CCTV, Street Lighting and Crime Prevention', *Crime Prevention Studies*, vol. 10, New York: Criminal Justice Press, 1999.

Pawson, R & Tilley, N., *Realistic Evaluation*, London: Sage, 1997.

Pease, K., 'Crime Prevention', *The Oxford Handbook of Criminology*, Oxford: Open University Press, 1994, pp. 659–704.

Pease, K., 'Repeat Victimisation: Taking Stock', *Crime Prevention and Detection Series, Paper no. 90*, London: Police Research Group, 1998.

Polsky, N., *Hustlers, Beats and Others*, Harmondsworth: Penguin, 1971.

Post, R. and Kingsbury, A., *Security Administration*, Boston: Butterworth-Heinemann, 1991.

Poyner, B., *A Study of Street Attacks and their Environmental Settings*, The Tavistock Institute of Human Relations, (unpublished), 1980.

Poyner, B., Warne, C., Webb, B., Woodall, R. and Meakin, R., *Preventing Violence to Staff*, London: HMSO, 1988.

Pratt, M., *Mugging as a Social Problem*, London: Routledge & Kegan Paul, 1980.

Rodriguez, P., 'Preventing Bank Robbery in Puerto Rico', *Paper to the ASIS Annual Security Exhibition and Exhibits, New Orleans*, September 1995.

Reid, P., *Train Robbers*, London: Cornet Books, 1977.

Reiner, R., *The Politics of the Police*, Hemel Hempstead: Wheatsheaf Books, 1985.

Rodger, W., 'Armed Bank Robbery: A Situational Approach to Reduction and Prevention', *MSc Dissertation*, Scarman Centre, University of Leicester, 1996.

Roebuck, J.B., *Criminal Typology*, Springfield: Thomas, 1967.

Short, E. and Ditton, J., 'Does CCTV Affect Crime?', *CCTV Today*, 1995, vol. 2, no. 2, pp. 10–12.

Simonsen, C., 'The Case For: Security Management is a Profession', *International Journal of Risk, Security and Crime Prevention*, 1996, 1, 3, pp. 229–232.

Skogan, W., *Weapon Use in Robbery: Patterns and Policy Implications*, Northwestern University Center for Urban Affairs, Illinois: Evanston, 1978.

Taylor, M., 'The Gun Club, Men, Firearms and the New Economic Order', *Sociology Review*, 1994, vol. 3, no. 4, pp. 10–14.

Tilley, N., 'Thinking about Crime Prevention Performance Indicators', *Crime and Detection Prevention Series Paper 57*, London: Home Office, 1995.

Tilley, N., 'Demonstration, Exemplification, Duplication and Replication in Evaluative Research', *Evaluation*, 1996, vol. 2.1, pp. 35–50.

Tilley, N., 'Whys and Wherefores in Evaluating the Effectiveness of CCTV', *International Journal of Risk, Security and Crime Prevention*, 1997, vol. 2, no. 3, pp. 175–186.

Trasler, T., 'Situational Crime Control and Rational Choice: A Critique', *Situational Crime Prevention: from Theory to Practice*, London: HMSO, 1986.

Trasler, G., 'Conscience, Opportunity, Rational Choice and Crime', *Advances in Criminological Theory*, New Brusnwick: Transaction, 1997.

Vagg, J., 'Armed Robbery in Hong Kong: A Consequence of Economic Change', *International Journal of Risk, Security and Crime Prevention*, 1996, vol. 1.2, pp. 103–119.

van Dijk, J., 'Towards Effective Public-Private Partnerships in Crime Control: Experiences in the Netherlands', *Business and Crime Prevention*, New York: Criminal Justice Press, 1997.

van Dijk, J. and de Waard, J., 'A Two Dimensional Typology of Crime Prevention Projects', *Criminal Justice Abstracts*, 1991, vol. 23, pp. 483–503.

van Voorhis, P., 'Delinquency Prevention: Towards Comprehensive Models and a Conceptual Map', *Criminal Justice Review 19*, 1986, vol. 11, no. 1, pp. 15–24.

van Koppen, P. J. and de Keijser, J.W., *Desisting Distance-Decay*, Netherlands Institute for the Study of Criminality and Law Enforcement (Niscale): Leiden, 1996.

van Koppen, P. J. and Jansen, R.W.J., *A Time to Rob: Variations in Time and Number of Commercial Robberies*, Netherlands Institute for the Study of Criminality and Law Enforcement (Niscale): Leiden, 1996.

van Koppen, P. J. and Jansen, R.W.J., *The Road to the Robbery: Travel Patterns in Commercial Robberies*, Netherlands Institute for the Study of Criminality and Law Enforcement (Niscale): Leiden, 1996.

Walker, N. and Padfield, N., *Sentencing, Theory, Law and Practice*, London: Butterworths, 1996.

Walsh, D., *Heavy Business: Commercial Burglary and Robbery*, London: Routledge & Kegan Paul, 1986.

Welsh, B. and Farrington, D., 'Value for Money? A Review of the Costs and Benefits of Situational Prevention', *British Journal of Criminology*, 1999, 39, 3, pp. 345–368.

West, D.J. and Farrington, D.P., *The Delinquent Way of Life*, London: Heinemann Educational Books, 1997.

Wiersma, E., 'Commercial Burglars in the Netherlands: Reasoning Decision-Makers?', *International Journal Risk, Security and Crime Prevention*, 1996, vol. 1, no. 3, pp. 217–228.

Wojcik, D., Walklate, S., Ostrihanska, Z., Mawby, R.I. and Gorgenyi, I., 'Security and Crime Prevention at Home: A Comparison of Victims' Response to Burglary in England, Poland and Hungary', *International Journal Risk, Security and Crime Prevention*, 1997, vol. 2, no. 1, pp. 38–50.

Wortley, P., 'Guilt, Shame and Situational Crime Prevention', *Crime Prevention Studies 5*, New York: Willow Tree Press, 1997.

Wright, R. and Decker, S., *Armed Robbers in Action*, Boston: Northeastern University Press, 1997.

Wright, R. & Logie, R., 'How Young House Burglars Choose Targets', *Howard Journal*, 1988, 27.2, pp. 92–104.

Wright, J.D. and Rossi, P.H., *Armed and Considered Dangerous: A Survey of Felons and Their Firearms*, Springfield, Illinois: Charles C Thomas, 1986.

Wyllie, B., *A Guide to Security Surveys*, Leicester: Perpetuity Press, 2000.

Index

Addiction
  addict robbers   149, 151
  alcohol   29, 31–2
  drugs   29–31, 32
  motivation for robbery   26,
    29–32
Alarms   52–3, 57, 171–2
  false activation   171
  silent   172
Alcohol   29, 31–2
Amateur offenders   20, 149, 150–1
  alcohol   29, 31–2
  planning   35, 54–5
  threat from police, perception of
    92
Armed police   77, 84, 168

'Buzz' see Excitement

Carrying out the robbery see Modus
  operandi
Case studies   110–47
CEPTED scheme   169
Choice of target   42–8, 55–6
  customer presence   44, 46, 47
  day   45
  design and layout   45–6
  escape route see Escape routes

Choice of target — continued
  expectations   68
  gender of staff   48, 174
  knowledge   43
  location see Location of target
  opportunistic   42–3
  repeat victimisation   53–4, 57,
    173
  revenge   43
  security measures   43, 44
    see also Security measures
  size   45
  visibility from street   46–7, 48
Closed circuit television cameras
    48–9, 56, 57, 58, 180
  disguises   49–50, 57, 172, 180
  false sense of security   49, 172,
    181
  poor quality images   49
  violent destruction   172
Community safety   9
Condemnation   176
Confidence   92–3
Control requirement   65, 66, 69, 70,
    83
  designing in surprise elements
    170–1
  hostages   69

Control requirement — *continued*
  weapons and   85
Crime, root causes neglected   8, 10
Crime facilitators   6
  control of   166–8
  knowledge of target   166–7
  weapons availability   77, 83,
    166, 167–8
Crime prevention
  classification   3–4
  community crime   4
  criminal event   4, 5
  criminality prevention   4
  definition   3
  displacement *see* Displacement
  distal causes   4
  identification of individuals at risk
    4
  law enforcement *see* police
  legislation   177
  negative consequences   7
  primary   4
  proximal causes   4
  removal of opportunity   5
  secondary   4
  situation *see* Situational crime
    prevention
  social *see* Social crime prevention
    and controls
  tertiary   4
Crime risk management   10
  assessment of situation   158
  avoidance of risk   158
  defence in depth   160
  definition   9
  education   22
  management techniques   158–9
  opportunity reduction   156–8
  people deployment   160, 161,
    173–4
  process   148, 156–77, 178, 179
  reduction of risk   158
  rewards
    eliminating and reducing
      174–5
    identifying property   175

Crime risk management —
    continued
  situational techniques   159–68
  social crime prevention and
    controls   162, 175–7
  spread of risk   158
  toleration of risk   158
  transfer of risk   158
  workplace   157
Crimewatch   34, 176–7
Criminal event
  lifestyle theory   5–6
  motivation   5
  removal of opportunity   5
  routine activities theory   5–6
Criminal justice agencies   4
  see also Police
Criminal justice process
  deterrence   12, 90
  intervention   12
  preventative functions   12
  rational offenders and   12–13
  reinforcement of moral order   12
  see also Likelihood of being
    caught
Criminality prevention   4

Day, choice of   45
Defence
  in depth   160
  principles   160
  see also Security measures
Demand for money   64–5, 71
Design and layout of target   160,
    161
  blind spots   171
  CEPTED scheme   169
  choice of target   45–6
  choice of teller   45–6, 161, 171
  doors   165
    revolving   46, 56, 85, 165
  entry screening   166
  escape route   169–70
    see also Escape routes
  external environment   169–70
  hostage taking   85, 166

Design and layout of target —
    continued
    internal environment   170–1
    music to spoil concentration   171
    open-plan layout   170
    passers-by   46–7
    queuing rails   56, 85, 161, 170
    'Secured by Design' scheme   169
    teller position   45–6, 161, 171
    visibility from street   46–7, 48,
        170
Deterrence   12, 90
    see also Likelihood of being
        caught
Disguises   57, 87, 180
    entry screening   166
Displacement   6–7, 11, 158, 180
Doors
    double   165
    revolving   46, 56, 85, 165
Drivers   66–7
    payment   67
Drop safes   174
Drugs *see* Addiction

Environmental design *see* Design
    and layout of target
Escape, priority   42, 45, 55–8, 85
Escape routes
    choice of target   43, 44, 45, 55–8
    drivers   66–7
    planning   42, 45
    redesigning external environment
        169–70
Excitement   70
    motivation for robbery   28–9
    weapons and   77, 85
Excuses
    removal   8, 162
    see also Motivation
Expectations
    method of robbery and   68
    see also Rewards

Facilitators *see* Crime facilitators
Firearms   62–4

Firearms — *continued*
    accidental injury   80–1, 82, 84
    armed police risk   77, 84, 168
    availability   77, 83, 167
    black market   77, 83, 167
    excitement   77, 85
    'have-a-go-heroes' injury   80,
        81, 82, 83
    imitations   74, 76
    numbers of robberies using   2
    replicas   74, 76, 99–100, 107
    sentencing and   99–100, 107
    to avoid violence   63
    types of target   74–6
    unloaded   74
    victim's perception of danger   76

Getaway cars   6
Great Train Robbers   1
Guilt   78–9, 80
    inducing feelings of   112, 162,
        175–6
Guns *see* Firearms

'Have-a-go-heroes'   56, 165, 173
    injuries to   80, 81, 82, 83
Hostages   65, 69, 85, 166, 174

Identification of property or money
    175
Identification of robbers   173–4
    see also Disguises
Imprisonment
    further crime after   103–4
    further robbery after   102–6
    negative experience   103
    planning and threat of   100–1
    removal of reason for offending
        102–3, 107
    'school' for offenders   105
    time for reflection   108
    see also Sentences
Information   55
    hot-lines   168
    planning robbery and   40–1
    staff members   40–1

Information — *continued*
   to police   94–5, 168
Injury
   avoidance of   82
   'have-a-go-heroes'   80, 81, 82,
      83
   offender fear of   80
Interviews with offenders *see*
      Research techniques
Intimidation   84–5

Law enforcement *see* Police
Layout of target *see* Design and
      layout of target
Lifestyle theory   5–6
Likelihood of being caught   100–1,
      108–9
   increasing   8, 160, 161–6
      design *see* Design and layout of
         target
      policing   168–9
      see also Security measures
   informants   94–5, 168
   luck   94
   negative thinking   93
   perception of
      after robbery   94–7
      by amateur offenders   92
      by professional offenders
         92–3
      prior to robbery   91–3
   see also Deterrence
Location of target   43–4
   accessibility   43–4
   corner positions   169
   corners   43, 44, 56
   escape routes   42, 43, 44, 45, 55,
      56, 57, 58
   main roads   43, 44, 56, 169
   pedestrian streets   56, 170
   planning   36
   redesigning external environment
      169–70

Management
   crime risk *see* Crime risk
      management

Management — *continued*
   security *see* Security management
Media
   copycat crimes   176–7
   encouraging robbery   33–4,
      176–7
   information flow to police   168
Modus operandi
   control requirement   65, 66, 69,
      70, 83
   demand for money   64–5, 71
   drivers   66–7
   expectations   68
   experience   67–8
   getting behind counter   65
   hostages   65, 69
   nervousness   70–1
   number of robbers   66–7, 149–50
   resources   69
   rewards *see* Rewards
   speed   69
   state of mind   68–9
   weapons *see* Firearms; Weapons
Money
   demand   64–5, 71
   identifiable bank notes   175
   see also Rewards, money handed
      over
Morality, reinforcement of moral
      order   12
Motivation   5
   addiction   26, 29–32
   excitement   28–9
   financial reasons   25, 26–7
   funding legitimate projects   28
   living expenses   27, 32–3
   materialistic   25
   media   33–4
   personal non-essential
      consumption   25, 27
   power   29
   reduction   162
   revenge   43
   safeguarding future   28
   unemployment   26
   see also Excuses

Muggings   1, 2

Offenders
   amateur *see* Amateur offenders
   interviews *see* Research
      techniques
   perspectives and   13–14
   professional *see* Professional
      offenders
   rational *see* Rational offenders
   sample   18–20
      bias   14, 15–16
      see also Research techniques
Opportunist robbers *see* Amateur
   offenders

People deployment   160, 161,
   173–4
   identification of robbers   173–4
Planning   20
   amateurs   35, 54–5
   escape route *see* Escape routes
   information   36, 40–1, 55, 181
   location *see* Location of target
   process   36–42
   professionals   35, 54–5
   security *see* Security measures
   surveillance of target   36, 40, 55
   target *see* Choice of target
   visits before offence   38–9, 169
Police
   armed   77, 84, 168
   illegal and oppressive tactics   95
   incompetence folklore   95–6
   information to   94–5, 168
   monitoring radio transmissions
      97
   not considered a threat   106
   planning robberies and monitoring
      91–3, 97
   preventative effect   4
   Rapid Response Units   96
   role   89–90
   security guards   168–9
   see also Likelihood of being
      caught

Power, motivation for robbery   29
Preparation   24–61
   choice of target *see* Choice of
      target
   motivation *see* Motivation
   planning *see* Planning
   security *see* Security measures
Professional offenders   20, 149,
   150, 151
   planning   35–42, 54–5
   threat from police, perception of
      92–3

Queuing rails   56, 85, 161, 170

Rapid Response Units   96
Rational offenders   6, 7, 152–6,
   178–9
   amateur and professional
      distinction   152–3
   bounded rationality   152
   criminal justice process and
      12–13
   indicators of rationality   153–5
   meaning   152
Recidivism   4
Remorse, inducement   78–9, 80,
   112, 162, 175–6
Removal of opportunity   5
Repeat offending   4
Repeat victimisation   53–4, 173
   need to improve security   54, 57,
      173
Research techniques
   accuracy of data   17–18
   approach to prisoners   16
   confidentiality   17
   false (forced) cooperativeness
      14
   interviews   17
      schedule   19
   issue identification   15
   numbers   15–16
   prison-based difficulties   14–15
   response rate   16–17
   sample   18–10

Research techniques — *continued*
  sample bias   14, 15–16
  supporting evidence   14, 15
  taking robbers back to scene   179
  tape recordings   14–15, 17
  validating data   14–15, 17–18
Revenge motivation   43
Rewards   71–4
  deception   87, 175
  disappointment with   86–7
  dividing and spending   74
  eliminating   174–5
  expectations   68
  money handed over
    deception   87, 175
    instructions and advice to staff
      73–4
    refusal by staff   72, 86
  obtaining no money   72–3, 86
  reduction   8, 174–5
  removal as security measure   163
Risk of capture *see* Likelihood of
  being caught
Risk of crime *see* Crime risk
  management
Robbers
  addict   149, 151
  alcoholic   149
  amateurs *see* Amateur offenders
  career   149
  casual   149
  compulsive   149
  identification   173–4
  numbers involved   149–50
  opportunist *see* amateurs
  professional *see* Professional
    offenders
  public perception   1
  rationality *see* Rational offenders
  typology   149–51
    usefulness   151–2
Robbery
  definition   21
  methods and styles *see* Modus
    operandi
  reward *see* Rewards

Root causes of crime neglected   8,
  10
Routine activities theory   5–6

Safes   173
  drop   174
  time-locks   53, 173
Sample   18–20
  bias   14, 15–16
Screens   50–3, 56–7, 58, 171
  firearms   62–3
  honest customer deterred   181
  refusal to hand over money   86
  rising   51, 164–5
  smashing   181
  steaming   52, 164–5
  violence increased by   52, 58,
    62–3, 164, 180
'Secured by Design' scheme   169
Security guards   168–9
Security management
  accountability   10–11
  care of staff victims   10, 11
  displacement   11
  education and training   11
  negative image   22
  professionalisation   11
  role   9, 158–9
  root causes of crime neglected
    10
  social problems excluded   10
  status   11
  subject area   9–10
Security measures   36
  access control   160, 165–6
  alarms   52–3, 57, 171–2
  cashless tills   163
  CCTV *see* Closed circuit
    television cameras
  delaying robber   162
  design and layout *see* Design and
    layout of target
  detection methods   160, 161,
    169, 171–3
  deterrent methods   160, 163–6
  entry screening   166

Security measures — *continued*
  environmental design *see* Design
    and layout of target
  false sense of security   49, 172,
    181
  increasing effort required   162
  increasing violence   52, 58, 180
  negative consequences   7
  not customer-friendly   86
  people deployment   160, 161,
    173–4
  physical   48–53
  removing reward   163
  safes   53, 173, 174
  screens *see* Screens
  surveillance   161, 169
  target hardening   161–6
  time-delay safes   53, 173
Sentences   86, 90, 107
  deterrence   4, 107
  irrelevant   97, 107
  mitigation   98
  prediction by robbers   98
  severity   4
  underestimation   97, 98–9, 107
  see also Imprisonment
Situational crime prevention   3–9
  examples of measures   7
  excuse removal   8
  rational choice *see* Rational
    offenders
  root causes of crime neglected
    8
  techniques   8–9
Social crime prevention and controls
    5, 162, 175–7
  change in conditions   177–8
  condemnation   176
  guilt   112, 162, 175–6
  increasing   176–7
  media   176–7
  reinforcement of moral order   12
  remorse   112, 162, 175–6
Staff
  bribes   158
  collusion   158

Staff — *continued*
  false sense of security   49, 172,
    181
  gender   48, 174
  handing over money
    deception   87, 175
    instructions and advice   73–4
    refusal   72, 86
  hostages   56, 174
  information from   40–1, 55,
    158–9, 181
  intervention by   174
  security measures and   86
  training   159
Steaming   52, 164–5
Street attacks   1, 2
Surveillance as security measure
    161, 169
Surveillance of target   36, 40, 55

Target
  design and layout *see* Design and
    layout of target
  hardening *see* Security measures
  location *see* Location of target
  rationality indicators by   154–5
  removing   174–5
  surveillance   36, 40, 55
  visits before offence   38–9, 169
Typology of robbers   149–51
  usefulness   151–2

Unemployment, motivation for
  robbery   26

Victims
  awareness of impact on   175–6
  handing over money
    instructions and advice   73–4
    refusal   72, 86
  inducing sympathy with   112,
    162, 175–6
  lifestyle theory   5–6
  perception of danger   76
  repeat victimisation   53–4, 57,
    173

Victims — *continued*
  routine activities 5–6
  security management
    responsibility 10, 11
  trauma 1, 78–9, 80
  weapons to reduce resistance
    77
Violence
  avoidance 57, 63, 82
  control and 85
  'have-a-go-heroes' 80, 81, 82,
    83
  intimidation 84–5
  limit on level 77–8
  offender fear of injury 80
  screens and increase in 52, 58,
    62–3, 164, 180
  victim response to 78–9, 80
  weapons carried to avoid 63, 77
Visibility
  choice of target and 46–7, 48

Visibility — *continued*
  marketing and security conflicts
    48
  passers-by 170

Weapons 6
  accidental injury 80–1, 82, 84
  avoiding violence 57, 63, 82
  compliance from victims 82
  control and 85
  excitement 77, 85
  intimidation 84–5
  limits on level of violence 77–8
  reasons for carrying 77
  underestimation of victim trauma
    78–9, 80
  use 62–4
  variation with target 76–7
  victim's perception of danger 76
  see also Firearms
Wheelmen 66–7